READING BETWEEN THE LIES

How to Detect Fraud and Avoid Becoming a Victim of Wall Street's Next Scandal

JORDAN E. GOODMAN

Foreword by Robert A. Olstein

Dearborn™
Trade Publishing
A **Kaplan Professional** Company

This publication is designed to provide accurate and authoritative information in regard to the subject matter covered. It is sold with the understanding
that the publisher is not engaged in rendering legal, accounting, or other professional service. If legal advice or other expert assistance is required, the services of a competent professional should be sought.

Vice President and Publisher: Cynthia A. Zigmund
Senior Project Editor: Trey Thoelcke
Interior Design: Lucy Jenkins
Cover Design: Design Solutions
Typesetting: Elizabeth Pitts

Published by Dearborn Trade Publishing, a Kaplan Professional Company

Printed in the United States of America

02 03 04 10 9 8 7 6 5 4 3 2 1

Library of Congress Cataloging-in-Publication Data

Goodman, Jordan Elliot.
   Reading between the lies : how to detect fraud and avoid becoming a victim
of Wall Street's next scandal / Jordan Goodman.
      p.   cm.
Includes index.
   ISBN 0-7931-6945-3 (hardcover)
   1. Finance, Personal. 2. Investments. 3. Capital market. 4. Corporations—
Corrupt practices.   I. Title.
   HG179.G6756 2003
   332.63′2042—dc21

                                                          2003006388

DEDICATION

To my wife, Suzanne, who supports all of my many activities, including writing this book, in a myriad of ways, and my son Jason, who also helped his dad complete the *Lies* book through his constant interest in understanding how the latest scandals on Wall Street might affect his financial future.

Contents

We believe that any investment philosophy requires a keen understanding of corporate reporting practices. For the past seven years, as president and head portfolio manager of the Olstein Financial Alert Fund, I have employed a philosophy and discipline that emphasizes financial statement analysis. Developed over the past 35 years, the cornerstone of my philosophy emphasizes that investment success is correlated with minimizing investment errors, as opposed to selecting companies with the highest appreciation potential without assessing downside risk.

My investment philosophy is based on the belief that an intensive inferential analysis of a company's financial statements, supporting documents, disclosure practices, and financial statement footnotes is the best way to analyze the capabilities of management, the economic reality of the information provided, the conservatism of the accounting and disclosure practices, the company's financial strength, and finally, the value of the company. I undertake a detailed look behind the numbers of financial statements to assess financial strength and screen for potential problems to assess downside risk—"defense first"—before considering a stock's potential for capital appreciation.

The first line of defense against investment errors is to select companies that generate excess cash flow after capital expenditures and working capital needs. Companies that generate excess cash flow have the potential to:

- Raise their dividend payments
- Repurchase company shares
- Make strategic acquisitions

- Ride out rough times without adopting short-term strategies not in the long-term interest of the company to alleviate cash shortages
- Be acquired because of their strong financial position

I believe that an equity security is worth the discounted value of the future expected cash earnings (excess cash flow) to be generated by the underlying company. However, Generally Accepted Accounting Principles (GAAP) requires that a company report earnings on an accrual basis, which has two basic premises.

First, accrual accounting states that revenue is recognized when a transaction occurs in which value has been exchanged. The revenue recognition may lead or lag the passing of cash.

The second basic premise of accrual accounting is that the cost of a transaction should be recognized over the same period of time that the revenue associated with the cost is generated. The cost or expense recognition also may lead or lag the passing of cash.

In reporting GAAP-based earnings, companies are given wide discretion within the rules. The numbers produced under GAAP rely on management judgment, leaving room for unrealistic assumptions and misleading numbers. In my opinion, most companies (including many companies in our portfolio) engage in some type of earnings management or make assumptions that may prove out to be unrealistic. Thus, to value a company according to a model of discounted excess cash flow, one has to be able to adjust reported earnings to arrive at we call true cash earnings (excess cash flow).

I believe that there is nothing wrong or illegal about earnings management within limits. However, some companies have far exceeded these limits. In cases such as Enron, Lucent Technologies, Boston Market, and Sunbeam, the financial statements may have been in accord with GAAP, but they were not in accord with economic reality. It is in management's best interest to report the best earnings possible to preserve financing alternatives, keep their stock options valuable and exercisable, and to keep shareholders happy via increasing stock prices. Thus, in instances when management identifies a problem, which because of bias and/or ego they deem temporary, management may adopt optimistic assumptions or accounting alternatives under GAAP to portray a positive picture until the problem is solved. Accounting alternatives used to delay reporting problems to shareholders include:

- Capitalizing costs based on unjustified optimism
- Reversing past reserves to earnings
- Realizing nonrecurring gains
- Lowering discretionary expenditures

Although earnings management is an everyday endeavor for most companies, the process makes it difficult to get a clear picture of the company's basic business without performing an intensive inferential analysis of financial statements. Therefore, even under GAAP (which I doubt Enron practiced), a true measure of the earnings power of a firm's basic business can be distorted.

It is important to pay attention to corporate reporting practices at all times to assess a company's ability to produce future excess cash flow. However, no portfolio manager, analyst, or investor can uncover everything. Despite an exhaustive inferential analysis of financial statements prior to purchase by my portfolio management team, once in a while even one of the stocks in our portfolio surprises us by disclosing questionable accounting. The objective is to keep these surprises to a minimum. Reading this book can go a long way toward that objective.

The 1998–2000 bubble markets, followed by the 2000–2002 market crash and its poster child, Enron, have created a political and media frenzy relating to the accounting and reporting games practiced by most companies. First, let's set the record straight. Whether or not we are in a bull, bear, or bubble market, most companies utilize financial accounting and reporting practices to their advantage in an attempt to put their best foot forward. As previously stated, a portfolio manager/analyst's job is to analyze the numbers in financial statements and to adjust those numbers and assumptions to reflect the economic reality of the company's basic business. The adjusted numbers should be utilized to value a company. It is just as important to assess the disclosure practices of a company and to determine whether information that is essential to the valuation of the company is omitted from the financial statements and supporting schedules. Over the years, I have found a high correlation between the omission of important information and the inability to disclose because of the repercussions. The risk of non-disclosed information must be factored into the valuation process by reducing the multiple of cash flow (even reducing the multiple as far as zero) you are willing to pay to purchase a company. Enron had limited disclosure as to the nature of the earnings being developed by their off balance sheet entities, yet these entities were material earnings contributors to Enron's bottom line.

So where to begin if every company engages in different financial reporting games? The key to Enron (which we would classify as an abusive game player) and other companies I have been publicly critical of in the past (Sunbeam, Boston Market, and Lucent Technologies), is the degree and extent to which the financial statements of such companies have deviated from the economic reality of their basic business. The recent accounting failures by major companies (e.g., Enron, Global Crossing, Xerox, etc.) have damaged investor confidence in the entire financial reporting system. Everyone wants to blame the accountants and corporate management, but I believe that the Wall Street financial community and especially the majority of security analysts and their supervisors are the biggest culprits. However, the investing public, intoxicated by the meteoric stock market returns, also has to accept its role in the eventual collapse of stock prices and the resulting mass destruction of trillions of dollars in capital.

The latest bout of Wall Street's lackadaisical acceptance of the numbers as presented, no matter how suspicious, is similar to many other financial and accounting crises I have experienced. The current period is reminiscent of the 1970s, when audit failures such as Equity Funding and Stirling Homex, as well as the accounting games played by the computer lessors and land development companies, wiped out billions of dollars of net worth as an economic boom turned into a recession. Like today, the investing public, the financial press, and government representatives called for more government regulation. Despite all of the current negativity, there has been a vast improvement in the disclosure practices of public corporations over the past 30 years. We understand that the financial reporting system can always use improvement, and new business practices will require constant modification of the reporting system. However, as previously stated, it is important to note that all reporting systems rely on management judgement, leaving room for potential abuse or unrealistic assumptions. The improvement in the disclosure practices since 1968 (when I started my career) has resulted in financial statement analysis becoming more difficult and time consuming. Today, a wealth of additional information that was not available 30 years ago is in the footnotes and management discussions of annual reports, for anyone who reads with a skeptical eye. The analytical community, including investors who select their own stocks, has the responsibility to assess new disclosures, adjust earnings for unrealistic reporting, and expose corporations whose disclosures are inadequate.

As early as May 2000, Enron's disclosures were sending out red flag alerts. The disclosures clearly stated that Enron's chief financial officer was personally sharing in the profits of the off balance sheet entities. Although the disclosures about the off balance sheet entities were generally inadequate, the percentage of Enron's profits being derived from these entities was materially increasing. If the security analysts had been doing their jobs and demanding more disclosure from management, perhaps Enron's stock would never have reached such lofty prices.

The problem is not the reporting system but the lack of independent (of corporate management) research by the Wall Street analytical community. If management was concerned about the analytical community rather than the analysts being concerned about their management contacts, a lot of these financial shenanigans would be nipped in the bud.

In conclusion, I believe that an investment discipline, where corporate earnings are adjusted for economic reality regardless of whether we are in a bull or bear market, provides the practitioner with a competitive advantage over others in seeking long-term capital appreciation. Although accounting and financial chicanery have always been a part of the Wall Street investment scene, bear markets create an increased awareness and call for reform. I doubt that any meaningful, permanent accounting reform is achievable via government mandate or legislation, so it is imperative for investment professionals and individual investors to assess the economic reality of financial statements. Further, the art of understanding financial statements must be practiced not only in a bear market but in all markets.

The Olstein philosophy values companies on the basis of their ability to create excess cash flow, rather than the ability of company management to create smokescreens. Let us reward companies that produce excess cash flow rather than companies's with creative accountants.

Failing to adjust reported results is a ticking time bomb with a high probability of eventually detonating. Cash flow analysis must be done in all markets at all times. GAAP and economic reality can, at times, be worlds apart, but an inferential analysis of financial statements will bridge the gap when it occurs.

I believe that the market, not legislation, is the best regulator. If the portfolio management and financial analyst community regularly adjusted reported corporate earnings for deviations from economic reality in all markets, the accounting crisis could end immediately. Under constant surveillance, management's engagement in financial chicanery would be regularly penalized and chastised for attempting to misrepresent the economics of the company's basic business. Understanding the concepts discussed in this book should go a long way toward explaining why it is important to take the time to read and understand financial statements. Ignorance of financial reporting techniques could be harmful to your financial health.

By Robert A. Olstein
Chief Investment Officer, Olstein Financial Alert Fund

Robert A. Olstein, chairman, founder and chief investment officer of the Olstein Financial Alert Fund, headquartered in Purchase, New York, has long been considered one of the financial community's most astute and original research analysts and money managers, and he is a recognized expert at looking behind the numbers of financial statements.

In the 1970s, Olstein and his partner, Thornton O'Glove, coauthored one of Wall Street's most influential research services, *The Quality of Earnings Reports,* a widely quoted newsletter, promulgated the belief that, "it is essential in stock selection to spend time with financial statements *looking behind the numbers,* rather than relying upon management contact."

In the 1980s, Olstein sold his interest in the service to pursue a career as an investment advisor at Salomon Smith Barney, applying the Quality of Earnings philosophy of utilizing financial statement alerts and error avoidance as the key to increasing one's chance of achieving long-term investment objectives.

Olstein founded the Olstein Financial Alert Fund in 1995. Since then, the Fund has consistently outperformed the market averages and its peer group of mutual funds over long periods of time. For more information on the Olstein Funds, or to receive a free prospectus, call shareholder services toll-free at 800-799-2113 or visit their Web site <www.olsteinfunds.com>.

Robert Olstein is a member of numerous professional organizations, including the New York Society of Securities Analysts and the Financial Analysts Federation. He has received a number of honors, including the prestigious Graham & Dodd and Gerald M. Loeb Research Awards, and has testified before the U.S. Senate Banking Committee. He is also frequently quoted in most major national publications including *The New York Times, The Wall Street Journal, Barron's, Business Week,* and *Money Magazine.* He appears frequently on financial television shows on Fox, CNBC, CNN, and many others.

Preface

The Investor's Dilemma

The entire structure of investing has changed. We have always believed that the institutions set up to protect our interests, at the very least, were above reproach. Thus, professional analysts, stock exchanges, corporate managers, regulatory agencies, and independent auditing firms could be relied upon to ensure that investors were receiving accurate information and that problems would be discovered as they emerged, rather than after it was too late.

Now we know better. The events of the early 2000s have demonstrated that the whole system requires a massive overhaul. The problems reported from WorldCom, Enron, Tyco, Cendant, Adelphia Communications, Informix, and Lucent Technologies, among many others, have shaken investor confidence and brought into question the very foundation of trust for the securities markets. This is nothing new. Reform of investment institutions has been necessary many times over the history of the United States and ultimately has led to a better and safer investment environment. So, as difficult as it is to go through a period like this, not to mention the shock of losing large sums of capital we believed safe, the outcome makes a better, stronger, and safer market in the long run.

This book explores the events that were widely reported in the early 2000s, as many publicly listed companies began to unravel. My purpose is not to dwell on the negative but to explain events in a context that will enable you to regain confidence in the markets, become a smarter investor, and know the kinds of risks you face in the ever changing investment marketplace. Certainly, many of the assumptions you used to hold have to be reexamined, and in some cases, abandoned. You cannot simply trust independent auditing firms or their report, until the relationship between management and auditing firms changes and reforms are enacted to fix the obvious problems. You also cannot trust top management to take care of investors' or employees' interests above their own just because they should. While the majority of corporate leaders would not cross the line into criminality, enough have done so that you need to evaluate management as carefully as you can. You also need to revisit your assumptions about analysis itself. Is it enough to study the fundamentals? If those fundamentals have been tinkered with or misrepresented, then your analysis will be flawed as well. So, in this changed environment, you need to develop new analytical tools and methods.

These major areas are just some that need reform, and you need to take defensive actions at once. You cannot afford to wait out the relatively slow moving pace of reform to protect your portfolio and financial future. Although initial changes in many rules and regulations were instituted as soon as the scope of the problem became known, investing now requires that you take a different approach. Unfortunately, some people in frustration, fear, and disgust with all the scandals, have simply moved their capital out of the stock market and will miss what continues to the best opportunity for long-term capital growth. Others—including you, the reader of this book—will profit by looking for ways to ensure the safety of your investments through more conservative selection, using revised tools for the study of companies and closely analyzing financial reports, management qualifications and actions, and a company's track record.

The first section of this book examines the corporate governance and stock market trading system and the abuses that have occurred in recent years, to show how you can protect and grow your capital through understanding how the system worked in the past and how it will work in the future. The second part of this book gives you new approaches to analysis in light of the changed environment, including ideas for research you can perform on your own. Finally, the third part offers a new series of strategies for investing and protecting your capital.

The market is volatile and fast moving. As more and more people use online trading, the pace of change and volume will continue to grow. The market has always been a risky environment, although many investors have failed to recognize this. I propose a combination of new approaches to investing, along with necessary reforms in corporate management activity and the regulatory structure (both for exchanges and government agencies), significant changes in the relationship between auditing firms and management, and a change in the whole market environment.

Investors are not lost in the market; however, you need to recognize that it does not make sense to be optimistic in *every* situation, even when brokers encourage that philosophy. Unfortunately, you also need to recognize that some of the sources of information you have trusted in the past—brokers, analysts, auditing firms, and management itself—cannot necessarily be trusted at all. At the very least, you should no longer assume that these resources are reliable just because many new rules and regulations have been imposed on them.

A central message must come out of recent experiences in the market. The lessons have been expensive and painful, but with greater care, proper analysis, more caution, and a realistic view of how the market works, you can proceed with greater confidence so you can make your capital grow to meet your financial needs for years to come.

Acknowledgments

Reading between the Lies: How to Detect Fraud and Avoid Becoming a Victim of Wall Street's Next Scandal would not have been possible without the generous contributions and extremely hard work of many talented people.

Foremost among these contributors are the staff of Dearborn Trade Publishing, who showed tremendous vision and professionalism in making this book a reality. Editorial Director Don Hull was the true champion of this project from day one, helping to conceptualize a book that would help investors cope with the new realities of a post–Enron, scandal-plagued investment landscape. Publisher Cynthia Zigmund also was an important supporter of the book from concept to publication. Sales Director Paul Mallon and Director of Marketing Leslie Banks were instrumental in making this book a reality through their enthusiastic support. Senior Managing Editor Jack Kiburz and Senior Project Editor Trey Thoelcke skillfully guided the book through the process from original manuscript to final published work. Paula L. Fleming provided copy editing assistance. Art Director Lucy Jenkins and designer Gail Chandler contributed their considerable expertise in overseeing the design of the book's cover, and typesetter Elizabeth Pitts created the book's pages. Buyer Judy Quinnert coordinated the timely printing and binding of the book. I also want to acknowledge the skillful contributions of Michael Thomsett, an experienced financial writer and author of several investment books, who was instrumental in shaping the organization and content of this book.

Robert A. Olstein, chief investment officer of the Olstein Financial Alert Fund, also deserves tremendous credit for his contributions to *Reading between the Lies*. Bob has been critically analyzing companies and their financial statements for decades, and he was extremely generous with his time in sitting down for a long interview, writing an impassioned and incisive Foreword. This is the first time that Bob has cooperated in a book project like this, despite mwany previous requests to do so. I would also like to thank Bill Bongiorno, vice president of the New York–based public relations firm of Mount & Nadler, who arranged for Robert Olstein's participation in the project.

Jean-Marie Eveillard of First Eagle Sogen Funds, David Rocker of Rocker Partners, and Charles Royce of Royce & Associates all were interviewed for this book, and I thank them for their valuable insights and expertise.

I also offer my heartfelt thanks to Elliot R. Goodman, my father and a professor emeritus of political science at Brown University, who meticulously reviewed the entire book and suggested many improvements, both in style and content. His contribution went far beyond the call of parental duty.

I have tried to make the book as complete and up-to-date as possible. With a steady stream of new laws and regulations coming from government agencies, stock exchanges, attorneys general, and trade associations designed to restore investor confidence in the wake of a massive number of corporate scandals, this chapter in America's financial history is far from closed. But the lessons you can learn from this book should arm you to be a much better investor in this new world—to profit while others remain bewildered at how to cope with the post–Enron investment landscape.

Part One

THE UNLEVEL PLAYING FIELD

1

THE LESSON PLAN
How Corporate Officers Shook Up the System

The news coverage tells the whole story. Federal agents move a handcuffed suspect from his expansive, million-dollar estate to a transport vehicle. We know it is early morning and the arrest has taken the man completely by surprise, because he is dressed in pajamas and a bathrobe.

This ultimate disgrace, variations of which have been taking place repeatedly, is a sign of the problems faced by corporate America and the ultimate victims—investors, employees, and stockholders who were robbed by high-level executives of publicly traded companies. The executive being taken off in handcuffs was, only a few months before, at the top of his game, running a huge company and using its resources as a personal piggybank. Therein lies the problem—the misuse of corporate funds by a few powerful individuals.

Is this an isolated problem, limited to a few crooked individuals, or only a symptom of a much wider and more pervasive problem in the back rooms of corporate America? More bombshells, not yet admitted or uncovered, may be yet to come. However, the abuses and illegal acts of the few do not necessarily represent the entire corporate world. The opportunities for misuse of funds and outright theft tempt many, but few are willing to cross the line into criminality, at least in the magnitude that some have, with outright theft in the hundreds of millions of dollars. Those are the headlines, but the real story goes back many decades before the recent news. In almost every case, the revelation of fraud, theft, and cover-up is only the latest chapter in a story that goes back many months, often many years.

Even though the well-publicized, multimillion dollar examples might be the exception, investors are aware that many problems regarding conflicts of interest, abuses of the system by analysts, and lack of oversight of management by boards of directors all contribute to a problem in the corporate world. A majority of Americans—63 percent—feels unprotected "against investment losses and accounting fraud."[1]

We are going through a period in which events demonstrate the need for reform, better oversight, and an overhaul of the corporate governance system. Auditing firms have become too cozy with management, and the boards of directors have become too complacent about their own responsibility to protect investor and employee interests. In virtually every case of abuse, the perception among those guilty of wrongdoing was that, in spite of the rules, no negative consequences would occur. Not only do those who have stolen have to be imprisoned, but they must be forced to pay a heavy financial penalty as well. Money people know that loss of personal freedom is a serious matter, but they understand far better the disaster of financial penalties—losing homes, bank accounts, and investments as a consequence of breaking the law.

THE SECRET LIVES OF ACCOUNTANTS

The acts of stealing money from a company, lying to investors and regulators, and destroying documents are not impulsive and do not occur suddenly. They are the culmination of a series of incremental decisions over a long period of time. The crossing of the line between legal and illegal does not happen in one giant step but is more difficult to pin down as to timing.

Accountants make decisions about how to handle specific transactions. Their judgment is tempered by management's directive, the pressure to meet expectations of investors and Wall Street analysts, and the desire of top management to produce positive results (and keep their jobs *and* large bonuses). One prevailing aspect of many scandals has been that fraud, deception, and falsification of financial statements often took place due to pressures from others. An accounting manager makes a classification decision at the direction of the CFO, or the CFO alters the books to conform to predictions made by analysts. A single incident of deferral or reclassification often can be justified on some basis, and corporate financial types have to be adept at finding justifications. As long as those decisions are minor or isolated, there is little concern; however, when such practices become the norm, the line is crossed and the resulting financial reports are fraudulent.

The accounting world (including not just the green-eyeshade types making the entries, but the CFO and the auditing firms looking over everyone's shoulder) operates in a strange and foreign land called GAAP (Generally Accepted Accounting and Auditing Principles), a series of rules and guidelines that specifies the proper classification of transactions and treatment of every financial matter. GAAP is complex and technical, but because of that very complexity, the rules are also flexible and allow for latitude in interpretation and treatment of assets and liabilities as well as revenues, costs, and expenses. No one "right" answer applies to every situation, and the decisions made in the treatment of financial transactions are a matter of how conservative or aggressive an approach is taken.

Because the decisions are so highly technical, many investors have little or no idea of the degree of interpretation that is practiced. The rules set down by the Financial Accounting Standards Board (FASB) provide only general guidelines, and a capable CFO or auditor can find a way to justify a decision with the right accounting assumption and still conform to the rules—to an extent. [2]

For example, a decision could be made to increase the current period's net income by deferring advertising and promotion expenses, amortizing those expenses over three years. Although the expenses relate primarily to the current year, an aggressive accounting assumption could justify the decision. It could be explained in a memo that:

> Advertising and promotion expenses are to be amortized over 36 months. The benefits expected to be derived from these expenditures will produce revenues over many years; accordingly, it is proper to amortize the subject expenses rather than to treat them as current-year expenses only.

This simple example makes sense, at least on the surface. Under the GAAP rules, an underlying principle states that revenues, costs, and expenses should be *recognized*—placed on the books—in the period where they properly belong. So many decisions refer to this principle. When those decisions are isolated, they usually have a benign result, but in many recent abuses, various forms of aggressive accounting, up to outright fraud, demonstrated that the line of legality was crossed, often in multiples of millions and even billions of dollars.

The open secret in the accounting world—one understood all too well at the top levels of corporate America—is that a lot of decisions can be justified *easily* without violating the general standards expressed under GAAP rules. You, as an investor, need to face this reality when studying the fundamentals of a potential investment.

Investors are not free of blame in this matter. The Wall Street establishment, including analysts, brokers, exchanges, and corporate executives, recognizes that investors prefer predictability over volatility. If you *know* that a company's reported revenues and profits will fall within a specific range, and if you *know* that dividends will be paid every quarter, then you invest with confidence. However, if revenues increase 500 percent one year and then drop by half the next, and large profits are followed by even larger net losses, then how do you make an informed judgment about investment risk? The fact is, both institutional and individual investors favor predictable reporting and are concerned with volatility, whether that volatility occurs in the stock's price or in the company's fundamentals. In this respect, investor pressure is a part of the problem. Many would even say that investors prefer a degree of financial tinkering to smooth out the ups and downs of competitive realities; they would rather see a slow but predictable increase in revenues from one year to the next, a corresponding growth in profits, and a decent, long-term growth in stock price and dividend payout.

Given the desirability of nonvolatility financial results, what is management's job? Some would suggest that the CEO and CFO are responsible for maintaining and improving the market value of stock (as opposed to the more mundane task of running the company). Also, maintaining and boosting the stock price often means making decisions that include accounting adjustments. In years of unexpectedly high revenues and profits, a portion of the windfall may be accrued for reporting in the following year, a practice known as "sugar bowling" revenues and profits. By the same argument, in more disappointing years, expenses may be deferred so that the net result is an even reporting of annual revenues, costs, and expenses.

One big-dollar example involved pharmaceutical giant Merck, which booked more than $12 billion in revenues (mostly patient co-payments at pharmacies) that it never collected. This is not petty cash; the improper revenue accounted for 10 percent of Merck's total revenue over the three years ending in 2001. Merck defended its actions, explaining that the revenues did not affect net profits, as the same amounts were backed out as expenses. The puzzling transaction, Merck claimed, conformed with GAAP rules; even so, the SEC investigated.[3]

Another company accused of questionable treatment of revenues was Halliburton. The company booked $100 million of revenues on projects with cost overruns. Because those revenues were disputed, the SEC questioned whether they should have been recognized. Halliburton changed its accounting assumptions from cost-reimbursable to lump-sum contracting, enabling more liberal revenue recognition.[4]

Tough penalties have been applied for some accounting misstatements. Former Sunbeam CEO Albert Dunlap agreed to a $500,000 fine and a permanent ban on ever again serving as officer or director of a publicly listed company. The penalties were part of a settlement involving the recognition of revenues prematurely and several other irregular accounting practices.[5]

Yet another case involved Adelphia Communications, the now bankrupt cable company that exaggerated cash flow for years 2000 and 2001. The cash flow overstatement was $54 million in 2000 and $28 million in 2001, resulting from improperly including nonrevenue payments as revenues. The company also capitalized its labor costs, artificially boosting net income by about $40 million each year. The company fired its auditing firm, Deloitte & Touche, when it suspended its audit of the company, citing possible criminal activities by corporate executives.[6]

Eventually Adelphia founder John Rigas, both of his sons, and other executives were indicted and charged with fraud. The indictment asked for $2.5 billion in damages. Rigas and the others were charged with taking hundreds of millions of dollars in loans and cash advances, as well as doctoring the books.[7]

The SEC has been expanding its investigation into the question of revenue recognition tactics. Ever growing revelations of wrongdoing by companies engaged in phony swap trades (paper transactions between affiliates that exaggerate revenues on both sides) and other questionable forms of aggressive accounting has supported the fear that such practices are commonplace. Companies such as Dynegy, Homestore.com, Hi-Speed Media, Reliant Resources, and CMS Energy were targeted for investigation of swap transactions. Charles Niemeier, of the SEC Enforcement Division, explained that, "we've seen enough problems that it concerns us." [8]

These financial alterations create the false appearance that all is well, and investors end up deceived that inflated stock prices are justified. Part of the problem lies with the fact that investors like to see low volatility and analysts crave it even more. When analysts' predictions are almost exactly right, analysts are perceived as being good at their job—even though corporate executives tend to "sugar bowl," or defer, so that outcomes fulfill the prophecy.

This is not to say that investors are to blame for the outright fraud that has occurred in some cases, nor that "the system" is to blame. Corporate officers made self-serving decisions for their own financial gain at the expense of investors and stockholders. However, this environment exists partially because the system requires and often demands certain outcomes in its publicly traded companies. The relatively benign act of tinkering with the books to create the expected outcome—without any glaringly obvious fraud—is only one step toward the more damaging decision to step over the line, falsify reports, and steal money from the corporation.

THE TIP OF THE ICEBERG

We tend to believe that a big news story is the starting point when, in fact, it often is only the first public disclosure of a story that has been developing for some time. The problems reported in the early 2000s can be traced back as many as five years, sometimes further.

Former chairman of the Securities and Exchange Commission (SEC) Arthur Levitt recognized the emerging problems in corporate America as early as 1998. In a speech concerning earnings management, Levitt offered a telling prophecy and warning:

> This process has evolved over the years into what can best be characterized as a game among market participants. A game

that, if not addressed soon, will have adverse consequences for America's financial reporting system. A game that runs counter to the very principles behind our market's strength and success.[9]

Levitt further defined the problem:

Too many corporate managers, auditors, and analysts are participants in a game of nods and winks. In the zeal to satisfy consensus earnings estimates and project a smooth earnings path, wishful thinking may be winning the day over faithful representation.[10]

The ex–SEC head cited an example of a major company that missed its earnings estimate by a penny, with the consequence that its stock fell more than 6 percent in a single day, making the point that pressure to "make the numbers" is a dangerous trend.

Such pressure has led many companies to go beyond the relatively simple practice of taking an aggressive accounting stance to the point of outright fraud. This is nothing new. For example, one of the earliest problems involved the large trash hauling company, Waste Management. In 1995, the company was reporting significant revenue and profit growth, but that growth was the result of aggressive acquisitions. Between 1993 and 1995, Waste Management acquired 444 other companies! While insiders and observers agree that mergers and acquisitions may be good business, in the case of Waste Management and others, the motive seemed to be to build up the numbers artificially.[11]

Waste Management used its acquisitions activity to create an artificial form of growth, but the problems didn't end there. The company also shifted current expenses to later periods, improperly capitalized maintenance and interest expenses, and depreciated assets over excessively long periods (reducing current-year depreciation expenses).

These improper practices should have been uncovered and disclosed by the required independent audit. The 1993 audit was the first opportunity for the company's auditor, the now-disgraced Arthur Andersen, to blow the whistle; but although the problems were discovered, Andersen did not question management's decisions.

The decisions concerning the treatment of expenses and the use of acquisitions should have popped up as red flags. However, the problems were not disclosed because of the close relationship between management and the auditing firm itself—one of the greatest problems in the auditing industry. Until 1997, every CFO and chief accountant at Waste Management had been recruited from the ranks of Arthur Andersen auditors. While it is not unusual for companies to recruit accounting personnel from their auditing firms, the consistency in this case contributes to the appearance of conflict.

Another problem was the level of financial relationship between auditor and management. For example, in 1997—several years after improprieties were known—Andersen billed more than $19 million in audit and consulting fees to Waste Management. An outsider should wonder about the motive here: were Andersen to condemn strongly accounting practices in the company, would the company look for a more favorable opinion from another firm? Would Andersen lose its lucrative $19 million client because Waste Management went opinion shopping? The question has to be raised, at the very least, in attempting to determine why the "independent" audit did not disclose, report, and fix the obvious violations of GAAP standards at Waste Management.

While independent audits are meant to ensure the accuracy of a company's reports, they do not always achieve that result. In some cases, a change in management leads to an internal discovery of improper practices. In the case of Cendant, a merger led to revelations of aggressive accounting and charges of outright fraud.

Cendant was created by a merger in 1997 between CUC and HFS. The newly formed company (best known for ownership of companies like Avis, Century 21, Coldwell Banker, Howard Johnson, and Ramada) soon reported that the previous entity, CUC, had inflated reported income. During 1996 and 1997, this amounted to $500 million in overreported revenues. Also, in 1996, the company began acquiring other companies to cover the accounting irregularities. The scheme was so large that investors lost an estimated $19 billion in market value when the stock plunged.[12]

The fraud committed by accounting executives at CUC included early recognition of income, nonaccounting for revenue cancellations or offsets, inflated reporting through acquisitions, altering reports to meet analysts' predictions, and disparate booking procedures (recognizing income in the current year and deferring related costs until a future period).

Auditing firm Ernst & Young settled shareholder lawsuits for $2.8 billion and also paid $335 million to settle a suit brought by the new Cendant management. In 2000, three former CUC executives pleaded guilty to fraud. They were former CFO Cosmo Corigliano, former controller Anne Pember, and former accountant Casper Sabatino.

During the same period, database management company Informix was making questionable accounting decisions as well. Revenues for 1996 were reported at $939 million, a 32 percent increase over the previous year. In 1997, the company admitted it was using barter arrangements with some of its larger licensees and that resellers were having difficulty selling products into the market. The company was forced to restate earnings when auditors uncovered side agreements in violation of contracts with vendors as well as other accounting irregularities. The total overstated revenue between 1994 and 1996 came out to $311 million, and overstated profits came to $244 million.

The violations at Informix were more sophisticated than the better understood practice of shifting numbers between years. Informix backdated some sales agreements, made side agreements with customers, accrued income from sources that were not creditworthy, recognized revenues even when disputes were not settled, and inflated license fees.

As serious as these violations were, independent auditors did uncover them, leading to a restatement of earnings. In this case, the audit system worked—it found violations and exposed them. You can never expect a system to anticipate and prevent fraud; however, the type of intentional deception at Informix could be curtailed if decision makers faced severe consequences, including enforcement of civil and criminal laws leading to financial penalties and jail time.

HIGH LEVEL DECEPTION

If $19 billion seems like a lot of money, imagine the relative size of $250 billion, or one-quarter of a trillion dollars. That was the loss to investors from accounting fraud committed at Lucent Technologies.

This AT&T spin-off started in 1996, and over the next four years, Lucent's stock price rose by more than 1,000 percent. Lucent became the most widely held stock in the United States. Investors enjoyed the impressive growth, supported by ever better reported revenue and income compared to relatively unexciting AT&T stock.

Then, in January 2000, management announced that it would not meet analysts' target revenues or profits. The stock immediately lost one-fourth of its market value. Matters continued downhill from there, and a year later, the company announced a $1 billion net loss for the preceding year. An SEC investigation was launched and uncovered many accounting irregularities that had taken place over the previous five years. These were not isolated incidents; they represented corporate accounting policy.

Violations included:

- Reducing liabilities by changing accounting assumptions
- Overstating accounts receivable and inventory levels
- Recognition of revenues not earned
- Reduction in bad debt reserves even though receivable levels had risen
- Reduction of inventory obsolescence levels even though inventory levels had risen
- Shifting of current-year expenses to later periods
- Improper reclassification of reserves into income

The violations that occurred at Lucent were so troubling because they were blatant and numerous—and because Lucent had been so highly regarded on Wall Street. It was perceived as a rock-solid, well-managed company, not a fly-by-night newcomer. The problems revealed in the Lucent case show that even a large, widely held company stock cannot be assumed to be safe just because it is so well regarded among investors and analysts.

These multimillion dollar losses could be curtailed if auditors discovered and reported them in time. The failure of auditing firms to provide the basic watchdog service expected of them is one of the more troubling aspects of today's market problems. The assurance provided through the unqualified opinion giving blessing to the books, as it turns out, often is but a shallow and automatic step conferred in spite of underlying, glaring problems. For example, shouldn't it have seemed suspicious to auditors of Tyco when, in 1997, the company moved its legal headquarters to the tax haven of Bermuda? By the year 2001, the company had formed over 150 subsidiaries, many in Barbados, the Cayman Islands, and other tax haven nations.

Auditors are not the only group at fault. Boards of directors have not only failed in these cases to exercise their "duty of care" standard; the boards themselves often have been guilty of abuses.[13]

In 2002, Tyco's board approved $20 million in bonuses to one board member named Frank Walsh for handling a large acquisition. The failure to disclose this inside deal led to litigation. However, a more serious offense was committed by former CEO L. Dennis Kozlowski. He was indicted in June 2002 for falsifying records in an attempt to avoid New York city and state sales taxes on the purchase of a $13.2 million personal art collection. He created false invoices and had empty boxes shipped to New Hampshire in an attempt to circumvent the sales taxes.[14] But there is more: Kozlowski and former CFO Mark Swartz were indicted in August 2002 for stealing more than $600 million by selling Tyco stock at inflated prices.

In the case of Tyco, the 10-K filed with the SEC disclosed neither the offshore subsidiary activity nor the questionable accounting gyrations involving those companies. In a complex scheme, the offshore subsidiary would borrow money and relend the funds to U.S. Tyco units, often at higher interest rates. The U.S. units were able to claim tax deductions for the interest. This went beyond good tax avoidance, because the purpose of generating loans through subsidiaries was to move tax benefits into the United States and other countries where taxes were assessed.

The abuses at Tyco certainly bring into question the role of the board of directors. Their job is supposed to be to protect shareholders' interests, but all too often boards function to enrich their own pals and themselves at the expense of investors. The much publicized troubles at Enron involve an array of abuses, but one of the more glaring was in 2000 when the board approved $750 million in cash bonuses to its executives. That represented about three-quarters of the company's profits for the latest year. At the same time, the board also approved a line of credit for CEO Kenneth Lay, allowing him to repay the loan with stock. This enabled Lay to defer reporting the sale of stock up to one full year.

Lay used the $7.5 million line of credit repeatedly, often maxing out the line and repaying it with stock on the same day. In one year, Lay managed to convert stock into $77 million in cash. The Enron abuses went on well before that, despite warnings that the board chose to ignore. In February 1999, Enron's audit committee warned the board that the company's accounting was "high risk." However, the warning was ignored by the board, and no further action was taken. Those high-risk practices included a phony $60 million profit created by a fake energy deal Enron entered into with Merrill Lynch.[15] The deal was canceled later, but accounting irregularities designed to cover Enron's ever growing undisclosed debts were standard practice in the company. Off balance sheet partnerships created by company president Jeffrey Skilling were complex and practically impossible to understand, but the problems they were designed to hide were substantial. By 2001, Enron had more than 800 offshore subsidiaries and affiliates, many in tax havens. Skilling created the complexities as part of an accounting and corporate strategy understood by few. The purpose of the complexity was to remove debt not only from the books but also from the financial statement's footnotes. It was described on the inside of Enron as "accounting nirvana."[16]

By December 2001, the debt overtook the company's ability to hide it. The debt level was staggering: $13.1 billion in direct debt plus another $18 billion for Enron subsidiaries and an estimated $20 billion off balance sheet debt—over $50 billion in all.

Former CFO Andrew Fastow was arrested on October 2, 2002, and indicted on a range of charges that could result in more than 100 years of jail time, including mail fraud, conspiracy, and a host of other securities violations. This was the first arrest of a former Enron executive, probably to be followed by many more.

The problems at Enron soon spread to include its auditing firm Arthur Andersen. In January 2002, partner David Duncan in Andersen's Houston offices admitted that documents concerning the Enron troubles had been destroyed in Andersen's offices. In March 2002, Andersen was indicted for obstruction of justice, and the auditing firm pleaded guilty in June. In August, the auditing firm agreed to pay $60 million to settle claims by stockholders and creditors.

The question of additional charges against individuals remains up in the air. The very complexity and scope of the Enron scheme delayed investigators' ability to pin down those responsible and make a legal case, and the destruction of documents made the case harder to investigate. The Enron story demonstrates that complexity makes a trail, but that trail often is difficult to trace. For example, it seems that no one knows for sure how much of investors' and employees' funds were misappropriated. Exorbitant bonuses and lines of credit authorized by the board are only a starting point; no doubt there is much more to the story than investigators will ever determine.

BROKERAGE CONFLICTS

Management and boards have failed to execute what should be their primary objective; working to protect and promote the interests of stockholders. Auditing firms have acted as partners to top management or have observed questionable practices without pursuing them.

Another group whose involvement is highly questionable is the world of Wall Street brokers and analysts. The dismal record of most analysts and money managers is well documented, and brokers often operate with severe conflicts of interest. When their firms serve as investment bankers for a company, should the same company's brokers advise clients to buy and hold shares? Brokers often continue giving optimistic advice, even when internal memos show that the companies involved were of questionable value. This happened frequently in the dot.com bubble and meltdown of the late 1990s and early 2000s.

Another, more recent example of questionable brokerage advice involves WorldCom, the telephone and Internet data company that filed for bankruptcy protection in July 2002—the largest bankruptcy in history.

In August 2002, Salomon Smith Barney telecom industry analyst Jack Grubman resigned, taking home a $32.2 million severance package. A series of investigations by the SEC, NASD, and the U.S. House Financial Services Committee centered on Grubman's recommendations to investors concerning WorldCom. Also in August 2002, WorldCom was one of a handful of companies that failed to certify its records as requested by the SEC. Former controller David Myers was arrested and charged with conspiracy and fraud after admitting that $3.85 billion in expenses were improperly recorded as long-term capital investments, artificially inflating earnings. In subsequent months, that amount was boosted to over $9 billion.

Steven Brabbs, former vice president for international finance and control, was warned by Myers in a January e-mail not to have any further meetings with Arthur Andersen auditors to discuss accounting practices.[17] Clearly, Myers knew at that point that there were matters worth hiding or he would not have demanded that his internal accounting people stop discussing accounting matters with the auditing firm. This order is damaging evidence against Myers as controller of WorldCom.

Former CEO Bernard Ebbers and former CFO Scott Sullivan also were targets of SEC investigations in 2002. Their involvement with improperly capitalizing over $9 billion in expenses to exaggerate profits is at the heart of the SEC question. Ebbers additionally is being investigated for taking $408 million in personal loans from WorldCom to cover margin calls. Sullivan, along with David Myers, was formally charged with securities fraud and conspiracy.[18]

Individuals as well as companies are being scrutinized. An investigation was carried out regarding Martha Stewart and her questionable timing for dumping shares of ImClone stock. While her case is a relatively small matter given the scope of Enron, WorldCom, and others, Stewart's high profile has attracted a lot of attention. Former ImClone CEO Sam Waksal, already in trouble for ordering documents shredded, creation of offshore accounts, and securities fraud charges (pledging shares he no longer owned as collateral for a bank loan), advised several people to sell ImClone shares on December 27, 2001. The FDA announced the following day that it was refusing to consider ImClone's application for approval of its cancer drug, Erbitux, causing ImClone's stock price to plummet.

Waksal was charged with advising his daughter and father to sell shares on December 27. Martha Stewart also sold 4,000 shares on December 27. She claims the sale was the result of a standing stop-loss order to sell if the stock's price fell below $60 a share—a claim that could not be substantiated with written records. Waksal faces possible penalties for conspiracy, perjury, and obstruction of justice from each insider tip he provided. Each count carries up to $250,000 and five years in jail. He also was sentenced to multiyear jail terms for securities and bank fraud charges. Stewart's high profile does not help in this matter. After several months of news concerning corporate misbehavior and record bankruptcy filings, what she claims as a coincidence did not impress the public or investigators. A second consequence of the negative publicity was a 70 percent drop in value of Martha Stewart Living Omnimedia stock. Although not directly related to the questionable trade, the stock is so closely associated with Stewart that its stockholders suffered mightily with a multibillion dollar loss in market value.

As other investigations emerge involving AOL/Time Warner, Adelphia Communications, and other potential abusers—not to mention continuing problems for the auditing industry—the story of corporate abuse and misuse of funds continues to develop. More than $700 billion in assets were listed among some of the largest bankruptcies in 2001 and 2002.[19] In 2001, the total bankruptcy count was $230 billion, a record 80 percent higher than total assets reported in bankruptcies for 2000, and involved 257 large companies. The total value of bankruptcies in 2002 was $368 billion, involving 191 public companies, according to BankruptcyData.com.

What will result from all of these scandals besides staggering losses to investors, former employees, and the American economy? Hopefully, we'll see improved accounting standards, including the expensing of stock options, better enforcement of existing rules, and better safeguards on the part of exchanges, auditing firms, regulatory agencies, and internal management. Whether behavior changes due to a sense of ethics or simply the fear of being imprisoned, I expect to see positive changes resulting from a troubling period of corporate abuse.

2

HOW THE SYSTEM
WAS ABUSED

The field of accounting is highly technical and not terribly interesting to outsiders. Thus, opportunities to abuse the rules abound. The complexities and scope of the rules allow decision makers latitude to tinker with the numbers without actually breaking the rules. The problem, of course, is that recent trends have demonstrated that some publicly listed companies operate in what ex-SEC chairman Arthur Levitt called:

> . . . the gray area between legitimacy and outright fraud—
> a gray area where the accounting is being perverted; where
> managers are cutting corners; and where earnings reports
> reflect the desires of management rather than the underlying
> financial performance of the company.[1]

Some accounting decisions are perfectly acceptable and a matter of individual interpretation. Some companies take a conservative stance and choose to err on the side of prudence. Others make more aggressive interpretations to favor booking higher profits now and defer losses to later years. As long as the decisions made can be justified by the broad accounting guidelines in use today, no laws are broken. However, some corporate officers have crossed the line and moved from aggressive interpretation into the more troubling realm of outright fraud.

In recent years, corporations have increasingly relied upon "pro forma" reporting of earnings, a practice that one study shows can mislead investors about profitability. According to a University of Michigan Business School study involving more than 12,000 quarterly earnings reports between 1988 and 1999:

> Pro forma earnings are an increasingly popular measure of earnings that excludes certain expenses a company deems nonrecurring, noncash, or otherwise not important for understanding the future value of the firm. Examples include restructuring costs, depreciation, amortization, losses on the sale of assets, and a variety of other miscellaneous charges.[2]

The problem with dependence on restated earnings using pro forma methods is that the method can be used, intentionally or unintentionally, in ways that are more accurate and reflective of real conditions. However, one of the researchers in the study, professor of accounting Russell J. Lundholm, explains:

> Prior research of pro forma earnings can be interpreted as supporting the position that investors are not misled by firms' use of such earnings. We come to a very different conclusion. The market does not appear to appreciate the future cash flow implications of the excluded expenses. Rather, the market appears to be systematically fooled by the firms' use of pro forma earnings."[3]

This study points out one unavoidable fact: if today's earnings are adjusted to make results appear more favorable, those results have to be paid for in the future. The systematic use of pro forma accounting builds in an illusion that earnings are greater than they appear, and the effect is felt in very severely reduced future cash flow. The study cited above concluded that on average, every dollar of excluded expenses in pro forma reporting resulted in 83 cents of reduced future cash flow.

The issue was explained by Bear Stearns in a September 2002 study, which began with this statement:

> The recent wave of corporate accounting scandals has given rise to a considerable amount of skepticism regarding the use of "pro forma" earnings measures. Much of this suspicion appears to stem from uncertainty about how pro forma numbers are calculated and when they form an appropriate basis for stock valuation.[5]

The problem is, in fact, a glaring one. Without specific accounting standards in play, analysts and corporations can adjust earnings on a pro forma basis any way they wish. Companies can make their numbers look promising, even when they lose money. Pro forma (as a matter of form) can be used to show what would have happened if the company did not have to pay income taxes, R&D costs, or payroll taxes—an unrealistic approach but one often used.[6] Comparing cash flow and earnings can reveal potential problems. If net income is far higher than cash flow—especially if the difference breaks with established trends—that may signal that the company is booking revenues aggressively or underreporting costs and expenses.

Forensic accountant Howard Schilit also mentions comparisons between earnings and cash flow as a valuable place to start. "One of the things I look for is a big drop in cash flow from operations even though net income continues to look very healthy."[7]

Other problem areas include questionable valuation. When Enron's PE ratio rocketed to 69 early in 2000, many investors failed to question why. Also in 2000, 16 members of Enron's top management sold off $164 million worth of shares by exercising stock options. At the same time, those same executives were claiming their stock was under-valued. Enron was also characterized by highly complex explanations of their financial transactions, to the extent that no one could understand the transactions or their explanations.[8]

It is unlikely that the origins of pro forma reporting or any other form of adjustment in accounting originated with the intention of deceiving investors. Rather, the problems of overstated earnings, aggressive accounting policies, and artificially propped-up stock prices have resulted from the gradual increase in questionable policies over time. It's unlikely, for example, that the decision to misrepresent the financial condition of a company is made suddenly. Once a stock's price is boosted using small, questionable steps, continuing the prac-tice from one quarter to the next becomes increasingly necessary. The practice builds as a series of steps in a longer course of action and even-tually becomes corporate policy. It occurs not only because the oppor-tunities are there but also because, traditionally, there was very little chance of getting caught and no one had really defined how far one could go. So someone who began by merely tinkering with the numbers via pro forma reporting, to meet Wall Street expectations, bent the rules for a few years, only to find that keeping up the appearance of financial success demanded more and more as time went by. Ulti-mately, corporate officers who became involved in this way seemed unable to stop for several reasons.

- *No one was questioning their practices.* Unfortunately for investors, regulators, boards of directors, or industry groups offered no oversight that effectively questioned the aggressive accounting decisions of CEOs and CFOs. Even independent auditing com-panies, whose auditors knew of the practices, often looked the other way because they were receiving large audit fees as well as consulting fees. Questioning or challenging corporate decisions could mean losing a big client.
- *Stopping could mean the whole scheme would unravel.* Those breaking the law and getting away with it built themselves into a box of sorts. Just as the small-time embezzler cannot take a vacation be-cause someone else would look at the books, the big-time corpo-rate thieves could not afford to retire or to stop their practices.

Because the deception involved ever growing misrepresentation of the numbers, any honest accounting would uncover the truth and require big adjustments, often in the millions or even billions of dollars. In fact, some of these schemes were finally uncovered when new management took over.

- *Compensation was tied to results, so the incentive was strong to keep the scheme going.* Traditionally, compensation for top officers has been tied to financial results. This has two aspects: fundamentals (sales, profits, dividends) and the stock price. While the two are related, they are different aspects of "results." So a CEO or CFO is expected to produce not only ever growing sales and profits, but also to keep investors happy with ever growing market value in the stock. If they succeed, their bonus and stock option package grows as well. If they fail, their compensation reflects disappointing results, and the executive might even be fired. The compensation packages have motivated some corporate officers to profit by exercising stock option grants for obscene rewards, often at the expense of shareholders.

- *The nature of greed dictates that there is never enough.* The level of bonuses, stock options, and other forms of compensation paid to CEOs and CFOs is downright puzzling in some of the more abusive cases. Deceptions continued well after hundreds of millions were taken, even artificially inflating the value of stock to earn more profits. The fact that these actions were clearly illegal did not seem to bother the officers. Once the schemes began, the amount of money was never enough. They wanted more and more, and simple judgment about risks seemed to disappear entirely. Money beyond rational needs becomes the abstract symbol of power. It appears that the power, added to the remote chance of being caught, led the abusers to notch up the theft to ridiculous levels.

- *Ego enters the picture, too, and stopping is no longer a choice.* At some point along the path, beginning with acceptable levels of aggressive accounting and ending up with fraud, conspiracy, and obstruction of justice charges, the individual ego begins taking over and the person's judgment becomes impaired. This explanation is the only one possible for the level and scope of theft in many cases. No doubt, the individual does not realize the degree to which the plan has veered from the original path until that cell door closes and locks behind them.

These factors add together to allow (and even encourage) corporate officers to abuse the system. While a minority of executives stepped over the line and broke the law, these motivators remain, and the system needs to be reformed. No one really knows specifically where that line is, and the whole system—involving outside auditors, boards of directors, regulatory agencies, accounting standards, compensation packages, and even Wall Street expectations—makes abuse of the system possible.

Not only numbers are falsified or miscommunicated; even visual aids published by companies mislead investors. For example, in Zales Corporation's 2001 annual report, a chart plotting net sales had a baseline of $1 billion instead of zero, showing a highly distorted view of what had actually occurred. In another case, the Dial Corporation reported a drop in earnings per share, but the chart used to supplement the report was scaled improperly, so that the drop was downplayed.[9]

Whether intentionally inaccurate or not, such charts are only an obvious form of poor communication. More troubling are the outright fraudulent schemes that started by adjusting results to comply with the predictions of high-profile Wall Street analysts. The market reacts to earnings reports, not so much for what they represent in terms of corporate performance but more for how they measure up to what analysts have predicted will occur. So, if earnings results are lower than expectations, the stock price is going to fall, at least in the short term. The CEO or CFO whose current year's bonus depends on the stock price has a compelling incentive to adopt an aggressive interpretation of complex transactions. Thus, the analysts' predictions are true, and the stock's price rises.

THE PRESSURE FROM STOCKHOLDERS

Some of the more capable corporate executives who broke the rules can be compared to those committing art fraud. A few highly talented artists have used their abilities to duplicate masterpieces—not trusting their abilities to create original work. Perhaps the money in art fraud is too good to resist. By the same argument, some executives have a real talent for accounting but have chosen to use their skills to obscure the truth, hide the deception, and enrich themselves at the expense of the stockholders. That is not the whole story, though. The environment itself allowed and even encouraged the deception, to a degree.

The truth is, once someone becomes a stockholder in a company, they expect that stock price to rise over time. They do not like losing money, and they do not like volatility. So a happy stockholder is one whose investment decisions were well timed, whose fundamental analysis was correct, and whose choices are rewarded with profits and ever growing equity in the market.

Knowing all of this, the capable executive who wants to keep his or her job is told that the year-end bonus and stock option package will be determined by "results." With this in mind, a hard question has to be asked: What is the executive's job? The traditional, but perhaps naïve, answer is that executives are capable leaders who take companies into more productive markets; cut costs and expenses to improve the bottom line; best competitors through deft handling of market forces, intuitive decisions, and exceptional acquisitions; and gain the respect and admiration of everyone from the board of directors down to the mail room.

That image certainly describes the majority of American business success stories. The capable executive possesses market and leadership qualities that take them to the top, and their performance often is measured via expansion in terms of sales and profits, employment, and market share. However, in a minority of cases, executives are self-serving and looking for ways to increase their own wealth, at the expense of the shareholders.

What is the executive's job? Do we expect a company's leadership to represent the interests of the shareholders, run the company well, and ensure ever growing market success? Can these goals be achieved while, at the same time, the executive is well compensated? Executive compensation packages are based on the idea that incentives will help everyone. Unfortunately, the pressure to perform well has led some to abuse the system.

Investors do not like volatility. If the stock price moves 5 to 10 percent every week, how can investors know what is going on or where the stock price is heading? Whether following the fundamentals or just charting the price, high volatility is a stock makes it impossible to predict its direction. However, while most of the analytical emphasis on volatility is on the stock's price, equally important volatility in the fundamentals is often ignored. While many investors claim they follow the fundamentals of their investments, they tend to pay more attention to technical indicators—market price and volume, index movements, chart patterns, and so forth—and largely to ignore trends in sales and profits.

Of course, the stock price and trend reflects what is happening in the fundamentals. So even the technician cannot really afford to ignore the overall picture, even though many do. In studying results over time, consistent trends in sales and profits should raise questions. However, rarely are even the most predictable results questioned. Why?

Just as investors dislike volatility in the stock price, they also are troubled by volatility in year-to-year financial results. Steady growth in the financial results is reassuring, letting one believe with reasonable certainty that the growth trend will continue. A conservative or moderate investor takes comfort in the analyst's predictions, because the results are easy to anticipate. Low volatility gives the investor a sense of security.

In practice, however, sales and profits may gyrate wildly over time. One year's sales could represent growth of 200 percent over the previous year, and then the year after that, sales could be 50 percent of the year before. Profits, too, may vary widely from one quarter or year to another, for a variety of reasons. The greater the variance, the more difficult tracking and predicting the trend becomes. Volatility in the fundamentals usually translates to volatility in stock prices as well, which is not desirable.

In this environment, where the Wall Street community of investors rewards stability and fears volatility, a great incentive exists to smooth out quarterly or annual variations. As long as profits are not falsified, the unspoken agreement between investors and corporations is that some fixing is allowable as long as it enhances the appearance of stability. The accounting rules allow for some accruing and deferring without such adjustments becoming violations of GAAP.

Opportunities are found within the rules, partially because of the highly technical nature of accounting itself and partially because corporations want to be able to control what is reported. This works for everyone as long as the results are not deceptive. However, when internal controls permit abuse, executives decide to enrich themselves by going over that line, and that is where the trouble begins.

The common factor in virtually every case of corporate misconduct is an environment of poor internal control. This most likely occurs where competition is so keen that getting results becomes more important than how they are achieved. When you see unusually fast growth in sales and profits or exceptionally high one-time charges, internal controls might be lacking, letting real problems remain undisclosed. How do we reconcile the turmoil of big change with the desire for stability in fundamentals and stock prices? In a well-controlled internal environment, one-time charges should not occur. The identification of proper accounting practices would ensure that, except for rare occasions, extraordinary items reflecting changes in past sales, profits, and valuation would not take place.

Another symptom of potential misconduct is unusually high levels of acquisitions. While acquiring smaller companies often is an effective method of achieving growth, it also enables the company to inflate its profits, reduce costs and expenses, and cause the stock price to rise artificially. While such practices are the minority, the scope of abuse in some cases (notably WorldCom and Waste Management) make the acquisitions game particularly troubling.

Two other symptoms worth noting: a relationship with outside auditors that is too close and involves high compensation for nonaudit consulting; and a board of directors lacking independent members.

In several instances of corporate abuse, the problems began when auditing firms knew of corporate practices but failed to blow the whistle. This misconduct took place over and over, and in some instances, one or more of the Big Five firms settled civil lawsuits because they knew, or should have known, of misleading practices or even outright fraud.

Boards of directors should provide an oversight duty, ensuring that operational management is conducting business in the best interests of stockholders and *not* profiting at the expense of the shareholder. Unfortunately, some boards are so inbred that they are not willing or able to protect the investor. Members may include executives from subsidiary companies, or corporate board members may sit on each other's board and rubber-stamp whatever the CEO wants. In some outright cases of abuse, boards are coconspirators in schemes to take money from investors and enrich their CEO and CFO pals. Perhaps the worst examples involved Tyco and Enron. The Tyco board authorized a $20 million bonus, without disclosing the decision, to one of the board members for handling an acquisition. Enron's board authorized cash bonuses representing three-quarters of the latest period's reported profits.

HOW THE NUMBERS LIE

False adjustments of corporate results can take place through a complex array of tricks and methods. These usually can be classified in five major areas:

1. Falsifying revenues
2. Recording revenues in the wrong period
3. Falsifying costs and expenses
4. Treatment of liabilities
5. Mergers and acquisitions and related accounting tricks

Falsifying Revenues

While some forms of aggressive accounting are considered acceptable within the rules of GAAP, the actual falsification of transactions clearly steps over the line. A defense of aggressive accounting does not justify the decision to make up numbers, and falsification requires a conscious decision.

This is achieved in a number of ways. One method is to overstate the amount of revenue. For example, a corporation may enter a contract to provide services to a customer. However, when the revenue is recorded, the amount exceeds the contractual level. If this practice is common, a company's annual revenue can be so far overstated, that the effect on its stock prices is false as well. A variation of this practice is the outright nonexistent revenue. When an executive decides to book revenue that does not exist, they are not even remotely connecting it to justifiable sales activity.

Some corporate officers have used a second method for inflating revenues, involving the reclassification of balance sheet items. For example, reserves or liabilities are moved over and reported as revenues without justification. An extreme variation of this is treating loan proceeds as revenue rather than as liabilities.

Other methods have been used as well. For example, one-time gains can be accomplished by selling undervalued assets. The problems occur when the incentive for selling assets is to inflate the numbers rather than for a legitimate corporate purpose. An example could involve the sale of real estate. Under GAAP rules, real estate is always reported at purchase price, and improvements are to be depreciated, usually over 31 years or more. However, if real estate was purchased many years ago when prices were relatively low, the balance sheet value could be significantly less than true market value. So selling that asset today would cause a capital gain.

The decision to sell in this case is augmented by the decision to classify proceeds as revenue rather than as a capital gain. It distorts the true picture with the motive of deceiving investors and inflating income. A similar distortion occurs when "other" income (nonoperating income from investments, interest, or overseas exchange rates, for example) is classified as operating revenues, with the result that operating profits are falsely inflated.

Finally, revenues are created fraudulently through fictitious sales between a parent company and a subsidiary for the sole purpose of inflating the dollar amount, or between affiliated companies when no services actually are provided.

Recording Revenues in the Wrong Period

A more popular trick is to recognize income before it is actually earned or to defer recognition of income until a future year. The decision depends on the desired outcome. If the idea is to inflate current revenue and profits, then revenues are recorded now even though they will not be earned until later. In an unusually good year, some revenue may be deferred for future use, so that revenues and profits will be evened out and less volatility reported. The practice of deferring revenue for later reporting is called *sugar bowling*. In a general sense, the practice of understating actual results in a current year is considered relatively benign. The practice of overstating current year revenues is far more serious, often crossing the line into outright fraud.

One of the standards of GAAP is that all transactions should be *recognized*—put into the books—in the proper period. Thus, accruing or deferring is a useful tool for matching up revenues, costs, and expenses in the appropriate period. That means that revenue should be booked in the period when customers have accepted the contract, when goods have been shipped, or when services have been provided. If revenues are prepaid, they should be deferred and then recognized later when the proper action has occurred—customer acceptance, shipment, or provision of services.

Falsifying Costs and Expenses

Costs and expenses also can be recorded in misleading ways, which usually involve pushing them into later periods or classifying them incorrectly in the books and records.

Accounting tricks involving the treatment of costs and expenses are among the easiest, most popular, and best understood methods for changing financial outcome and valuation. In the case of corporate executives, one of the most difficult tricks to catch was payment in stock instead of cash. The same approach—providing stock as a substitute form of payment—also has been used in merger and acquisition activity, payments to service providers, and others, all as a means of keeping costs and expenses off the books.

Another form of falsification is simply deferring expense recognition to a later period. A cost or expense related to current-year sales is set up as a deferred charge on the balance sheet and later moved over to the proper classification. Under GAAP rules, costs and expenses are supposed to be recognized in the same period as related income. If corporate CEOs and CFOs can direct adjustments in violation of GAAP without limit, then ultimately the value and accuracy of financial statements is destroyed completely, and outcomes can look like anything, including steady growth in profits even when business is falling off.

The opposite technique can be used as well—prerecognition of costs or expenses. This lowers current-year costs, a variation on deferring income and another way of sugar bowling profits in anticipation of disappointing results in future periods. Companies subject to cyclical economic changes might use this technique during highly profitable years to even out reported results. Like income deferral, prerecognition of costs and expenses is not frowned upon to the same degree as falsely reporting profits that don't exist, because the real situation is "better" than reported. The purpose of prerecognition is to stabilize results and reduce volatility. Similar forms of prerecognition of costs and expenses involve writing off research and development costs, retiring prepaid expenses and acquisition costs, and other methods for piling expenses into the current year instead of amortizing them over future periods, as would be more correct.

More troubling is the reduction of current-year costs and expenses by one method or another. A favorite has been to change accounting assumptions. For example, the company might liberalize its policies concerning accounts receivable bad debt reserves, or it reduces reserves for writing off obsolete inventory, with the result that related costs and expenses fall as well. Even though the newly formed reserves are inadequate for the realistic level of losses, the desired result is achieved: lower costs and expenses, thus higher profits. One advantage to using this method is that it often involves accounting complexities that most people do not understand, so the abuse is not questioned by the typical stockholder.

Another way in which expenses are reduced in the current year is by capitalizing them. This creates a variation on the more direct deferral method. By setting up costs and expenses as assets and then amortizing them, the current-year charge is spread over several future years. Again, by increasing profits, the result is likely to be artificially inflated stock prices and the deception of stockholders—plus higher bonuses and stock options to executives.

Treatment of Liabilities

One of the more difficult methods to trace involves booking revenue in the current period but failing to record related liabilities. In some instances, a particular type of revenue has an associated cost or expenses that will be paid out later. For example, a commission liability accrues when sales are made on a commission basis. So the corporation increases its margin by accruing the income but leaving off the commission that relates to it.

Accounting assumptions also reduce liabilities. Setting up reserves for future losses is typical, and those reserves can be lowered even when increases would be more appropriate. The result is higher net income than should be accurately reported. Recording too-low reserves for bad debts, for example, not only reduces bad debt expenses but also understates the liability for those debts.[10]

Legitimate debts are sometimes not even recorded on the books of the company. This practice is fraudulent not only because it overstates profits, but also because it enables the company to create the illusion of continued growth where the opposite might be true. The extreme example of this was Enron, where the smoke and mirrors were so complex that the billions of debt disclosed in the 2001 bankruptcy came as a surprise to most observers. Enron used its hundreds of offshore subsidiaries and partnerships to achieve a complex scheme of asset swaps and off-the-record liabilities.

Liabilities can legitimately exist off the balance sheet without breaking GAAP rules, but they are still supposed to be disclosed in footnotes. When liabilities are left out of the footnotes or the footnotes themselves are misleading, then it is impossible for investors or analysts to value the company properly. Typical of these so-called contingent liabilities would be pending lawsuits, in which the liability consists of the potential loss in the case of an unfavorable judgment against the company, and obligations under long-term leases. While the company is obligated for lease payments, that liability is not recorded as a liability on the books. It is disclosed via a footnote.

A fraudulent method for overstating profits is to reclassify liabilities as income. The previously mentioned technique of classifying debt as income is one example. A legitimate deferred credit relating to a future year may also be reclassified as current income with the same result: overstating this year's revenue and profit.

Mergers and Acquisitions and Related Accounting Tricks

By far the most complex schemes—and the most difficult for most people to understand—involve the magic tricks that are worked with mergers and acquisitions. Companies often find continuing a healthy expansion program difficult when they saturate their primary market. Selling a single product or service, or having a finite customer base, eventually causes saturation, even for sector leaders. Profits can be expected to level out as well. In this situation, companies can continue to expand by branching out into other industries, diversifying their product or service base. The most efficient way to do that is by acquiring smaller competitors or merging with them.

A well-structured merger achieves great advantages for the newly enlarged company. The joining eliminates competition while increasing working capital and equity base. The traditional point of view among analysts has been that mergers and acquisitions are good for everyone and that stockholders on both sides of the transaction probably benefit—and that was true until some unscrupulous CEOs and CFOs figured out how to take advantage of the system. Waste Management and Cendant, among others, used several accounting adjustments to falsify true results, mergers and acquisitions being their primary means of deception.

One method is a corporate-level pyramid scheme involving payments in stock, called the *roll-up*. The company buys up a lot of small competitors, making payments in stock, and turns around and sells inflated-value shares to the public. This creates short-term profits so that earlier investors make a lot of money (assuming they sell in time) but those coming in later buy at highly inflated prices and lose most of their capital.

Another trick is to inflate profits by treating current expenses as acquisition expenses. These are piled up and written off just before the acquisition, rather than amortized over future periods. This has the effect of inflating future profits (as well as stock prices) and making the acquisition look more profitable than it actually was.

Shifting losses into short years (also called *stub periods*) is another trick. When the fiscal year of an acquired company is different than that of the acquiring company, its final year is shortened to bring its reporting into line. By piling up expenses in the stub period rather than spreading them over several years, a one-time loss shows up in the short year, and full-year profits are inflated.

Similarly, corporations set up reserves at the time of acquisition to be amortized over many years. By releasing those reserves early into revenues, companies can control their reported growth. However, as their rate of reported growth increases, it becomes necessary to inflate revenues more and more, which explains the need to acquire more companies. The activity's purpose is to keep the ruse going rather than to improve real long-term corporate growth.

Writing off acquisition costs can be altered as well, by reassigning part of the tangible costs to goodwill, an intangible asset. For example, if a large company acquires a smaller one and pays 110 percent of the smaller company's tangible net worth, then the additional 10 percent is called goodwill, the value of name recognition and reputation. So, if the acquiring company reassigns part of the tangible growth to goodwill, which is not amortized, then the amortization expense is underreported in the following years.

Another trick is to compensate customers in stock, in exchange for future purchase commitments, and then assign the stock payment as a form of goodwill. Before the acquisition, the target company asks customers to sign future purchase agreements and in exchange, gives them shares of stock. Upon acquisition, the stock is exchanged for parent company stock. The value of the purchase commitment is recorded as revenue, often before the applicable period, and the stock paid out is treated as goodwill and never amortized.

These are the major tricks of the trade used by some of the now infamous executives. The inability or unwillingness of the auditing companies, the government regulatory agencies, and boards of directors to identify and stop these activities led to their unprecedented growth. Often individual stockholders saw large portions of their portfolios destroyed. The next chapter examines the intended and actual roles of the Securities and Exchange Commission and looks at how that organization needs to be reformed.

3

THE ROLE OF THE SEC

The process of making sausage, Otto von Bismarck once remarked, is something best not seen. This adage may well apply to the process of reforming the rules and regulations at the federal government level. The political, legal, and market implications of making radical change are not simple, yet clearly some drastic changes are needed.

Just as the securities laws of the early 1930s prevented some forms of market abuse practiced in the Roaring '20s, we are faced today with a similar situation, and, perhaps, a more complex political world. The post–Depression laws were sweeping and changed the market forever; today, though, the working relationship between the federal executive and legislative branches has changed. More power has shifted to Congress, meaning that a consensus (or a compromise) is virtually required for any new laws. The result, of course, is that any strong proposed legislation is likely to be weakened before it can be passed and signed into law.

A philosophical question concerning the free market further restricts the type of change that an investor can expect. For example, at first glance, it seems logical to restrict greatly the ability of corporate leadership to abuse the system, to curtail and better define the activities

that auditing firms can perform for their corporate clients, and to demand far-reaching disclosure on the part of financial officers as well as
improved oversight by boards of directors. However, there is another
consideration as well: all of these steps adversely affect the free market.
They take away some of the competitive advantages that American companies hold in what has become a truly international market (again compared to the early 1930s, which was a period of political and market
isolationism). So we should expect that opposing forces of political and
free market interests will come into play. The way that corporations operate in the future will certainly change in many ways. However, it is not
realistic to expect the federal government, specifically the Securities
and Exchange Commission (SEC), to impose the types of change that
can *guarantee* that investors' capital will be better protected.

THE RESPONSIVE REGULATORY APPROACH

The SEC requires publicly listed corporations to submit quarterly
and annual reports, and it exercises an oversight function designed to
(a) prevent misrepresentation and fraud in financial reporting and (b)
to respond when such abuses are discovered, by imposing civil or criminal penalties when appropriate.

The first function—prevention—is, of course, most effective if it
serves to protect investors before a problem causes bankruptcy. Unfortunately, a skillful program of fraud and deception, if not discovered in
time, often is revealed only after the true value of the corporation's
stock has fallen below the artificial market value. At that point, all the
SEC can do is attempt to punish the abuse through civil or criminal penalties, or both. SEC ex-chairman Harvey Pitt advocated a four-point reform to the agency's approach and to the industry:

1. *Stronger enforcement of laws and regulations.* Stronger enforcement would require, of course, an expanded investigative staff
   supported by a larger annual budget.
2. *Stepped-up penalties.* These would include both civil and criminal
   penalties for misusing public funds; a requirement that companies work with the Justice Department; and in some cases, the

prosecution of individuals under RICO, which includes tougher penalties.[1]

3. *Guidelines and clearer financial disclosure.* It remains to be seen whether the SEC will be able to develop guidelines that are effective and practical.

4. *Structural reform of auditing practices.* This idea is complex because the relationship between corporations and "independent" auditing firms involves far more than audits. Millions of dollars in consultation fees change hands every year, ultimately affecting an auditing firm's ability to remain independent.

For ex-chairman Harvey Pitt and the SEC, the challenge was not merely one of changing regulations and laws, nor the enforcement of those laws; it also involved larger questions of whether changes would be politically viable. In the final analysis, we also have to question whether increased oversight will actually protect investors more. Considering that the abuses that have occurred are relatively small in number, the question should be asked about any proposal: "Would that change have prevented what happened?" The skill with which many corporate officers worked the system demonstrates that as regulations are tightened, corporate officers—with the help of their financial experts—are likely to change the way they operate. Just as tax laws designed to close loopholes often open new ones, changes in auditing standards, corporate disclosure, and enforcement standards and practices might only shift the problem from one arena to another.

REFORMING THE METHODOLOGY

Almost certainly, the demise of Arthur Andersen will have some influence on how other firms operate. It's reasonable to assume that, fearing the same consequences for their firms, management in the other "Big" accounting organizations will retreat from any practice that could be seen as aggressive or overly cooperative with management at the expense of investors or employees. It is also likely that, because Andersen's aggressive marketing compromised its audit objectivity, the remaining Big Four firms will yield much of their business to second-tier accounting firms, so that a broader range of independent firms—

operating in a more controlled (and conservative) environment—will become involved in both auditing and consulting with their publicly traded clients.

The SEC's Pitt went beyond the suggestion for greater oversight as well as structural change in auditing firms. He also advocated more disclosure of 8K reports, including reports of off balance sheet partnerships and subsidiaries, more details on transactions involving officers and directors, and faster reporting of material write-offs (under the present system, corporations can delay reporting write-offs until the following quarter). Pitt further advocated a stepped-up schedule for reporting insider stock trades, with a tough 48-hour deadline.

The former SEC chairman also said he supported disclosure of "critical" accounting issues and major business risks as well as a discussion by management about accounting decisions that were considered and rejected and what the resulting changes would have been in the final report. These ideas would be of little value in practice. They would make corporate officers more sensitive about discussing any ideas that might have to be disclosed under such broadly defined requirements. The SEC would be highly unlikely to achieve greater disclosure of accounting decisions by requiring that reports include discussions that took place but were rejected.

Pitt was closer to what is needed in his ideas about what investors should get in the way of information beyond audited financial statements. He said in one interview:

> Investors should get a wider range of data than just the standard financial statements. In the end, investors should see the company through the same reports, the same eyes, as managers and directors.[2]

That is exactly the point. As long as investors see a sanitized report without being exposed to the alternatives or decisions that went into that report, they don't know whether they are getting the full range of information. Traditionally, the investing community (including both institutional and individual investors) has depended on the integrity of management and oversight of the independent audit, with the basic belief that the system worked and, for the most part, prevented serious misrepresentation. Clearly, in some instances, this belief has not been well founded, and the whole system has been called into question. However, everyone has to ask: is the solution to increase oversight and regulation, or should reform occur in a market-driven environment?

Increased regulation has to be a part of the solution. Obviously, the SEC's mostly reactive role has not served the public well, failing to identify or prevent big-money abuses over the past few years. The fact that auditing firms got too close to their clients only added to the problem. However, even though more oversight is clearly needed, that will not bring investors back to the market and it will not improve confidence. Only a voluntary series of changes, in conjunction with regulatory changes, will result in the needed overhaul.

Pitt was criticized in his short tenure at the SEC for being reluctant to take a tough stance in chasing down corporate and market industry abuses. He was embarrassed, for example, when New York's attorney general, Eliot Spitzer, took the bull by the horns (figuratively speaking) and slapped a $100 million fine on Merrill Lynch, whose internal documents proved that analysts knew securities were of low quality even when recommending them to their clients. Pitt saw Spitzer's actions as encroachment, whereas Spitzer viewed the SEC as passive and slow moving, not to mention reluctant to impose sanctions on wrongdoers.[3] By early 2003, all of the regulators finally got together and extracted a $1.4 billion settlement from ten of the largest Wall Street firms.

Even while the debate between New York State and the SEC continued, the mood for reform was studied at the New York Stock Exchange. In a June 6, 2002, report of the New York Stock Exchange Corporate Accountability and Listing Standards Committee, a number of recommendations were offered. This report was, in part, a response to a request from Harvey Pitt on February 13, 2002, that the NYSE review its corporate governance listing standards. Among the changes recommended for the SEC, the report included:

- A requirement by the SEC that public accountants should be regulated by a new private-sector organization funded by the accounting industry
- Required certification by publicly listed companies's CEOs that financial reports to shareholders are accurate
- Required disclosure of GAAP-based financial information before pro forma or adjusted changes, with a reconciliation between

GAAP and pro forma reports made a part of the report to share-holders

- Prohibition of relationships between independent auditing firms and clients that would impair the effectiveness or objectivity of their reports
- Greater oversight by the SEC over the Financial Accounting Standards Board (FASB) with a focus on improving GAAP quality
- SEC improvement of the Management's Discussion and Analysis disclosure requirements
- Requirement of more prompt disclosure of insider transactions
- An evaluation of the impact of Regulation FD[4] on corporate behavior, specifically the degree to which frequent reporting adds to the pressure on management to "manage" reported earnings
- Increased budgeting by Congress to enable the SEC to improve its monitoring and enforcement activities
- Congressional change enabling the SEC to bar officers and directors from holding office if they fail to comply with regulations
- Congressional change creating a public/private panel to review stock concentration in 401(k) plans[5]

These suggestions affecting the SEC, and the ideas for improved oversight of the auditing industry and over corporations, would provide investors with solutions to many of the problems encountered in the recent past. These ideas also address a broad range of issues: corporate disclosure, accounting practices as well as weaknesses in standards, problems in the auditing industry, and the need for greater budgetary and oversight support from Congress.

CONNECTIONS BETWEEN THE SEC AND CORPORATIONS

Among the formidable problems faced by SEC ex-chairman Harvey Pitt, one was a perception in some quarters that he might not have been the right man for the job. This perception was due to a combination of his leadership style and his connection to the corporate and auditing worlds. Pitt resigned his post on election day, 2002, after he failed to advise fellow SEC commissioners that his choice to head up the Accounting Oversight Board had connections to a company accused of fraud. William Webster, former CIA and FBI chief, had led an audit committee for U.S. Technologies, and while Webster had disclosed the potential conflict to Pitt, Pitt's judgment was not to pass on the information to fellow commissioners. The resulting controversy led to Pitt's demise.[6]

Pitt had been highly qualified but controversial as SEC head. He came from Brooklyn, New York, and earned his law degree from St. John's University. He first joined the SEC in 1968, and in 1975 at the age of 30, he was appointed the SEC's youngest-ever general counsel. Three years later, he left government service and became a partner in the Washington, D.C., law offices of Fried Frank. In 1986, he represented Ivan Boesky and, as part of a negotiated plea bargain for his client, pointed the SEC investigation to Dennis Levine and Michael Milken. President Bush appointed Pitt to head up the SEC; however, during his years in private practice, his client list had included at various times such names as Merrill Lynch, America Online, the New York Stock Exchange, the AICPA, and all of the Big Five public accounting firms.

With Pitt's extensive background in both law practice and with the SEC, he certainly was qualified for the job, at least on paper. However, many—notably Democrats in Congress—were critical of his style and even suggested that he should resign, especially as corporate scandals came to light. However, anyone as qualified to head up the SEC as Pitt would be likely to have similar connections.

When he first took the job—before the big scandals hit the news—Pitt favored a low-key approach and proposed that voluntary compliance on the part of corporations and auditing firms was the most appropriate way to proceed. Pitt later changed his tone. One fact had become obvious: the problems recently disclosed had been accumulating for many years, and Pitt faced the task of having to make reforms to restore investors's confidence without violating the politically conservative philosophy that excessive federal regulation is bad for business. Not only did Pitt need to placate Congressional critics and investors, but he also had to be concerned with publicly traded companies, stock exchanges, and auditing firms, all of whom would resist any moves that would affect their operations and, potentially, limit economic growth.

Pitt began his program early in 2002 with a large increase in SEC audits of publicly traded companies's books—a move designed to accelerate enforcement of current accounting rules. At the same time, preventive action was occurring behind the scenes, discouraging companies from using questionable accounting practices.

Another important change was Pitt's support of an idea, put forth by former U.S. Treasury Secretary Paul H. O'Neill, to require CEOs be held personally liable for financial reporting. He favored increased penalties for accounting irregularities, and the new requirement would also make it easier for stockholders to file suit against corporate executives, who have been generally exempt from personal lawsuits under the protection of the corporate umbrella. Beginning in 2002, companies were required to disclose in their annual reports which accounting decisions had the greatest impact on earnings, key risks faced by the corporation, and other disclosures designed to provide investors with more information than just financial statements and an optimistic message from the CEO.

One of the more interesting trends in SEC enforcement is their attempt to get repayments of money generated by the exercise of stock options in cases where inflated earnings reports boosted the underlying stock price. In March 2002, the SEC filed suit against executives at IGI Inc., a publicly traded chemical company. Pitt said in that case, "We are going to go after compensation packages whenever we think the facts show disservice to the shareholders."[7]

THE POLITICAL PROBLEMS OF REFORM

The challenge of reforming the SEC and its approach to enforcement was only the tip of the iceberg for Harvey Pitt. He also needed to contend with the volatile political climate in Washington, where the distinction between proper response and partisan conflict is difficult to identify at times. Pitt was known to be politically tone-deaf, so in that respect he probably was not the right man for the job. As a starting point, Pitt asked for approval of a budget increase of $91 million; the administration originally had proposed a $15 million increase for 2002. The General Accounting Office reported that the SEC workload has grown 80 percent since 1993, but the agency's staffing has changed very little. SEC appropriations for 2003 were authorized as part of the Sarbanes-Oxley Act of 2002, including an additional $98 million for oversight and auditing costs.[8]

Beyond the budget fight, the SEC's reform programs will have to satisfy the public demand for tougher standards as well as Congressional criticism, without going so far that they interfere excessively with the free market—a difficult balancing act. Pitt took the approach that the solution was "to make disclosures more meaningful, and intelligible, to average investors."[9]

Pitt also stated that it is illusory to believe that a foolproof system can be achieved, but his emphasis on improved disclosure and up-to-date financial reports included nine key elements:

1. A system of current disclosure, including updates of previous reports
2. Disclosure of trends in financial information
3. Clear and informative financial reporting
4. Identification of critical accounting principles, their application, and their effect
5. Private sector standard setting for financial reporting
6. Change in the reporting environment aimed at changing how companies and auditors view the SEC; encouraging communication with the SEC on complex accounting questions *before* mistakes are made
7. Self-regulation in the accounting profession that is "effective and transparent"
8. Protection for investors on the part of corporate audit committees
9. Changes in the way that analysts make recommendations, based on financial data rather than corporate presentations[10]

The effectiveness of any SEC-generated reform will ultimately be judged by market reaction, industry cooperation, and political support for change. President Bush, in supporting the new reform efforts by Congress, set the tone by promising to "end the days of cooking the books, shading the truth, and breaking our laws."[11]

With support—both political and budgetary—the SEC is poised for action. With Harvey Pitt's resignation on election day, 2002, one controversy is out of the way. The most effective role for the SEC of the future, under SEC Chairman William Donaldson, will be to lead voluntary reform while enforcing the law and proactively to prevent future problems from becoming huge financial disasters.

4

THE AUDIT
Can You Trust the Accounting Firm?

Perhaps the most shocking revelation in the recent corporate scandals was that one of the Big Five accounting firms was implicated in wrongdoing.[1]

For decades, American investors, institutions, exchanges, and regulators have viewed the independent public accounting firms as the incorruptible protectors of the truth. We were assured that, at the very least, corporate flaws would be discovered and corrected by the independent audit before numbers were released. The unqualified approval was the final word that, even given the flexibility allowed under GAAP, the financial statements were within the acceptable range and were correct, complete, and true.

As we now know, such reporting was not necessarily true.

SETTING THE RULES: THE FASB

Accounting rules and guidelines are published by the Financial Accounting Standards Board (FASB), a private sector organization formed in 1973 to develop rules governing financial reporting. The

SEC has recognized the authoritative power of FASB rules, and the American Institute of Certified Public Accountants (AICPA) has also recognized that the FASB *is* the final word on how accountants are supposed to conduct audits, interpret financial information, and guide their clientele in reporting results.

FASB defines the need for consistent, conforming standards on its Web site:

> Accounting standards are essential to the efficient functioning of the economy because decisions about the allocation of resources rely heavily on credible, concise, transparent and understandable financial information.[2]

Given this clear guideline, what has gone wrong? Obviously, the mission of the FASB is well-intended and its purpose clearly defined. The problem, however, is that when a self-regulated industry listens to its clients rather than following its guiding standards, then those standards have little value. If FASB lacks enforcement capability, then the concept of "self regulation" falls by the wayside. It only works as long as the members of the organization are willing to apply those standards to their methods of operation.

Further complicating the problem is the scope of the rules themselves. Walter Wriston, former CEO of Citicorp (now Citigroup) explains by way of example that, ". . . there are over 800 pages now from FASB on how to account for a derivative . . . we have thousands and thousands of pages that are very difficult to interpret."[3]

In the case of Arthur Andersen, the whole idea went terribly wrong. A year earlier, it would have been impossible to imagine that one of the Big Five accounting firms would disband in the middle of a scandal involving shredding documents for a large client. Many believe Andersen's aggressive marketing (i.e., attracting and keeping big client accounts) clouded its judgment. Others contend the problem was a senior partner in the Houston office whose decisions were contrary to Andersen's mandate, not to mention the FASB rules. A combination of these factors—poor judgment, ambition, aggressive marketing—may have contributed to the problem.

David Duncan, who headed up Andersen's Houston office, pleaded guilty to obstruction of justice charges in the Enron case in April 2002.

Duncan, an ambitious, competent, and widely respected career partner with Andersen, had been partner-in-charge of the Enron account for five years, and he was close to the client; his office, in fact, was located in Enron's Houston building. Right after Duncan was informed that the SEC had requested documents, he ordered his staff to "get in compliance with the document-retention policy." Translation: shred documents, including many requested by investigators. Of course, Duncan's career with Andersen rested on revenues from accounts like Enron. Total fees exceeded $50 million per year. However, the close relationship that develops over time between a senior auditor and a big client defines the problem: the loss of objectivity and potential conflicts.[4]

The structure within a big accounting firm such as Arthur Andersen no doubt aggravated that problem even further. The company has been described as "a loose confederation of fiefdoms covering different geographic markets . . . unable to respond swiftly to crises or even to govern itself decisively."[5]

Fallout from the Andersen matter has affected the remaining Big Four firms to some degree. The well publicized troubles of Adelphia Communications and the Rigas family led to the company's dismissal of Deloitte & Touche, citing the auditor's failure to notify the audit committee about accounting irregularities. Deloitte was let go in June 2002, a month after its refusal to complete their audit of the company's 2001 financial results. They cited mistrust of many senior executives, many of whom were still with the firm. It is questionable whether notification would have mattered; both founder John Rigas and former CFO Timothy Rigas sat on the audit committee at that time.[6]

Also on the hot seat in 2002 was KPMG, auditor for Xerox Corporation. Under subpoena, KPMG accountant Ronald Safram was questioned by SEC investigators back in March 2001. A year later, when much publicized accounting questions arose concerning Andersen, KPMG's work with Xerox was still being investigated. The SEC had found Xerox documents concerning the use of different accounting methods to meet earnings targets. At issue when the investigation began was whether KPMG knew of the internal discussion when it performed the audit.[7]

Following a decline from a 1999 high of $60 per share down to less than $10 by mid-2002, Xerox restated its revenues for the past five years. The company admitted that it booked $6.4 billion in revenue improperly, which exaggerated its pretax profits by $1.41 billion. SEC and legal questions focused not only on the company but also on KPMG's role over the five-year period. Also caught in the regulatory scrutiny was Xerox's new auditing firm, PricewaterhouseCoopers. Xerox agreed to settle the SEC matter by paying a $10 million fine for the misleading financial reports.[8]

Another investigation concerning PricewaterhouseCoopers involves the Tyco matter. By September 2002, the Manhattan district attorney's office was questioning the audit firm's management to determine whether it knew of wrongdoing by Tyco CEO Dennis Kozlowski or CFO Mark Swartz. PricewaterhouseCoopers's position was that they were cooperating with investigators as well as performing an ongoing interview with Tyco itself and, at the same time, completing the fiscal 2002 audit. The big question involved $170 million in unauthorized compensation and $430 million from sale of stock—both significant enough that, "accounting for the bonuses appears so egregiously wrong that a thorough audit should have caught it."[9]

The reviews of work by all of the major auditing firms also led to a review of past audits. The firms were "identifying those companies most likely to draw unwanted attention from regulators and plaintiffs' lawyers."[10]

The decision by Andersen and other auditing firms to increase business beyond auditing work defines a part of the problem. As revenues from consulting matched and surpassed audit fees, a glaring conflict of interest became institutionalized within the industry. How can a firm remain "independent" when it also earns hundreds of millions in consulting fees from the corporations it audits? The answer, of course, is that it cannot. The rather simplistic move of forming separate subsidiaries for auditing and consulting achieves separation in name only. The conflict is as serious in the accounting occupation as the equally glaring conflict of interest for brokers and analysts whose firms also serve clients as investment bankers.

Andersen was auditor and consultant for Enron and WorldCom, among others. By 1999, Enron was paying more than $50 million per year to Andersen, split about equally between audit and consulting fees. Andersen had classified Enron as a "high risk" audit client, clearly a classification of questionable accounting practices. Internal disagreements in Andersen about whether or not even to keep Enron as a client preceded the public revelation of trouble, and Andersen knew that there was trouble. In early 2001, the Chicago-based firm sent a senior partner, Carl E. Bass, to audit the auditors in the Houston office and specifically to review the Enron situation. Bass visited with Enron executives and, while Andersen has not admitted any connection, he was removed from his oversight post a few weeks later—at the request of Enron.

This sign of trouble was merely the latest in a series. In 2001, the firm settled Sunbeam Corporation stockholders' lawsuits for $110 million, another $100 million went to investors of Waste Management, plus $7 million in fines settled an SEC case involving fraudulent Waste Management audits. Andersen's retired partners also have filed suit to protect $800 million in benefits.

The June 15, 2002, conviction of the firm for obstruction of justice was the last straw and spelled the end for the long-standing accounting firm. It raised new questions among investors and Wall Street experts: were other problems out there involving the remaining four public accounting firms? Considering that the revelations to date seem to be centered on Andersen, more than likely their practices were exceptional, and if anything, other firms will be more conservative in their future audit practices. PwC (PricewaterhouseCoopers) could possibly be tainted to a degree by the Enron scandal. In 1999 and 2000, PwC certified the fairness of an exchange between Enron stock and partnerships controlled by CFO Andrew Fastow. The SEC opened an investigation into the complex transactions in February 2002. PwC's involvement likely will end up as a minor embarrassment in comparison to Andersen's problems.

CHANGING THE INDUSTRY— AND THE CULTURE

The conflicts and reporting problems associated with auditing firms developed over many years and did not occur suddenly. If nothing else, the Arthur Andersen case will be credited for long-needed reforms in the industry. Former SEC Chairman Harvey Pitt described the problems of the accounting profession as a whole:

> Today, disclosures are made not to inform, but to avoid lia-
> bility . . . there is a need for reform of the regulation of our ac-
> counting profession. We cannot afford a system, like the present
> one, that facilitates failure rather than success. Accounting
> firms have important public responsibilities. We have had far
> too many financial and accounting failures. The Commission
> cannot, and in any event will not, tolerate this pattern of grow-
> ing restatements, audit failures, corporate failures, and investor
> losses. Somehow, we must put a stop to a vicious cycle that has
> been in evidence for far too many years.[11]

Pitt correctly identified the loss of confidence among investors as one of the more serious problems to come out of recent events. He called for a fully transparent disciplinary system within the industry, including a newly formed public body concerned with both discipline and quality control. The ultimate question is whether such a body would prevent a repeat of the abuses found at Enron, involving not only corporate practices but also abuses by the auditing firm's senior part-ners—abuses that were known in advance and allowed to continue unchallenged. Pitt called for a needed series of reforms. However, for them to work, a new system within the new laws will be necessary to ensure that audits of publicly listed companies should be trusted and believed—and that is going to take a lot of work.

In June 2002, the SEC proposed a framework for a Public Account-ability Board (PAB) that includes some reform ideas worth consider-ing. Provisions in the original SEC proposal included the need for SEC oversight of the board; required membership on the board by auditing firms (failure to join would mean the SEC would not accept financial statements from a firm's clients); nonaccounting membership on the PAB; strong oversight and quality review by the PAB over accounting firms; disciplinary powers including fines, censures, removal from cli-ent accounts, or suspensions; and audit standard setting.[12]

Some of the proposed terms of the SEC idea did not make sense. For example, asking such a board to set audit standards would dupli-cate and possibly contradict standards set by the FASB and adopted by the AICPA. The solution is not to create a new layer of regulation but to strengthen the existing layer and monitor how auditing firms conduct their business. Initial reaction to Pitt's proposal by the accounting industry was negative. The PAB's proposed mandate to audit the auditors and even to censure, fine, or prevent firms from serving their clients did not go over well with the industry, which would prefer an improved self-policing system and, agreeing with Pitt, a more effective FASB system for enacting changes in GAAP. Many in the accounting industry as well as in the American Bar Association believe that the proposed broad scope of authority Pitt proposed for the PAB would not stand up in a court challenge. The proposed eight part-time board members who would govern the PAB would lack subpoena power and would have great difficulty functioning effectively. In addition, Pitt suggested that three board members would be from the accounting profession; clearly, their knowledge of the industry would provide them far more say than other members would enjoy. The idea as originally proposed by Pitt was modified to a degree in legislation that did pass in 2002. Ultimately, the effectiveness of new legislation and Board has to pass the test: would the new laws and their application have prevented the corporate problems revealed in the recent past?

THE FLEXIBILITY IN GAAP

Whether reform addresses future problems in a preventive way or changes GAAP rules to restrict how much companies can alter their books, the basic GAAP rules themselves are part of the problem. In many respects, the GAAP rules allow so much flexibility, that considerable tinkering can occur within the existing rules.

GAAP rules are understood, to some degree, beyond the accounting and auditing professions. Rather than a hard-and-fast set of specific rules, GAAP is closer to a collection of guidelines and standards with a lot of flexibility.

For example, GAAP sets down the *types* of items that should be disclosed, but it does not offer any rigid rules about the language of disclosures, nor even how disclosure is supposed to be utilized to clarify financial reporting. To the contrary, a lot of so-called disclosures in financial statement footnotes tend to obfuscate rather than to enlighten. Robert Olstein warns, "Don't look to GAAP to bail you out."[13]

T h e   E x p e r t s   S p e a k

Robert Olstein, manager of the Olstein Financial Alert Fund and an expert in accounting concepts, cautions that, "There is no specific formula for GAAP, as GAAP reporting gives management wide discretion within the rules to apply their own judgement. People misunderstand this, so it's critical to monitor the financial reports for the appropriate disclosures which enable you to analyze the reality of the assumptions behind the reported numbers. There is a high correlation between nondisclosure and the inability to disclose."[14]

In other words, investors are supposed to be protected regarding the accuracy of the numbers, and, clearly, that assumption has been shaken severely. But even if the system works well and reporting is done within the rules, GAAP rules cannot realistically provide foolproof protection against manipulation of the numbers.

There exists no single, authoritative rule that reflects GAAP; rather, it is a broader technical description of a series of standards:

The phrase *generally accepted accounting principles* is a technical accounting term that encompasses the conventions, rules, and procedures necessary to define accepted accounting practice at a particular time.[15]

The development of GAAP "rules" is complex itself. A 2002 article explains that, "Accounting rules come from numerous sources, so it is understandable that nonaccountants have difficulty becoming fluent in—or even finding—the rules." In fact, five separate levels in the hierarchy of GAAP make the whole system very complex indeed, containing approximately 20 separate pronouncement sources and 10 issuing bodies.[16]

The premise behind the GAAP system is a sensible one. Corporate managers and their auditors have to be able to work within the rules in an environment where circumstances change—not only from period to period, but also from case to case. In one matter, a conservative approach and interpretation may be justified, but in another, more caution will be called for. The degree of flexibility is comparable to real estate appraisal. An appraiser can decide a home's value within a broad range of possible comparisons. The real level and approach is dictated by the purpose of an appraisal. If a bank hires the appraiser to ensure that the property is worth the sales price (and if the bank wants to write the loan), the appraiser has the task of verifying that the house is worth that price (assuming it is not so overvalued that it cannot possibly be appraised for the price). However, if the appraiser is hired by someone going through a divorce, then the desired result might be to appraise the house at the low end of the possible spectrum. "Market value" is a range of possible prices rather than one, specific amount.

In accounting, the same is true. An accounting opinion about value of a company's assets is going to be different in the case of bankruptcy, for an initial public offering, or as part of a financial statement in the annual report.

An uncomfortable reality is that—within the rules—the outcome of accounting decisions can present a broad range of valuation. This flexibility exists for good reasons, but it also leaves the door open for possible abuse. This is not theoretical only. Recent events have shown that those abuses do occur, and the consequence to stockholders is not just in the thousands or millions of dollars but often in the billions.

For example, accountants deal with estimates continually. The establishment of reserves for future bad debts or for inventory obsolescence requires a decision about how to set up the reserves. If the reserve is set high, that increases current expenses and reduces earnings. If the reserve is set low, it could be inadequate to cover future debts, affecting working capital and cash flow. In the decision of how to set a reserve, the accounting process is also influenced by management's desire to meet earnings estimates. Falling short results in a drop in the stock price. Some of those very same managers pressuring accountants to modify their reserve estimates will also earn bonuses based on reported earnings—thus, the problems begin.

This relatively simple example demonstrates how various forces determine how an accounting estimate is made. The pressure to meet analysts's estimates, the desire by executives to earn a healthy annual bonus, and an accounting manager's career ambitions all add to the complexity of the problem. The independent auditor, in reviewing those decisions, also faces an array of pressures: the desire by the auditor's managers to keep a big client because of lucrative consulting revenues from the same source, the field auditor's own ambition to rise in the ranks and one day become a senior partner, and finally, the flexibility in the GAAP rules that enables the decision to stand within a broad range on justifications.

If a reserve is lower than it should be, the all-important *assumption* backing up a change is often enough to satisfy the auditor that all is well. For example, an accountant with modest writing skills could reduce a reserve for bad debts by arguing that:

> Reserves for future bad debts have been lowered even though projected future revenues are expected to rise. This decision is based on recent improvements to internal collection procedures and policies limiting lines of credit to new clients, designed to prevent major bad debts from developing and to limit nonpaying client levels through periodic account examination. The reserve has been lowered 15 percent, while estimates of actual bad debt reductions due to improved internal controls is expected to result in a reduction of 20 percent in actual bad debts to be written off.

In this made-up example, the assumption explains the reasoning for reduced reserves. It even supports the decision by arguing that actual bad debts probably will be even lower than the reduced reserves, indicating that the decision is conservative rather than aggressive. Such arguments—whether valid or not—may placate a conservative auditor, whose conclusion would be to allow the change. The astute accountant, anticipating further examination of the facts, might even write up proposed internal procedure changes for more aggressive monitoring of accounts receivable, supporting the contention that internal controls have been approved. The proposals might never be implemented, but the existence of the memo (often approved by the CFO) give coverage to everyone. The company reduces expenses, and the auditor is satisfied that the change is reasonable.

In many instances, a range of adjustments like this, along with carefully worded assumptions, constitutes the culture of what former SEC Chairman Levitt called "nods and winks."

The **E**xperts **S**peak

The problem of accounting reports, according to Jean-Marie Eveillard, copresident of First Eagle Sogen Funds in New York, is, "the disparity between accounting profits and true economic profits. Even if the rules say it is all right to change the numbers, it is simply unethical to do so."

THE NEED FOR BASIC CHANGE

The culture itself is a big part of the problem, and it needs to change. Accountants are judged, from the departmental level to the executive suite, by their ability to manage the numbers, to make results come out the way everyone wants, and to protect the corporation and its members with ironclad documentation—even if it has to be spun.

A long-standing joke in the accounting world involves three candidates for an accounting job. The interviewer asks each one, "What is two plus two?" The first answers, "Four;" the second says, "Twenty-two;" and the third—who gets the job—replies, "What do you want it to be?"

Even though the GAAP rules allow accountants great flexibility to manipulate the numbers, and even though the law itself recognizes that this takes place and is not considered a crime, is such manipulation right? Perhaps the larger the gap between what is reported and the true economic profit, the greater the problem, both legal and ethical.

The pressure to force the numbers comes from several quarters. Wall Street analysts project earnings, often based solely on what they are told by corporate management. The pressure on management is to meet or exceed those earnings estimates, and if they are missed then the stock price will fall, at least temporarily. Top management also exerts pressure, and these are the very people whose bonuses and stock options are tied to results. Finally, stockholders themselves demand low volatility and predictability. Investors do not like volatility, and to some extent, they accept the idea that earnings are accrued or deferred to even out ups and downs. That has the effect of keeping the stock price predictable, too, although in the real world, sales, costs, and profits are chaotic and uneven.

So, given this range of problems, how can the accounting world be changed, and to what degree does it need to change? These questions must be addressed by regulators, the accounting profession, and investors. Clearly, the functions of independent auditing and consulting need to be separated and even restricted, so that the auditing firm will no longer depend on big consulting fees from a particular client. How to achieve separation is a problem, and the industry and its trade group, the AICPA, are likely to resist any such restrictions.

Another idea, now part of the Sarbanes-Oxley Act but originally opposed by AICPA, is a requirement that auditors be rotated off accounts at least once every five years. AICPA's CEO, Barry Melancon, responded to that idea by saying, "The more I understand about a business, the better able I am to be critical in an audit."[17]

The problem with that point of view is that, in an objective audit applying GAAP, it is not as important to be familiar with a particular corporation as to apply sound principles in judging management's accounting decisions, especially those about valuation and current-year profits. In some respects, knowing *less* about management and the business could make an auditor more objective and capable in auditing the financial results.

Melancon has recognized that a true separation between auditing and consulting is the only way to save the profession. Whether accounting firms or trade groups like it or not, complete separation of those functions makes sense. Auditing should be conducted in a completely independent environment in every way possible, and even though big fees will continue to be involved in audit work, excluding consulting from the same firm will help keep the audit as independent as possible.

The mere separation via subsidiary companies will not do the job; that is a token move designed to present the appearance of objectivity by two arms of the same company, but in practice it would not make a difference. Even at the business school level, accounting should be taught with an entirely different emphasis, perhaps as much as a law course as a course on managing numbers. The recent announcements by some business schools that courses in business ethics will be added— as though they alone will solve the problem—is laughable. As Lynn Turner, former chief accountant with the SEC, has pointed out, "Curriculums are not designed today to provide the student with sufficient training . . . [about] whether the management judgment being made is right or wrong."[18]

Internet **R***esources*

The Web pages for the three major accounting trade groups are:

- <www.aicpa.org> American Institute of Certified Public Accountants
- <accounting.rutgers.edu/raw/aaa> American Accounting Association
- <www.imanet.org> Institute of Management Accountants

Change takes time, however, and it will be many years before accounting education is able to fully address the cultural problems of accounting itself. Past emphasis on the technical aspects of GAAP needs to be expanded to include managerial judgment, analysis, research, and communication. The required changes are being made in the CPA exam and at several schools in cooperation with industry groups, including the AICPA, the American Accounting Association, and the Institute of Management Accountants.

Regardless of what the trade groups say to business magazines, these organizations know that they need to change their approach to their industry to survive. AICPA's Melancon summarized the problem well in a 2002 address:

> What is needed is not just reform of the accounting laws, it is a rejuvenated accounting culture—both internally in corporate finance offices and externally in audit firms. The culture must build upon the profession's traditional values. We are determined to demonstrate that auditors can and indeed do say "no." Because only if auditors are fully prepared to say "no" to management will investors be fully prepared to say "yes" to the markets.[19]

The future will demonstrate whether this position will be backed with real change. However, investor confidence will depend on such changes, not only in the accounting culture but also in regulatory oversight and the structure of corporate management, boards of directors, and internal accounting practices.

Change on the regulatory side began with passage of the Sarbanes-Oxley Act of 2002. On July 30, President Bush signed the new law, which drastically changed and restricted the ways in which accounting firms are allowed to operate. This new law created a Public Company

Accounting Oversight Board to set rules and enforce provisions of the Securities Exchange Act of 1934.[20]

Section 103 of the 2002 Act defines auditing, quality control, and independence standards and rules. Among the big changes is the board's right to inspect auditing firms and their practices and enforce compliance. Another significant change is found in Section 201, which prohibits accounting firms from performing nonaudit services while also involved in audit work. Prohibited services include bookkeeping, systems design, appraisal or valuation services, actuarial services, internal audit outsourcing services, management functions or human resources, investment-related services, or legal help.

A higher level of disclosure of relevant accounting decisions is included as well as audit partner rotation every five years. This addresses the long-standing problem of "independent" audit partners becoming too cozy with a client's management. The Act, in Section 207, also proposes to study a requirement that companies rotate auditing firms on a mandatory basis.

Traditionally, companies have recruited top accounting and executive talent from their auditing firm. The 2002 Act restricts this practice, forbidding a CEO, controller, CFO, or chief accounting officer from being employed by the company's audit firm during the past year. While companies might try to get around this restriction by hiring ex-auditors as consultants or giving them nonfinancial titles, this section does send the message that the conflict of interest associated with crossover from auditor to corporate officer will no longer be allowed.

One of the big changes for corporate management is a requirement that the CEO and CFO must certify the financial results being reported. Also, if officers have to restate financial results due to "material noncompliance," they will be required to reimburse their bonuses and other incentive compensation, as well as any profits from selling company stock.

In addition to subjecting officers to the penalties defined in the 1934 Act and other federal legislation, the new law also enables the SEC to bar directors or officers—in some cases, permanently. Many other provisions of the new law give real teeth to reform, including making personal loans to executives illegal, increasing disclosure rules, and increasing criminal penalties for destroying documents, mail and wire fraud, and tampering with records. As long as the SEC enforces this sweeping new law, the culture—both accounting and corporate—will change in very significant ways.[21]

THE GAAP PROBLEM

The new law will address the non–GAAP problem—management misrepresentation and conflicts of interest on the part of auditors. However, another problem remains—the latitude in the rules themselves.

GAAP provisions include lists of rules and guidelines but allow for liberal interpretation of how to treat certain items. In comparison, European auditing firms operate under International Accounting Standards (IAS), which require auditors to look not only at whether decisions comply with the law but also at the results, intended or not, of those decisions. So auditors operating under IAS might have asked management about off balance sheet liabilities, prebooked revenues, and capitalized costs and expenses—not so much to determine whether they were appropriate but whether the results mislead investors by misrepresenting the value of corporate assets and, ultimately, of the stock itself.

While the distinctions to those outside of the accounting profession are technical at best, it is important to realize that many economies have chosen IAS as the system of choice. These include Australia, Singapore, and Hong Kong. In the United States, where tightening the rules appears to be called for, IAS is viewed as being too ill defined. It may give individual auditor judgment too much weight instead of less judgment and more clearly defined compliance standards.

Reform has been accepted, and perhaps the most significant change because the big scandals began to make news has been in the accounting industry itself. Before 2002, the industry fought even minor reforms such as separating audit and consulting and doing away with an obvious conflict of interest. Now the industry, without Arthur Andersen, has recognized the need to accept sweeping change for its own survival. Even Harvey Pitt had resisted ex-chairman Levitt's proposal for separating out audit and consulting, arguing that it was not necessary—before the big news hit in 2002. Pitt, whose ex-clients included all of the

Big Five firms at one time or another, became a leader in shaping the needed reforms.

To move from a culture of "nods and winks" to one in which auditors will be required to look beyond manipulated quasicompliance is a big step. The auditing industry will be required to operate forms of forensic auditing to uncover misleading accounting entries. A truly independent audit can and should reveal practices of recognizing revenues in the wrong period, deferring or capitalizing costs and expenses inappropriately, manipulating reserves, and using acquisition activity to falsify the true earnings picture, and an audit can reverse such practices so that financial results can once again be trusted by investors.

Will fees for audits be higher? They certainly will, because the auditing firms will have to document everything, ensure proper disclosure, and face higher legal and insurance costs themselves. However, it makes more sense to pass on these higher costs to the consumer through higher prices than to allow continued deception and huge stock portfolio and pension plan losses—while corporate executives run off with millions in excessive compensation.

READING BETWEEN
THE LINES

How can you analyze and study
financial reports of publicly traded companies? If your goal is to discover the truth, find potential problem areas, and even adjust reported
results to arrive at a fair picture, you face a formidable task. There are
solutions, however. Even the nonaccountant can perform simple tests
to identify red flags and find good value investments worth pursuing.

EVALUATING COMPANIES

Considering that financial statements are prepared by teams of
well-trained accountants, it is not reasonable to expect to understand
them on the highly technical level of accounting discussions. However,
as an investor or potential investor, you do have the right to well-ex-
plained and documented reports. If an annual report or financial statement's footnotes do not make sense, the failure is on the part of the
reporting company. Their task should be to make sure that you, the investor, more often than not untrained in finance, understands what is
going on and the impact on stock value. Anything short of that degree
of clarity is unacceptable.

Publicly traded companies are being required to confront this problem. Whether by way of regulation or through voluntary effort, financial reports are improving. High-level corporate officers are now required to certify personally that financial results are accurate, and misrepresentation can mean they have to pay back bonuses and other forms of incentive compensation. They also face potential criminal penalties.[1] Without any doubt, this requirement alone will go a long way toward making disclosure clearer, more detailed, and more accurate, so that investors will be able to understand better what financial statement footnotes really mean.

For many individual investors, trying to understand complex financial statements is daunting. However, as reform progresses, this long-standing problem is changing for the better. In addition to the severe penalties that executives now face for misleading their stockholders, the simple public relations problem is causing real reform at the reporting level. As financial officers are forced to live with real and personal liability, using questionable accounting practices has become increasingly unrealistic, and deceiving stockholders is viewed as extremely poor public relations practice.

The annual report is a good place to start. It provides financial reports as well as disclosures by the executives. It will be especially interesting to compare annual report disclosures from past years to postreform annual reports. You will see more carefully constructed messages, clearer explanations, and more detail—even if the motivation is to cover the officers. As an investor, the important benefit is that you are getting better information and can make more informed investment decisions.

In that regard, the recent bad news about corporate abuse has been expensive in many ways, but it is leading to substantive change in the way that corporations, auditing firms, and even regulators conduct business. All of these changes are benefiting investors by protecting them from deceptive reporting practices, as well as providing clearer financial reports.

This is not to say that understanding complex transactions will be easy. However, one trend that is emerging from the corporate mess is a widespread recognition of the corporation's responsibility for explaining financials to investors: what the numbers mean, how they came about, business risks, and realistic expectations about the future.

Management's often misleading claims in the discussion portion of annual reports have added to the confusion. For example, the claim that revenues are rising can often mean that revenues are being booked prematurely, that some revenues are not really revenues, or that many customers are not likely to pay the company. The claim of higher profits could be accompanied with low quality of earnings, generous accounting assumptions, or capitalization of current year operating expenses. Improved cash flow could mean the company is no longer paying its bills on time. In other words, investors need to analyze the numbers rather than trust in the self-serving and misleading statements in many annual reports.[2]

Experts cite obfuscation in financial reporting as a warning sign in itself. If you don't understand what management is saying, avoid the company. Roger Lowenstein of *The Wall Street Journal* said it well before Enron's demise, noting that, "If you haven't learned that confusing financial statements are to be avoided like the plague, check out Enron's stock, now fetching 26 cents a share. Nothing obscure about that."[3]

Investors, too, need to reevaluate the way they rate companies and the way that they receive information. In recent years, many companies projected growth in double digits for the future, a rate that is virtually impossible to sustain. However, such projections often went unquestioned. As Wall Street expert Robert Olstein suggests:

> Stop looking at these 25 percent growth rates. Very few companies can do it. You're lucky if you can even get companies doing 15 percent long-term growth rates; they're few and far between.[4]

Another source of information is the SEC reports that every publicly listed company is required to file. These include:

- *Form 10-K.* An annual filing, it includes the audited financial statements (balance sheet, statement of operations, statement of cash flows, and explanatory notes), management discussion and analysis, and auditor's report. The form is due 90 days following close of the fiscal year.
- *Form 10-Q.* A quarterly report filed 45 days after the close of each of the first three quarters, it contains a full set of unaudited financial statements plus management discussion and analysis.
- *Form 8-K.* A disclosure report, this is filed to report changes in control over stock, acquisitions or mergers, changes in auditing firm, board of directors resignations, bankruptcy, and other major events. Changes are reported within 15 days (exception: a change in auditing firms has to be reported within 5 days).

A review of reports filed with the SEC should serve as a good beginning. Wall Street expert Robert Olstein has said, "We would rather spend one night with a 10-K report than two days with management."[5]

What should you look for when reviewing a company's information? Perhaps the most valuable test any investor can perform is the test of reasonableness. Are the numbers realistic? How do they compare to last year's report? Are disclosures clear and understandable? Is management discussing problems and concerns? Every company has problems and concerns.

Looking beyond the official reports, what is the tone of the annual report? What message does the corporation send to stockholders? Do projected growth rates make sense? Do the trends look right, considering the past? Also, look beyond the numbers. Be cautious of corporate executives who seem to be saying more to hype the stock's value than they are saying about their operations, quality of product or service, competitive stance, future growth in sales and profits (as opposed to stock price); and be cautious if the message is unclear. An obscure message from a corporate executive is a red flag.

LONG-TERM TRENDS WORTH STUDYING

Financial analysis, on either the technical or the layman's level, comes down to one point: it is all about trends. Projections about the future have to be supported on a solid base, and the past can reveal a lot about where a company's markets are headed. Losing sight of the fundamentals—the basic financial information—when so much emphasis is placed on technical indicators like stock price. Of course, price is important to the investor in terms of investment growth, but a lot of emphasis is put on short-term price movement, which reveals little of value. The real value is in determining a company's true profit picture and in comparing today's stock price to what the realistic value should be, not estimates of near-term growth. For serious investors, more emphasis should be placed on realistic estimates of value (often a discount of current market value) and less on the word of so-called Wall Street insiders who often do not have any idea of what value really means.

It does little good to take the word of an analyst predicting future earnings per share if that analyst is simply saying what management tells them. If management hypes their stock to the analyst, and the analyst then conveys that message to the investment world (where the estimate of earnings has reigned in the past), what good is the message? The trouble begins at that point, especially if management has exaggerated their future outlook when speaking to the analyst.

Today's experts talk about a different approach than that used in the past, in which the reported earnings are only the starting point. From there, discounts are applied to arrive at the true intrinsic value of the company. That means removing deferrals for tax liabilities, doing away with entries designed to inflate current earnings, and removing any items that change the report in a nonrecurring way. The analysis ends up with an estimated value per share that reflects what the company is really worth. Robert Olstein explains, "We look at the amount of cash we could take out of the business as an owner, if we owned 100 percent of the company."[6]

That estimate is accomplished through a series of analytical methods. While some are fairly technical, others can be performed by anyone and involve working directly with one of three sources: reported numbers on the financial statements, explanations provided in the footnotes, and disclosures provided by management.

Studying the numbers themselves and looking for trends (discussed in detail in the next chapter) has always been the starting point for fundamental analysis. The corporate scandals brought into question the very value of performing fundamental analysis at all, because if the reported numbers are false (and if auditing firms allowed them to go through), then how dependable is any analysis? The new laws, which affect not only corporate officers but auditing firms as well, are designed to prevent deception as much as possible.

However, investors need to understand that, even after reform, GAAP rules will never ensure absolute accuracy or catch every form of aggressive accounting or misrepresented results. Reform will prevent a repeat of many of the problems that had built up in the 1990s and early 2000s. The revelations in recent years were the culmination of a series of decisions made in a corporate cultural climate where deception was not all that unusual, and some companies went over the line between GAAP flexibility and outright fraud. While that culture can be changed, and has already started to change, reform will take time. However, even with changes that improve the overall situation, every investor needs to understand that placing money into the stock market will always involve risk that cannot be removed completely.

The second area of study is the financial footnote (more on this topic later in this chapter). Footnotes have always been used to disclose off balance sheet items affecting value and potential value. While an investor's concern should be to discover emerging problems revealed in the footnotes, a large number of footnotes does not necessarily indicate an excessive number of problems. Many standard disclosures have always been handled via footnotes.

The footnotes often are highly technical, and a red flag in one company might be business as usual and no cause for concern in another. So it is not always a simple matter to translate the significance of footnote disclosures. However, as reform moves ahead, corporations should begin to explain their disclosures to investors. In the new mood of financial transparency, footnotes should be augmented with plain English explanations of risk, financial impact, and the effect of accounting decisions on the bottom line. A general rule for investors should be that unclear footnotes should not be shrugged off; if you don't know what they mean and management's discussion and analysis does not clarify the matter, you should not buy the stock. If all investors, especially institutional investors, would apply this commonsense rule, corporations would have to make the financial information easier to read.

The proposal is not a hardship for a company. With the accounting, public relations, and other corporate resources at its disposal, explaining financial matters to investors should be an easy matter—assuming that the corporation *wants* to tell what is really going on. Many companies have boosted their earnings significantly—in ways that might raise questions among investors. For example, IBM's 2001 net income included $824 million in pension fund income, or 7 percent of its earnings. If this were highlighted in a discussion for investors instead of left to a footnote, it could lead to a discounting effect. However, from the investor's point of view, that is exactly the kind of information needed to make valid comparisons and, ultimately, the decision to buy, sell, or hold shares of the company.

A more troubling example of how pension income affects net profits is found on the 2000 financial report from Qwest. Its pension income added $319 million to income; however, the company reported an overall net loss for the year of $81 million. So the true operating picture was far worse than it appeared and could only be figured out by reading the footnotes. The use (or misuse) of footnotes to hide the facts is a chronic problem in the way financial statements have been put together. Pension income reporting is one example of how corporations distort the picture of what is really taking place. To present a fair picture of operating net income, pension profits should be uniformly excluded and reported in a separate, nonoperating format.

The problems at Qwest were augmented by its increase of expected return on pension fund assets of .8 percent over the prior year. Justification for this increase is difficult to understand; in some cases, estimates appear designed to improve the report rather than to reflect the reality of the situation. Many of the accounting decisions made at the corporate level involve estimates. Pension income is a prime example, where assumptions about rates of return can have a big effect on net income. Two changes could help to clarify pension-related financial reporting. First, pension income should be deducted from operating net income, because the income is not actually a part of the corporate generation of sales. While defined benefit pension plans have to show up on the statements, they should be reported separately from operating income to provide greater reliability and accuracy. Second, the method used to establish reserves for future pension payments should be formalized by a formula that everyone is required to use. This method should be set up in much the same way as reserves are reported by insurance companies, in which actuarial assumptions are based on mortality rates more than assumptions about future net investment income. This area is only one needing reform, and the FASB needs to provide auditing firms and corporations with specific guidelines to accomplish uniformity in reporting pension profits.

Robert Olstein proposes a change not only to make reporting uniform but to the way that pension accounting is done:

> I think we should change our generally accepted accounting principles and have pension expense (which assumes no more than Treasury bond returns) in operating income above the line and . . . the income produced in excess of ten-year Treasury rate returns by the pension portfolio below the line.[7]

The complexity of reporting of pension income can be summarized with one fact: those companies providing deferred benefit pension plans to their employees also have complete control over the accounting assumptions that affect the bottom line. Because pension income has been a large source of profits in recent years, the bigger the pension asset, the bigger the potential for distortion. For example, between 1999 and 2001, General Electric's pension plan provided $4 billion in pretax income, making the GE pension plan the largest single source of profit for those years. However, at the same time, the asset value fell by $5 billion due to investment losses.[8]

Corporations use footnotes for matters beyond pension income reporting. For example, those companies owning real estate often include footnotes to report estimated current m'arket value, sometimes requiring a large adjustment. Improvements to real estate (including buildings themselves) are depreciated over time, so that the balance sheet value of real estate declines. However, in real terms, the actual market value of real estate could be rising, so the difference between reported book value and actual market value of real estate has to be explained in a footnote.

Another common use for footnotes is to explain assumptions supporting reserves. For example, companies set up reserves for future bad debts, which should be calculated based on historical trends in bad debts written off, adjusted by changes in accounts receivable levels currently shown on the books and also by anticipated increases in future revenue. The same argument applies to other reserves, such as the reserve for obsolete inventory. Any reserve level should make sense in terms of growth in sales and cost activity and trends comparing sales and inventory levels. Footnotes are used to explain how reserves are set up and why they were increased or decreased.

Footnotes are also used for standard disclosures that are not reported directly on the books of the company. These include terms of long-term leases, which represent a liability that is not shown on the liability section of the balance sheet, even though the amount of obligation might be significant. Other disclosures include so-called contingent liabilities that might or might not become actual liabilities in the future. For example, if a lawsuit has been filed against the organization, the amount being claimed in the lawsuit is a contingent liability. Depending on a future court hearing or settlement, the company might incur a liability in the future.

The footnotes are only the starting points of disclosure. The whole industry of accounting involves big-number estimates, accruals, and deferrals often based on best estimates, and other accounting decisions, so that no "one true answer" is ever possible. In fact, if an accountant can document a reasonable assumption for a decision, that often is justification enough. The task of the auditing firm is to examine the books and records and to ensure that the assumptions and estimates made by the company fall within the rules. Thus, a secondary form of disclosure will be found in future reports: management's discussion of accounting alternatives, special risks, and perhaps most important of all—a disclosure about what the financial reports really mean.

Accounting is a highly technical field, but that does not excuse unclear or misleading reporting. In the future, the successful publicly listed company will not be the one whose stock performs best in the market (as has been the case in the short-term view of the recent past), but it will be the company that is able to communicate well with its stockholders about the significance of its numbers, in nontechnical language.

SPECIAL ADJUSTMENTS

One of the more troubling areas of abuse in the recent past has been the tendency to include special adjustments and nonrecurring items—so often that the nonrecurring items became a regular feature of the financial report. Companies with especially high activity in acquisitions, for example, took so many adjustments for restatements of earnings, one-time write-offs of reserves, and other fixes, that it became virtually impossible for the nonaccountant to figure out what was really going on. In fact, acquisitions became a trick to falsify and inflate revenues from one year to the next rather than a sound business practice.

An important new guideline for every investor is: if you do not understand what the numbers mean, and if management's explanations do not help, that is a red flag. The numbers should be clear, their meaning explained effectively by management.

Companies have to report extraordinary items, of course, such as one-time losses from sale of assets or loss of inventory, gains or losses in foreign exchange rates, and other, easily explained nonrecurring items. However, when companies are heavily involved in acquisition activity, restated earnings are difficult to follow, especially when accompanied with a lot of write-offs of reserves, so that it becomes increasingly difficult to identify the real growth rate of the company. One purpose of analyzing financial reports is to identify a company's recurring earnings base by eliminating items such as earnings inflated by transactions with affiliates, by making overpriced acquisitions (the purchase of CUC by Cendant, who overpaid according to Olstein), by otherwise masking deteriorating future earnings through other forms of acquisition activity. The purpose in seeking out trends like these is to define the *quality of earnings* of a company. You should measure the quality of earnings by how realistically financial statements reflect economic reality. This information helps determine whether the current market value of stock is realistic or inflated.

In the past, the stock's price has always been considered a true reflection of a company's value based on the market's opinion of its future growth potential. However, the value investing approach endorsed by Robert Olstein and others calls for a different analysis—adjusting reported earnings for unrealistic accounting and valuing companies according to a model of estimated discounted future cash flow.

Amazon.com is an example Olstein likes to cite. Amazon CEO Jeff Bezos shrugs off the importance of accounting, and Olstein is amazed that analysts continued to recommend the stock at a market capitalization of $38 billion with no earnings and none expected in the foreseeable future. This example raises an important question: how do you evaluate a company that does not show a profit and whose business model indicates negative cash flow for the foreseeable future? What is the quality of earnings when there are no earnings? Buying stocks is not an intuitive or a metaphysical exercise; it should be based on science and analysis—in other words, hard work. Olstein properly identifies the problem as one of the Wall Street establishment. He sums it up: "No matter how many more Enrons explode, Wall Street will never do the grunt work needed to look behind reported numbers to assess the true economic reality of financial statements. A bull market is intoxicating."[9]

Amazon's CEO shrugs off GAAP profits as an exercise his company doesn't bother with. Not only CEOs disdain the fundamentals. Jack Grubman, formerly of the big Wall Street firm Salomon Smith Barney, has said that accounting has "no bearing" on valuation of companies and is a "backwards-looking" method.[10]

It should strike anyone as incredible that a CEO of a listed company or an analyst in a major Wall Street firm would dismiss the fundamentals in this manner. Ignoring accounting means that analysis is based entirely on nothing of substance. The fundamentals are the only method for realistic valuation of a company. Lacking that, the analyst or investor is shooting from the hip or depending on some kind of momentum on the part of the market to continue pushing stock prices upward. Anyone who went through the late '90s dot.com bubble market knows by now that artificially inflated stock prices eventually come crashing down. The false promise of ever increasing profits is simply an appeal to greed and is not based on any kind of reality. To ignore the fundamentals is irresponsible.

READING THE FOOTNOTES

Assuming that every investor should use fundamental analysis as an analytical tool, where do you start? It is true that comparative reporting serves as a basis for determining whether currently reported results (as well as projected future results) are realistic. However, before proceeding to detailed fundamentals and trends, first make sure that the financial statements disclose all that you need.

Some adjustments might be called for, and these should be disclosed in the footnotes. This is perhaps the most overlooked section of the financial report, because so much valuable information is found there. Footnotes may serve as the basis for deciding not to invest in a company, especially if one or more are unclear. Jean-Marie Eveillard of First Eagle Sogen Fund gave one example:

> Analysis begins with reading public information. If you take the example of Enron, the footnote concerning off balance sheet partnerships was incomprehensible. Anyone who tried to reach the CFO found no one who was willing to explain it, because it was deliberately incomprehensible.[11]

The footnotes are supposed to clarify and provide *more* information than is given in the financial statements. Those statements conform to GAAP rules; so, for example, the market value of real estate is not reported, just the depreciated book value. A footnote is needed to reconcile and explain the difference, which can be material. In the Enron example, however, footnotes were provided but did not clarify what was being reported. The purpose was, perhaps, to conform to the law by presenting the appearance of disclosure but also to use such language that no one could understand what was being said.

Footnotes can be used to adjust the reported results in an attempt to identify the *intrinsic value* of a company—what the business is worth not in future potential but in today's dollars. Jean-Marie Eveillard describes the adjustments as intended to identify "core earnings" of the business, also known as the *true economic profit*. This number is not easy to pin down given the complexities of accounting; however, the material elements can be identified and used to adjust reported earnings.

The core earnings should begin with operating profit, then remove pension income and any other forms of nonoperating profits included in that section. This includes any income derived from nonrecurring or extraordinary items, all of which are supposed to be spelled out in the footnotes. A lot of confusion has arisen in the past over distinctions between cash flow and earnings, and between reported versus cash-based or economic earnings. Because these terms are not used consistently in all quarters, it is impossible to apply them universally.

For example, one of the favorite gimmicks is EBITDA (Earnings Before Interest, Taxes, Depreciation, and Amortization), which was developed in the 1980s when leveraged buyouts were the rage. Originally intended to allow comparisons between industries and to identify a company's cash-flow and debt service capabilities (e.g., current and likely future working capital), EBITDA has been used in many other situations to distort reported earnings or to put an otherwise dismal earnings report in a positive light. While EBITDA often is intended to mean the same thing as "cash flow," it is not a dependable measurement of how working capital will change in the future. Thus, if you are analyzing footnotes to identify working capital strength, references to EBITDA can be misleading rather than clarifying, because the calculation ignores the actual changes in working capital over time.

In the aggressive accounting mode of the recent past, companies with questionable quality of earnings have been able to pump them up, even as reported under the EBITDA calculation. So deceiving the analyst who depends too heavily on this cash flow income calculation is easy. Another serious flaw is that the EBITDA calculation does not account for noncash revenues and their effects on cash flow. If a company is understating bad debt reserves, booking revenues that are not likely to be received, or accruing sham transactions, EBITDA does not capture these practices (in comparison to reported sales).

In other words, a study of the footnotes is not adequate if the test of cash flow is limited to the EBITDA calculation. There is no substitute for a trend study of cash flows that looks at working capital changes over time, especially with accounts receivable and bad debt reserves considered as a big part of the equation. Watch out for companies whose footnotes merely cite techniques of recalculation like EBITDA but do not actually expand on the information in the financial reports.

Footnotes, in other words, can clarify and expand information, or they can obfuscate and confuse the analyst. Footnotes, of course, involve much more than explanations of cash flow and working capital, but these examples serve to show the type of information you can expect to find in the footnotes and how the company can use (or misuse) that information.

A likely trend for future reporting will be an effort on the part of management (whose increased personal liability requires them to disclose more) and independent auditing firms (now on notice that their audits have to be of the highest possible standards) to improve the use of footnotes in their reports. Future footnotes should not disclose in name only but rather educate the investor or analyst as to what specific items really mean. Hopefully, the footnote will become an educational and clarification disclosure tool, as originally intended, and less of a highly technical device used by accountants and executives to confuse outsiders.

FINDING THE INFORMATION: NEW REALITIES

C h a p t e r

6

THE FUNDAMENTAL
GAME PLAN

With the new environment on Wall Street, the importance of fundamentals—the financial information about companies—has once come again to everyone's attention. It is clear now that fundamentals are the key to identifying value as well as to seeing red flags.

Because virtually all forms of accounting transgressions show up in the fundamentals, it is impossible to ignore financial statements and related information. Even technicians—those who follow nonfinancial indicators—need to recognize the importance of studying information beyond stock price. Because one of the primary motives for aggressive accounting has always been to inflate the stock price, limiting analysis just to the stock price is unrealistic. After all, if that price is not realistic, how can you find out? In practice, technical analysis should be used as one of many tools for the analyst. Stock pricing certainly can be used to test volatility, compare value (especially in identifying differences between estimated true value of the stock and current market value), and watch the market in general. However, the serious analyst will recognize that, if anything, analytical work has to be expanded beyond the traditional two camps—fundamental and technical—and modern analysis will have to be done on a higher level.

Must the average investor become skilled in financial and analytical skills? No, they do not. Certainly, any skills you develop to improve your understanding of numbers and financial trends will be helpful. However, a needed cultural change is happening at the corporate level. The corporation has its own army of accountants plus outside auditors, a bank of accounting and analytical talent that few individuals could ever hope to possess. If corporations are to respond to the needs of their stockholders, cultural change must include not only improved disclosure but also clearer explanations of:

- How the numbers were developed
- Alternative methods and assumptions and how those would affect valuation
- Risks associated with the company's markets
- Incentive-based executive compensation and how it would change under different accounting assumptions

Realistically, the individual investor will not be able to perform the tests to adjust reported operating income, for example, and find the intrinsic value of the company. The majority of market volume reflects activity by mutual funds and other institutional investors, and the individual—especially one working alone or with substandard brokerage advice—is at a severe disadvantage. So, given the fact that institutional investors should perform their own analytical work and that corporations are armed with their own accounting departments, how can the individual get a fair opportunity?

For some, the solution will be to abandon direct ownership and entrust their money to a well-managed mutual fund. However, how do you know that the fund is doing its job? Many of the large funds bought Enron stock and did not act cautiously when reviewing indecipherable footnotes (not to mention suspiciously high growth rates and other signs). If mutual funds were unable to recognize problems in the past, why trust them in the future?

The corporations themselves need and are undergoing a significant change in attitude toward investors, and they are accepting responsibility for reporting their results in an entirely new way. In the past, many corporations adopted an adversarial attitude toward investors, replacing responsible reporting with the desire to meet analysts's predictions and keep stock prices up. In some cases, they adopted accounting policies to make the picture as rosy as possible. The new laws and regulations requiring corporate executives to disclose more *and* to certify their reports will lead to more carefully communicated messages to stockholders and to the Wall Street establishment. That whole establishment, represented by large brokerage firms also engaged in investment banking, has been largely discredited as a part of both the late '90s dot.com debacle and disclosures of corporate accounting abuses. Not only corporate executives but also brokers hyping stock added to the problems. So it is time to recognize that, until significant changes are made to the way brokerage firms operate, a covenant is required between corporate management and investors to reestablish confidence in the markets.

You as an individual investor, even in an improved environment of disclosure and reporting, remain responsible for developing analytical tools to monitor stocks and make intelligent comparisons. Even though corporations will improve their reporting and the majority of companies remain on the right side of the law, you should adopt the policy, *trust but verify,* in your analysis of financial reporting.

THE BASIC VALUE OF FUNDAMENTALS

Analysis begins with an understanding and appreciation of the numbers. In business, the financial strength of a company and its results of operations (profits and losses) are the major arena for making judgments about the corporation itself. How else would you come to a conclusion about one or more companies? With so much emphasis historically on stock price, short-term technical indexes like the Dow Jones Industrial Averages, and number of points of change in daily stock prices, the fundamentals have gotten lost in the shuffle. Unfortunately, the shoot-from-the-hip Wall Street attitude often is that fundamentals are backward-looking, out of date, uninteresting, and somehow irrelevant. In practice, though, the fundamentals, while backward-looking, are the sole indicator of likely future growth and so are extremely interesting and relevant to investors.

The fundamentals include a broad range of information, essentially anything having to do with financial information, either directly or indirectly. So, in addition to the obvious tests involving working capital, capitalization, sales, operating profits, and earnings per share, the fundamentals also include dividend yield, quality and effectiveness of management, cyclical factors that will affect corporate results, economic factors (e.g., the effect of interest rates on high-debt industries such as public utilities), labor relations, competitive situations within as single industry, new product developments by a company or its competitors, and world and national politics. While some of these factors are very indirect and even esoteric, they should be kept in mind, as a means of comparison if nothing else. Investors considering buying stock in several companies may use the less direct elements to choose one corporation over another.

Fundamentals provide not only a numerical test; they also identify and quantify degrees of market risk and other forms of risk. The obvious fundamental test is to compare financial results from one period to another or between companies and to attempt to equate those results with growth in the future of the investment. This means, of course, that a company with strong fundamentals should be able to produce long-term yields for investors, which is the basic premise in performing the tests.

Along the way, however, fundamental tests also provide investors with the means to compare risks. The basic *market risk*—that risk of the stock's price over time—often is expressed in terms of volatility. Market risk in that respect is a technical indicator (see the next chapter). However, market risk can also reflect the corporation's market and associated risks and, for the purpose of making the distinction, should perhaps be given the different name of *business risk*.

Risk analysis—that makes the fundamentals interesting—is where you ultimately define value in a stock. In a nutshell, a value stock is one that is selling at a discount, a bargain based on a study of fundamental or intrinsic value, or a stock that is not only a worthwhile long-term hold stock but also one having strong fundamentals. Ron Muhlenkamp, manager of the Muhlenkamp Fund and a midcap value manager, advises that investors should, "forget the popular image of value managers as white-haired old men in bow ties and suspenders sleepwalking through reports on cement producers, insurers, and paper makers. Value stocks are anything but boring."[1] He cites the year 2000, in which value stocks rose 15.3 percent while typical growth stocks fell 45.7 percent.[2]

One of the great mistakes investors make is confusing fundamental analysis and technical analysis. The study of market risk is a good example. In studying how the fundamentals work from one period to another, it is easy to slip into the confusing gray area. Watching earnings per share—a valid fundamental test—invariably transitions to a study of the stock's price and, from there, to concern about price volatility. Business analysis—as practiced in corporate accounting departments—is quite different from the types of technical analysis performed by Wall Street analysts. To the degree that corporations estimate their earnings and convey that information to analysts, the exercise itself has little to do with actual business forecasting. In practice, estimating future operating revenues, costs, expenses, and profits is an exercise in building market-based assumptions in great detail. The budgeting process as practiced in companies is quite different from the earnings estimates most investors see and hear about.

This disparity has come about for several reasons. First, the budgeting process is of little interest to anyone but the back room accounting folks. Second, the budgeting process may be used for internal monitoring and evaluation of controls but has little, if anything, to do with investment marketing (the effort to get investors to buy and hold stock). Third, it would be difficult to explain the budgeting process in a way that would make it interesting to nonaccountants. Thus, corporate America has accepted the disparity between the way it operates internally and the message it conveys to Wall Street.

Investors may accept and understand this disparity without having to know the details, but they may still gain insights by performing some fundamental tests. However, it is also important to remember the distinction between fundamentals and technical indicators—whether in tests performed individually or in the messages sent out by corporations.

If corporate messages to stockholders emphasize stock price too much and not financial or market information, you need to recognize this as a problem. As part of changing its culture, corporate management must focus on maintaining financial health. Most publicly listed companies do this most of the time; the danger signals arise when so-called management actually functions as a cheering section for the buy-

K e y P o i n t

Some of the messages investors get from corporations are more technical than fundamental, and the wise investor needs to remember the distinctions. Confusing the two distracts you from the fundamental tests that are crucial to making informed decisions.

ing and holding of stock rather than as corporate officers. Investors need to recognize the two, often contradictory roles of management. On the one hand, managers theoretically report to the board of directors, and the board theoretically works for investors; this textbook structure is how corporations operate. The other role of management, which has been self-serving in too many cases, is to keep stock prices and profits up, even if that means having to use aggressive accounting tricks. This role of management, built upon the incentive compensation system, is not only nonoperational in the corporate world but potentially damaging to investors looking for long-term, sustained growth.

Wall Street insiders have long recognized the relationship between ever-growing earnings and stock prices. This has led to an unrealistic rule: you have to improve earnings each period, or your stock goes down. For executives, an earnings setback means loss of incentives like stock options—or even being fired. The problem is not just at the corporate level; it permeates the whole market. One major change that needs to occur is cultural; investors need to recognize the inaccuracy that has dominated analysis, both fundamental and technical. The scope of the problem is described by one expert as fiction:

> Over the years, an entire earnings infrastructure has developed, including corporate executives and directors, accountants and analysts, fund managers and kitchen-table stock players. These interested parties are mutually reinforcing roles in sustaining the fiction that continuous profit growth is either possible or desirable.[3]

THE PE RATIO AND ITS LIMITATIONS

Given the modern-day adversarial role between management and investors—a situation that has to change—everyone needs to (a) track the fundamentals, (b) develop and follow trends, and (c) try to recognize the signs that those trends are changing. All of this needs to be achieved through analysis that is easily and quickly performed. Not every investor has experience or training in accounting, so the analysis has to be nontechnical enough that anyone can use it.

With that in mind, the price-earnings ratio has become a popular tool for investors. It is a single number, lends itself to comparison quickly, and is easily calculated. Most investors understand what the PE ratio represents, even though some have difficulty equating PE to actual value or safety features of a particular stock.

Like all forms of analysis, the PE ratio is accurate and useful *only* if you first have faith in the fairness and consistency of the financial results reported by the company. This ratio is interesting because it includes two elements, one fundamental and the other technical. The price (a technical indicator) is divided by earnings per share (a fundamental indicator) to arrive at the PE ratio (usually rounded to the closest whole number). Also called *a multiple of earnings*, PE represents the market's current perception of future earnings potential for a particular company.

For example, if the current price of a stock is $28 per share and latest reported earnings per share are $1.42, you can determine the PE:

$$\frac{\$28}{\$1.42} = 20$$

Current market price is at a multiple of 20 times the latest reported earnings per share. So the higher the PE ratio, the more in favor the stock. That is to say, the greater optimism for the stock, the higher the price will be driven, and that relationship between price and earnings is reflected in the PE ratio.

PE is a useful comparative tool for investors and should be used as a measure of relative safety. The higher the PE ratio, the greater the market risk. Once PE ratio reaches triple digits, the current price of the stock may be far out of line with reality. Ironically, some investors view a growing PE ratio as a positive sign and look with disdain at low-PE stocks. The PE for stocks tends to rise overall as markets rise, so broader market PE ratio can also be used to measure the mood of the market. However, for individual stocks, low PEs translate to low risk, while high PEs signal high risk.[4]

While some investors view PE in an upside-down manner—viewing a high PE as a positive and a low PE as a negative—the precise value of PE is not that clear, either. Just because the current PE ratio is low does not mean the company's stock is a better investment. Making comparative studies within specific industries is no more, because typical earnings per share vary widely from one industry group to another. Comparing PE ratios between, say, the construction and retail industries is not valid.

Another problem associated with PE is that of relevance. Price is always up to date within 24 hours, and today's published PE ratio for a company will be based on yesterday's closing price. However, the last known earnings per share could be three months old. So the more time has gone by since earnings were reported, the less reliable the PE ratio. This problem is further aggravated when a company's revenues and earnings are seasonal. Imagine the distortion for a corporation depending heavily on retail sales for the holiday season, whose latest earnings reflect December 31 results, when the PE ratio is reported in March (before the current quarter's earnings have been published). Making this timing problem even a greater concern is the fact that the three interim quarters are unaudited.

PE ratio, when applied to a single stock, can be used as reliable measurement of change in the relationship between price and earnings, remembering these points.

- The timing of latest reported earnings makes PE less reliable when the last report was significantly long ago.
- You need to assume that earnings have been reported consistently and accurately.
- The desired PE ratio will differ between industries, so stock-to-stock PE comparisons are not reliable.
- This ratio combines fundamental and technical information, so it will vary not only with regard to the fundamentals, but also

due to temporary aberrations in the market. Thus, to be useful as an analytical tool, it should be applied in the longer term.

Finally, remember that PE should not be thought of as a simple measurement of a stock's current value or safety. The implications are far broader and involve many factors beyond the relatively simple "high" or "low" comparison that reassures investors and analysts all too often. It is wise to follow this guideline from *Smart Money Magazine:*

> . . . interpreting a stock's PE is a complicated matter. To decipher it, you have to know the stock's historical PE range, the historical range of typical stocks in that industry, interest rates, debt loads, margins, and profit growth patterns. Only then will you know if the PE is telling you that the stock is too cheap or too expensive.[5]

STANDARD RATIOS

While the PE ratio has been a useful and quick indicator (often for marketwide studies), it is of limited value in a purely fundamental application. Because the financial purist tends to limit the investigation to the financial information alone, current price is seen as a factor outside the range of interest. This is not to say that technical indicators, including price, can be ignored; however, the fundamentals should not be confused with price or other technical indicators, notably market indexes like the DJIA.

A study of the numbers is most reliable when done as part of a long-term trend. The real methods for finding out what is going on in a company—and for identifying when the numbers are being misrepresented—involve moving averages. Also useful is to study not just singular dollar amounts but relationships between a series of related results. When a company's reported results are altered inaccurately, trend analysis and ratios ultimately uncover the problem.

Balance sheet ratios are a starting point; these refer to relatively simple tests comparing items on the balance sheet alone. Useful ratios help you to locate evolving problem areas or areas that should be questioned. The valuable ratios include:

Current ratio. This number is an old favorite among accountants. It is a comparison between current assets (cash and assets that can be converted to cash within one year) and current liabilities (debts owed and payable within one year). The current ratio, as a generalized standard, should be 2:1 or better. Thus, current assets should exceed current liabilities by a 2:1 ratio. This ratio is a broad indicator of the health of a company's working capital. If you see the current ratio declining over time, the organization may be experiencing a decline in working capital, often leading to difficulties in the near future.

Quick assets ratio. Also called the *liquidity ratio,* this is the same as current ratio except that inventory is excluded. This variation makes sense when a company has exceptionally high inventory levels as a matter of course. A general standard is that the quick assets ratio should be at or above 1:1.

A problem with current ratio and quick assets ratio is that they do not always present a clear picture. For example, exceptionally high inventory levels could be financed through long-term debt. In that situation, the current ratio appears healthy when, in fact, the company may be relying too heavily on debt capitalization to fund operations. With this in mind, more reliable measures of working capital are needed.

Working capital turnover. Working capital is the net difference between current assets and current liabilities. By dividing sales by working capital for the latest year, you can judge the level of turnover (the number of times, on average, working capital is replaced during the year).

$$\frac{\text{Sales}}{\text{Current Assets} - \text{Current Liabilities}} = \text{Turnover}$$

While assets and liabilities are not actually replaced in the sense of being removed and then built up again, turnover is a device enabling you to spot emerging trends over periods of time. Working capital is essential to funding operations, so a comparison between working capital and sales is valid. It can also help to spot artificial current ratio trends. As current assets such as inventory or accounts receivable grow with long-term liability offsets, the working capital turnover will begin to decline.

Inventory turnover. This is another popular measurement of how well companies manage their balance sheet accounts. Inventory levels may be higher than they should be or financed with long-term debt; the inventory turnover ratio will uncover both of these potential problems. A slowing turnover rate indicates excessive inventory, and when turnover grows, inventory levels may be unreasonably low. While some analysts like to compare inventory to sales, it makes more sense to perform the comparison between inventory at cost and the cost of sales (also reflecting a cost basis). Because sales are on a marked-up basis, turnover could be distorted when different lines of business are combined together. To calculate, divide the cost of sales by inventory at cost.

$$\frac{\text{Cost of Sales}}{\text{Inventory at Cost}} = \text{Turnover}$$

Accounts receivable to sales ratio. The receivable balances carried on a company's books are one area where some aggressive accounting decisions have been made. By booking income in advance of when it is earned, revenues can be inflated in the current year. This invariably shows up in the form of higher accounts receivable.

A ratio comparing accounts receivable to total revenues over time is useful in trying to spot questionable accounting practices. For example, as sales volume grows, accounts receivable dollar amounts will probably grow as well. However, in a properly managed program, the percentage relationship between accounts receivable and revenues should remain fairly consistent. Some increase would be reasonable but not an ever growing percentage. For example, if accounts receivable range consistently between 40 and 45 percent of sales, that range might be seen as healthy and consistent (depending, of course, on the industry). However, if revenues are expanding rapidly and accounts receivable represent a growing percentage of sales, that could be a red flag.

Bad debt reserve ratio. The accounting standard for treatment of bad debts is to set up a reserve in the asset section of the balance sheet. The reserve is a *negative asset* in the sense that it reduces the total balance of accounts receivable. The reserve is supposed to be established at a level estimated to cover future bad debts. As average receivable dollar balances grow, you would expect to see a corresponding percentage increase in bad debt reserves. It is not realistic to expect that bad debts should remain stationary or fall when sales volume is growing. Tracking the bad debt reserve trend can reveal that a corporation is understating its future losses to increase net operating profit.

Diluted earnings per share. The primary earnings per share is a simple calculation in which the reported earnings for a year are divided by the outstanding shares of common stock. However, this figure is not necessarily the most accurate reflection of earnings. The earnings and number of shares should be adjusted for a number of factors. For example, if the company carries convertible preferred stock or bonds, one form of dilution involves increasing the number of outstanding common shares of stock to the number that would exist in the event of conversion.

The net profit should also be adjusted to arrive at a realistic operating profit number. Thus, extraordinary items and nonrecurring forms of revenue like capital gains should be removed from reported earnings before calculating adjusted earnings per share. By the same argument, current-year earnings from acquired subsidiaries should be removed to make valid year-to-year comparisons. The trend toward high-volume acquisitions has clouded analysis for many large companies, so adjustments are essential to ensure valid comparative information.

Reported earnings should be based on after-tax operating profit. This might require a series of adjustments. Any deferred taxes should be put back into the picture and current earnings reduced to reflect tax liabilities. Any nonoperating income included above the line of after-tax profits should be removed. This includes interest income, foreign exchange gains, capital gains, and net income from pension funds. The collective total of these adjustments can be substantial.

To evaluate a company on as realistic a basis as possible, additional adjustments may help. These would include the effects of changing accounting methods, writing off reserves to income resulting from past-year acquisitions, and increasing expenses for depreciation and amortization when the company is deferring those expenses over longer periods than they should. Such adjustments, however, become highly technical and even subjective in nature, because understanding the transactions and accounting assumptions is no easy matter. Hopefully, as corporate officers begin to disclose more and certify their operating results, publicly listed corporations will accept greater responsibility for explaining their accounting methods and decisions, making it easier for the average investor to understand what is going on with the numbers.

Capitalization ratios. Corporations fund their operations and growth through two primary methods: equity and debt. Equity is another word for stock, meaning that growth is funded through selling stock on the market. Debt consists of long-term and short-term loans and issuing bonds. One important trend to watch for is an increase in debt capitalization over time. As a corporation comes to rely more and more on debt, especially fixed-rate, long-term bonds, it has higher annual interest expenses and less money available to fund operations or to pay dividends to stockholders. The relationship between bonds and total capitalization (equity plus debt) is worth monitoring carefully.

During periods of growth, several things occur. Not only do you expect increased sales but, hopefully, increased profits as well. If growth is profitable, corporations often finance that growth by issuing bonds. The justification is that selling more stock permanently commits the company to paying dividends, whereas bonds will eventually be redeemed and the corporation will end up being more profitable. However, if the profitability of growth is lower than projected over many years, then the debt commitment of bonds (as well as long-term loans) can become a severe burden. As the ratio of debt to total capitalization increases, the danger increases as well. If the percentage of debt increases while earnings per share remain the same or falls, capitalization may be relying less on equity and more on bonds and other long-term debts. Ultimately, profits suffer due to ever growing interest, and in the long term, lower profits will be reflected in weaker stock prices as well.

Interest coverage. Another way to measure debt capitalization is by comparing interest on bonds to operating profit. The multiples of bond interest monitored over time can reveal a trend. As bond interest rises, the coverage ratio will fall. The coverage ratio is computed by dividing net operating earnings by annual bond interest. Net profits might be rising and even earnings per share, but if the interest coverage ratio is falling at the same time, the corporation is becoming increasingly dependent on debt.

Return on equity. Most investors understand earnings per share and net profit as a percentage of sales; these are popular measurements of business performance. However, one little-used ratio that holds significance for investors is the measurement of profitability based on *equity* rather than on sales.

Whereas net margin is valuable because it shows how effectively corporations manage costs and expenses, return on equity reflects a more accurate return on investment. Ironically, investors understand return on equity for their own portfolios, but they rarely apply the same test to corporate results. Most tests of earnings are based on business activity rather than on investment value. From the point of view of the corporation itself, which is financial in nature, this makes sense. However, investors take risks in the hopes of realizing a good return on their money. So, as a means for judging results, it makes sense to study how well corporate profits are yielding a return on investment.

An interesting form of trend analysis is to compare net margin (earnings and sales) and return on investment (earnings and equity) on a side-by-side basis. You can not only monitor how each form of return changes over time but also spot trends in the difference between the two forms of return. For example, if the net margin typically ranges between 6 and 8 percent per year, while return on investment ranges between 2.25 and 2.5 percent, there is a correlation between the two forms of return. However, if return on investment begins to fall, while net margin remains the same, what does that mean? The trend may be justified by stabilization in dividend yield during a period of growth, or it could mean that the corporation is retiring older debt. A study of other trends in financial strength can be generated by recognizing gaps between these two forms of yield.

To compute return on equity, divide net income by the *average* value of equity. This changes from year to year due to (a) increased retained earnings from profits (or decreased retained earnings from operating losses), (b) purchase and retirement of stock as treasury stock, which reduces outstanding shares, and (c) the sale of new and additional classes of common or preferred stock. Some expenses end up as adjustments to retained earnings because they are not legally deductible, and other minor changes may occur as well. For the sake of simplicity, you can find the average by adding together the beginning and ending balances of the equity accounts, then dividing the result by two. (This calculation may need to be weighted if significant changes to equity occurred near the beginning or end of the year, such as new stock classes issued, for example.) The net profit is then divided by the average equity value to arrive at the percentage return on investment.

Increase in sales. An important measurement of expansion is found in sales volume. However, merely comparing one year's sales to the next is not accurate; a number of factors need to be taken into account. First is the question of acquisitions. It is not accurate to compare this year's sales to last year's if the current year is distorted by acquisition activity. This activity adds a special complexity to year-to-year comparisons, especially if a corporation has engaged in a large volume of acquisitions, or has merged with another corporation.

The quality of earnings becomes ever more important when a corporation is expanding its sales. Thus, any study of sales growth should be accompanied by a trend analysis of gross profit (revenues less cost of goods sold) as well as a trend analysis of net operating profits.

Gross profit may change as corporations grow into dissimilar lines of business, perhaps through acquisitions. Different types of operations are likely to contain inconsistent ranges of costs. Thus, comparing reported cost of sales and gross profit may be puzzling unless one can separate out different sources of revenues, costs, and gross profit—not always an easy task with the summarized information corporations provide in their financial reports. If nothing else, corporations should reconcile aberrations from one period to another to aid investors in their fundamental analysis.

As to net earnings, tracking sales *and* earnings together makes a lot of sense. By the same argument above, different industries tend to experience a diverse range of potential net returns on revenues, so acquisition activity can cloud the trend. However, assuming that the trend is reasonable, what should you expect to see as the result of growth?

A lot of emphasis is placed on ever growing sales, but often as sales increase, the percentage yield falls. This is a negative sign if sustained over time. Some falling off in yield might be expected during the first year of expansion (although it should be minimized because exceptional expenses are properly amortized over several years). As a general observation, expansion on the top line—revenues—should be accompanied by, at the very least, a consistent yield percentage. So if a company typically earns a 6 percent net profit, it should continue to earn 6 percent on revenues when those revenues increase. If the margin falls off, either the quality of earnings has fallen (a red flag for investors), or the corporation is failing to exercise internal controls and costs and expenses are growing out of proportion (another red flag).

It is not realistic to expect ever growing earnings per share or net margin. These factors are naturally limited and will not exceed a reasonable level. Maintaining is enough in most cases, and given growth in sales volume, the dollar amounts of a consistent net margin will grow with time, representing good quality of earnings. This translates, of course, into a good prospect for long-term investment growth. From the traditional point of view on Wall Street, dominated by analysts who do not understand corporate accounting and financial reality, a corporation is succeeding only when net margins continue to grow year after year. That is simply unrealistic. It can be compared to an investor who earns 6 percent on stock investments one year and sets a goal to earn 7, 8, and 9 percent in the next three years—which makes no sense. Not only is the goal impractical, but it implies that the investor is willing to increase risk exposure year after year.

You can use many other potential ratios to judge the reasonableness of a corporation's balance sheet and income statement. For example, you can track the relationship between capital assets and accumulated depreciation to spot accounting decisions that are not realistic. (Some companies wrote off capital assets over longer periods than under recommended methods, resulting in higher profits in the current year.) However, the range-of-ratio tests provided above serves as a good basis for most people; moving beyond these basic tests requires a greater accounting background and, perhaps, more financial information than is usually available in published financial statements.

TREND ANALYSIS

One of the problems companies face is investors's expectations. Investors like reliable, consistent, and predictable financial reports. Corporations, recognizing this, are inclined to alter their books so that sales and profits are evened out over time. In the real world, outcomes are chaotic. They are affected by cyclical economic forces, internal changes, the very process of expansion itself, and numerous other factors that belie the desired state of low volatility.

Just as investors take comfort in less volatile stock prices, they also seek less volatile fundamentals. So a company whose sales rise gradually over time, corresponding with small but consistent increases in dividend payments and a strong and steady rate of net profit, is reassuring to investors, both institutional and individual. Beneath the surface, it is possible that some "cookie jar" or sugar bowl accounting is going on. The company may be deferring sales above the previous years' average and recognizing them in future years so as to report steady and consistent results.

In one respect, adjusting results in this way is dishonest, because it is done in the knowledge that it is not accurate. In another respect, it is at least partially a response to expectations on the part of the Wall Street establishment and investors. Given the fact that the GAAP guidelines allow flexibility in reporting, the astute corporate accountant can certainly arrive at logical justifications for referring some portion of revenues. The same accountant can use other devices, such as setting up reserves that are on the high side, for example, to increase current-year expenses and reduce profits. If these actions are intended to defer good news until later, they are benign compared to inflating results artificially by overstating revenue and deferring expenses—especially with the intention of inflating executive incentive compensation. That is done at the expense of stockholders.

With the mood for reform and disclosure beginning to unfold upon the market, future reporting will involve a greater degree of fundamental volatility, meaning reported revenues and profits being more erratic and more difficult to predict. However, these outcomes also will be more realistic. Perhaps investors are unreasonable to deceive themselves into believing that multiyear consistency in revenues, dividends, and profits is a good thing.

In the likely future of more erratic reporting, investors will have a more difficult task. The fundamentals are easier to track when results are consistent, because trends are relatively simple; however, if the results have been altered by the corporation in advance, then everyone—analysts, investors, and auditors—is working with a set of numbers that do *not* tell the real story.

So financial trends must be discovered using statistical methods that deal with unpredictable results. A few basic statistical tools will help in this effort.

The first statistical rule is to remove aberrations from your field of study. In the case of financial results, this means that any unusual and nonrecurring items should be taken out before trying to compute averages. Unusual items distort. Some corporations acquired other companies to inflate revenues and deceive investors, so extraordinary and nonrecurring items, while having a real effect on financial reports, should be removed. What's left are the "core earnings."[6] The same is true in the other direction. If a corporation paid out a large settlement in a lawsuit this year, that expense would not be recurring and—only for the purpose of trend watching—should be removed.

Remember, the purpose of the trend is neither to identify the intrinsic value of the company nor to judge the fairness of the stock's price. Those efforts are valid for the purpose of trying to decide whether or not to own the stock. The purpose in analysis is to isolate core revenue and profits and to develop a moving average—to spot where the company is going in terms of revenues and future profits. As companies grow, eventually revenues tend to flatten out, and profits follow. One of the primary motivations for long-term analysis is to identify the gradual weakening of market control, even if it has only begun to appear. Most long-term investors, are likely to realize real growth and return on investment by buying stock in companies whose star in just beginning to rise. While older, established companies often are safer investments, they will not experience the same level of growth as newer, more aggressively growing companies.

Given the desire to identify companies in terms of their long-term growth curve, the purpose of analysis is to (a) identify core earnings and profits, (b) track movement of those results over time, (c) identify any material changes in the trend, (d) determine what, if any, actions should be taken in response to a changing trend (e.g., buying shares for the first time, or selling shares currently owned), and (e) continuing to monitor and compare companies you consider investment prospects or that you currently own.

The following section explains briefly how to compute various averages useful for investment analysis. The first is the simple average, where a series of results are added together and then divided by the number of entries. If you are tracking a ratio for ten quarters, you would add up the ten outcomes and then divide by ten.

Example.   You are following the current ratio for a company over ten quarters. Results have been:

Quarter	Current Ratio
1	3.3:1
2	3.2:1
3	2.7:1
4	2.7:1
5	2.4:1
6	2.2:1
7	2.5:1
8	2.4:1
9	2.1:1
10	2.2:1

FIGURE 6.1 *Current Ratio Trend*

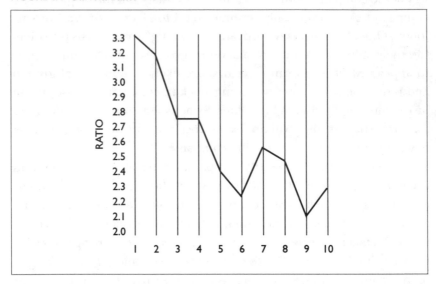

Attempting to draw any conclusions from this trend would be difficult. Even placed on a chart, the results do not necessarily identify what is occurring here.

Reviewing these results in the form of an average is far more helpful. To average each of these outcomes using a simple method, divide first two outcomes by two, the first three by three, and so forth.

Quarter	Current Ratio	Average
1	3.3:1	3.3
2	3.2:1	3.25
3	2.7:1	3.1
4	2.7:1	3.0
5	2.4:1	2.9
6	2.2:1	2.8
7	2.5:1	2.7
8	2.4:1	2.7
9	2.1:1	2.5
10	2.2:1	2.6

The outcome now is significantly different, showing less volatility. The longer the period being averaged, the less volatile the shape, or appearance, of the result. Thus, using two or three fields in the beginning has a certain effect, but by the end of the study, all ten quarters are being used and tend to flatten out the averages.

FIGURE 6.2 *Current Ratio Trend–Averaged*

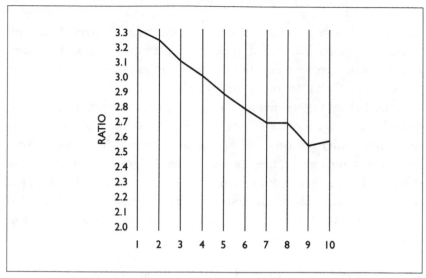

Alternatively, analysts like to use the moving average—a simple average applied to the same number of fields but moving through time. For example, in studying the trend in the current ratio, you might decide to use a four-quarter average. At the end of the fourth quarter, you would take the average of the first four; for the fifth quarter, you would use quarters two through five, and so forth through the range of quarters.

Here is the outcome for the same study using a four-quarter moving average (note that we have added an additional three preceding quarters to provide the full range).

Quarter	Current Ratio	Moving Average
-3	2.8:1	—
-2	3.0:1	—
-1	2.8:1	—
1	3.3:1	3.0
2	3.2:1	3.1
3	2.7:1	3.0
4	2.7:1	3.0
5	2.4:1	2.8
6	2.2:1	2.5
7	2.5:1	2.5
8	2.4:1	2.4
9	2.1:1	2.3
10	2.2:1	2.3

This method evens out the results even more, as shown in Figure 6.3.

The variation in outcome should not confuse the analyst. Using different averaging methods will produce different results, and the purpose is not to affect outcome but to find a method that is efficient, easy to use, and reflects outcomes consistently.

Another averaging method is to give greater weight to the latest period, on the theory that more recent information has greater significance than older information. For example, using the previous four-quarter moving average, the latest entry may be given a weight value of three, and the previous three quarters remain at one. In this case, the moving average would involve four quarters, but the outcome is divided by six because the latest quarter is included three times (weight value of three).

Quarter	Current Ratio	Weighted Average
-3	2.8:1	—
-2	3.0:1	—
-1	2.8:1	—
1	3.3:1	3.1
2	3.2:1	3.1
3	2.7:1	2.9
4	2.7:1	2.6
5	2.4:1	2.6
6	2.2:1	2.4
7	2.5:1	2.5
8	2.4:1	2.4
9	2.1:1	2.2
10	2.2:1	2.3

Note that this method produces results very similar to the use of a simple moving average, so it would be reasonable to conclude that weighting the average in this particular case does not add enough value to make the extra step worthwhile. This remains one of several methods available for managing data and may be useful when greater volatility is involved and, perhaps, when a larger field of study is included. Calculations for a moving average are performed easily using spreadsheet software such as Microsoft Excel, in which you can preprogram the calculations with little effort.

FIGURE 6.3 *Current Ratio Trend—4-quarter moving average*

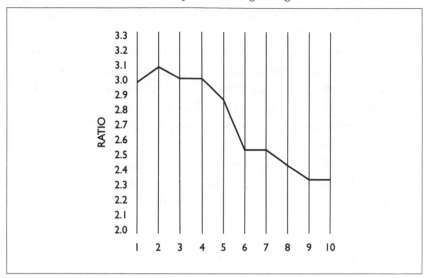

The calculation of an average is only the beginning phase in the analytical process. From there, you need to interpret the information. Here are a few questions worth asking, especially when studying sales and profits for a company.

- *Has the rate of growth changed?* Typically, and most statistically likely, a growth pattern established over many years will tend to slow down and level out. This doesn't mean that growth ceases altogether, but a high rate of growth is unlikely to be sustained for many years; certainly such rates will not continue forever. Thus, you may draw two conclusions from a long-term study. As the growth rate begins to slow down, you may identify the emerging height of a growth pattern. However, if an exceptionally high growth rate in sales continues without slowing down, you might also become suspicious and question how realistic the ever growing revenues are.
- *Is the trend overly predictable?* One of the motives in tinkering with accounting outcomes is to reduce fundamental volatility and reassure Wall Street analysts as well as investors. Astute investors are highly suspicious of an overly predictable outcome, remembering that the world of competitive business is chaotic, often cyclical, and unpredictable. When outcomes are so predictable that analysis produces no surprises, you should be suspicious.

- *Can you confirm the outcome in some way?* Even though trends might change from one period to the next, a turn in direction does not signal a permanent change. One of the principles in trend analysis is that a change in an established trend should not be considered permanent unless subsequent indicators confirm it. This is why watching two or more different indicators is useful. If you see revenues slowing down, you confirm the trend when you also see reductions in working capital, lowered inventory and receivable amounts, and lower costs and expenses.

- *How should you act on changes in trends?* When a trend establishes some fact or signals a change in previously assumed facts, you do not necessarily have to act in some manner. This year's slowdown in sales does not dictate that it is time to sell your stock. A big surge in a company's revenues does not always signal that it is time to buy more shares. The purpose of analysis is to put together pieces of the puzzle rather than to look at one or two outcomes in isolation. The decisions you make to buy shares of a company or to sell shares should be made by considering a number of factors.

- *Are the underlying assumptions valid?* Everything can change, potentially. For example, today you might consider sales growth the major factor in whether or not to hold a stock. Next year, you might be concerned if the ratio of debt to total capitalization is growing and dividend payments have leveled out. So, even when earlier assumptions continue to support your original conclusions, be ready to change your conclusions as other trends become apparent.

- *Is the range of analysis necessary?* You could end up studying so many different fundamental indicators that coming to a conclusion will be impossible. You need to limit what you follow. A handful of relevant indicators covering revenues, profits, capitalization, and working capital gives you a good sense of what the company is experiencing, and they tell you how the financial results compare to other companies. Limit your analysis, and be willing to do away with some indicators when calculating them becomes time consuming. Critically evaluate what numbers you are following in terms of information yielded.

Chapter

7

HOW COMPANIES CREATE GROWTH

Investors are attracted to the idea that expansion is positive, that growth means progress. The opposite side of this belief is that once sales stop expanding, the company has come to the end of its value as an investment.

These beliefs are only partially true. In fact, growth has to be defined before it can be called a positive trend. So many companies fail in their attempts to expand, that a program aimed at growing market share (or moving into new markets) is perhaps one of the most dangerous phases in a corporation's life. Well-managed growth is profitable, while growth that is not managed well is easy to recognize by a lack of profitability and deterioration of cash flow.

Key Point

Often, growth on the top line translates to decline on the bottom line, where it really counts. Investors can define quality of earnings during growth phases by checking ratios and dollar amounts.

The concept of quality of earnings is a great standard for investors to adopt in analyzing companies. This is more true in the analysis of expansion than anywhere else, and the ratios are easy to apply.

REAL GROWTH AND THE APPEARANCE OF GROWTH

A general assumption, promoted by Wall Street analysts more than by anyone else, is that a corporation *must* have ever higher sales or it has not met expectations. This belief is very destructive, because it does not place value on the profitability of revenue. It is a great disservice to investors to emphasize expansion while dismissing a decline in profitability. Excuses are commonplace. They include three old favorites:

1. *Expansion always costs money, and lower profits are part of the process.* This explanation contradicts reality and also flies in the face of accounting conventions. Expansion does cost money, but GAAP provides that expansion costs are supposed to be set up as assets and amortized over several years. Any expenses that apply to more than one fiscal year are spread over several years in this manner—the very reason why those expenses do not belong in the current year.
2. *Lower profits represent an investment in greater market share.* This, again, is double talk and a poor excuse. An examination of lower profits usually reveals expenses that have outpaced sales, a sign of poor internal controls rather than an investment in the future.
3. *The decline in profits is due to nonrecurring expenses, changes in accounting methods, or internal reorganization.* This argument does not fly and represents another form of explanation designed to obscure rather than to explain. Nonrecurring expenses can be isolated and an operating improvement demonstrated. However, when profits really have declined, it is easier to blame the numbers on nonrecurring expenses than to show what actually happened. Likewise, changes in accounting method can be explained by showing how profits would have been reported without the changes; this explanation, given without support, is another poor excuse for poor controls. The use of terms like *in-*

FIGURE 7.1 *Attributes of Earnings*

High quality of earnings	Low quality of earnings
Revenues are real, so that accounts receivable balances do not edge up as revenues are posted.	Reported earnings are accompanied by ever growing balances in accounts receivable.
Revenues are achieved through actual transactions for products or services, not via journal entries and closing of reserves.	Growth does not consist of sales but comes from adjustments from mergers and acquisitions, accounting accruals, and reserve adjustments.
Costs of sales remain steady and constant.	Costs of sales begin to inch upward. Gross margins begin to fall.
Operating expenses are not affected by higher revenues. They remain steady or grow only minimally.	Operating expenses begin to rise even in accounts not affected by higher revenues. As a consequence, net margins fall.
High quality of earnings growth is achieved in a controlled corporate environment. Management is always in control.	Low quality of earnings occurs in a chaotic environment. Management has lost control and cannot identify the cause of ever growing losses.
Cash flow remains strong, as demonstrated by consistently healthy ratios and appropriate debt levels.	Cash flow declines, represented by declining working capital ratios and increasing dependence on debt to fund operations.

ternal reorganization might have another meaning. For example, the corporation may have closed unprofitable divisions, cut back on internal staff and other expenses, or taken other steps to cut losses. Often, top management recognizes their failure to control costs and expenses and will tighten the belt next year.

The problems of low quality of earnings are easily defined. Expanded earnings *should* have several attributes, and a low quality of earnings contradicts them. Figure 7.1 summarizes these attributes.

Testing ratios is a fairly easy task that investors can perform on their own. The following methods are recommended for testing quality of earnings and defining the effectiveness of sales expansion:

- *Current ratio.* Is the corporation maintaining a steady current ratio? (The general standard is 2:1 or better.) A comparison between current assets and current liabilities may reveal a gradual shift in the relationship, which may indicate that management's control over cash is slipping during periods of expansion.
- *Debt ratio.* As working capital declines, corporations may depend increasingly on borrowing to fund operations. That means interest expenses begin to rise, affecting profits this year and in the future.
- *Gross margin.* A low quality of earnings can be discovered by monitoring gross margin from one period to another. This margin (revenues minus the cost of goods sold) represents operating profit before operating expenses. Its percentage of revenues should remain constant, or profits will be affected. Causes of declining margins may include carrying obsolete inventory or incurring unreasonably high labor and other direct charges. If a corporation expands into different lines of business with lower realistic gross margins, that move will take the whole operation's average down. However, in that case, the separate sources of revenue and gross margins should be broken down and reported separately, so that investors can understand why margins have fallen.
- *Net margin.* The all-important measure, profitability, ultimately defines quality of earnings. If net margin falls, so that the percentage of profit is less than in previous years, the company has a severe problem and a decline in quality of earnings. In comparing net margin, be sure to include and exclude the same factors. In the past, some corporations have distorted the true profitability picture by including some items in operating profits that do not belong there. Decide how to treat net pension income, deferred taxes, restatements, nonrecurring and extraordinary items, income from acquisitions and mergers, and changes in accounting methods.

- *Accounts-Receivable-to-Sales ratio.* The relationship between accounts receivable and sales should remain fairly consistent, even when growth occurs. In fact, one sign that quality of earnings is slipping is a distortion in this ratio. If receivable balances begin to rise, earnings may be exaggerated with accruals representing soft earnings (money that will never be received), or the company may have relaxed internal controls. In either case, cash flow will begin to deteriorate.

SALES AND PROFIT EXPANSION— UNREALISTIC EXPECTATIONS

In past years, Wall Street relied on analysts' predictions rather than on corporate reality. If the analysts predicted a certain earnings outcome, that became the standard against which market value of stock would be measured. If the corporation missed the mark by even one penny per share, the stock's market value suffered. If the corporation's results came in above analysts's predictions, a momentary euphoria ensued, and the stock was likely to soar.

Both cause and effect were out of line. The very fact that analysts have had such sway on Wall Street is itself a significant problem in the way that investors make decisions. Wise investors shy away from the predictions game, now aware that analysts often do not base their predictions on accounting analysis, instead repeating whatever they have been told by management.

The fundamental reality of reporting earnings is far different than the favored Wall Street method. If anything, the reason that established brokerage house analysts achieved influence was that simply believing what they said was easy. The fact that earnings often came in at or close to the predictions added to the legend that analysts were good at their job, never mind that corporations themselves often told analysts what to say. When some companies altered earnings to meet market expectations, they added to the illusion that investing in the stock market was an orderly science.

In the real world, sales and profits do tend to occur more chaotically than many investors believe. True accounting often involves struggling with fundamental volatility, natural limits to growth, and competitive forces that move cyclically. Evening out the results is not only deceptive, it also creates an illusion of predictability and low volatility in the very fundamentals that are given such lip service on Wall Street.

Sales growth curves cannot reasonably continue at the same pace each year without change. Not only is growth more chaotic than often reported, it also will tend to level out after an expansion period. Statistically, no trend continues forever without change. Leveling out occurs because, as the base becomes larger, the rate of increase cannot be sustained. Even if the annual dollar amount of sales growth remains the same from year to year, the growth curve will level out.

For example, if a corporation had $10 million in sales last year and its sales growth is $1 million per year, consider what happens over a six-year period.

Year	New Sales	Total Sales	% Growth
1	$1 million	$11 million	10.0
2	$1 million	$12 million	9.1
3	$1 million	$13 million	8.3
4	$1 million	$14 million	7.7
5	$1 million	$15 million	7.1
6	$1 million	$16 million	6.7

This growth trend is summarized in the chart in Figure 7.2.

Note that, while sales dollar amounts increase steadily (dollar amount scale at left), the rate of change (percentage scale at right) declines. Statistically, the rate of change in sales will decline as the base grows, so sales increases are not sustainable when reported as a percentage of change. In practice, it is also difficult for a corporation to sustain the same dollar amount change of sales as well. Every market is finite; given the fact that competitors claim some percentage of the whole, it is not realistic to expect one company's growth to continue without change from one year to the next.

The same argument applies to net profits. As stated before, you need to define profits before attempting to perform comparative analysis. Are you using net operating profits or net profits after nonoperating adjustments, are you including or excluding taxes, and are you making adjustments for nonrecurring changes? These are big questions, especially if the corporation changes how it reports these items from year to year.

FIGURE 7.2 *Sales Trend*

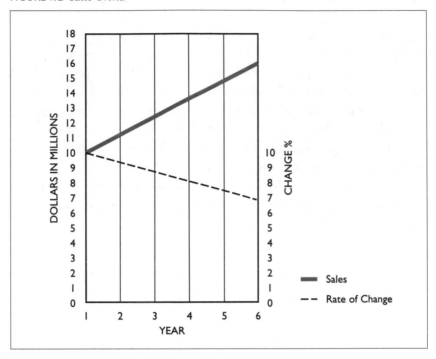

Certainly, a cultural change will demand that corporations provide investors with better disclosures, less confusing accounting, better explanations, and consistent year-to-year comparative data. However, investors also need to improve diligence in the way they adjust and use that financial information.

That said, let's look at some realities about net profits. Earnings margins cannot be expected to continue growing. However, dollar amounts of earnings should expand annually as long as sales growth is taking place. As previously explained, expansion should be accompanied by higher net profits, not by lower profits or net losses.

In a given industry, a *range* of net profit margin is reasonable, and that range cannot be expected to grow indefinitely. For example, in some industries with high dollar volume but exceptionally high cost of sales, a relatively small net margin is expected. So a 3 percent return on sales would be reasonable, and you cannot realistically expect margins to grow to 4, 5, 6, and 7 percent in the next four periods. Other industries may experience net margin in the 8 to 10 percent range, for example, but it would still not be realistic to demand that net margins move beyond that range.

This general rule is distorted when companies diversify into dissimilar product and service lines. If significant distortions occur, corporations should report by line of business as well as on a consolidated basis, and they should provide investors with the information needed to perform relevant analysis and make a decision. During a period of expansion, you should expect to see higher dollar amounts of sales (but a declining percentage increase from year to year), steady cost of goods sold and gross margins (allowing for dissimilar outcome for separate lines of business, especially in a diversified company), very little change in operating expenses (indicating a carefully controlled internal corporate environment), and increasing dollar amount of sales but steady net margins.

LATERAL GROWTH

One of the areas where much abuse occurred in recent corporate scandals was in acquisitions. Using a variety of accounting tricks, companies used acquisition reserves to overstate revenue. In fact, some companies acquired hundreds of smaller concerns.

The purpose of acquiring so many companies and setting up dozens of offshore subsidiaries, partnerships, and offbalance sheet divisions was to hide assets and liabilities and misstate revenues and net income. So one warning sign for astute investors is a high volume of acquisitions. That said, to acquire competitors or to merge with them remains a valid business strategy, for several reasons.

- A competitor is eliminated.
- Instead of duplicating advertising and other overhead, a merged concern can more efficiently serve a larger customer base.
- Combining resources (personnel, facilities, geographic presence, and cash) aids cash flow as well as competitive control.
- Acquisitions and mergers may be the best way to create and sustain growth while also maintaining high quality of earnings.

The last point is worth more discussion, because it is the key to long-term growth.

When a company with a primary line of business is not likely to acquire more market share, revenue growth begins to dry out. There is only a finite amount of market share to go around, and the customer or client base is finite as well. Both a limited customer base and competitive forces limit how much real growth a company can expect over the long term.

One solution is to develop related new products. A company involved with film and cameras might add a new line of digital cameras, for example. A pharmaceutical company will develop new drugs to increase revenues. A food company might develop new cereal products. However, even within an industry, growth will always be limited.

Lateral growth often is the solution. By this, I mean expansion into lines of business other than the primary or original lines. So a tobacco company like Altria Group (formerly Philip Morris), recognizing the limitations of tobacco alone, purchased Miller Brewing and Kraft Foods, both profitable companies with long-term track records. They provided Altria with high quality of earnings and long-term growth. When Miller Brewing's growth slowed, Altria sold the business to a South African brewing company, SABMiller, plc.

The combined revenues of the company add to the top line *and* to the bottom line, because the company and its subsidiaries are designed to produce profits consistently. In addition, lateral growth provides a company with diversification, which is all-important for long-term growth. Altria Group provides another good example. Everyone knows that the tobacco industry has been plagued by significant litigation in recent years, part of a process of gradual restriction in tobacco sales and product evolution. As tobacco becomes more obsolete as a product, tobacco companies face the possibility of extinction, unless they shift away from their primary, original market. Thus, acquiring subsidiaries in food and beverage industries makes a lot of sense. While acquisitions of high quality of earnings companies is expensive, it is also economically sensible. It adds to long-term expansion of earnings and helps the company to diversify its product lines as well.

How do you evaluate a big company's acquisition activity? In the case of many of the abuses seen in recent years, the acquisitions were made to set up and use reserves, with no long-term business purpose.

When Waste Management acquired over 400 smaller companies by 1995, the intention was obvious. That level of acquisitions does not make sense by any accounting standards, and even the most aggressive, growth-minded executive would question the value of so many acquisitions. The problem was apparent to Waste Management's auditing firm Arthur Andersen, but they did not question the transactions. In 1996, the company admitted to overstating profits by $1.43 billion, and Andersen paid $220 million to settle stockholder lawsuits.

If Andersen had been in business to protect investors, it would have blown the whistle on the unseemly level of acquisitions. Clearly, Waste Management was out of control—thus, the lawsuits. Assuming that future auditing firms will be more inclined to qualify their opinions and to highlight these types of problems, investors should look at high-volume acquisition activity as a very big red flag.

The distinction between abusive levels of acquisitions and sensible lateral growth comes down to motive and earnings. If a company acquires at ever growing volume, and if those acquisitions do not make economic sense, then there is probably an underlying accounting problem that should alarm you as an investor. However, a well-considered acquisition of a company with high quality of earnings makes sense and can add to future profits.

Another point about acquisitions: a company being acquired should be complementary in some manner. In the case of Altria Group, acquiring high-quality companies with unrelated product lines represented a form of diversification. It was the very quality of those companies that defined the move as a smart one. Altria Group also recognized the importance of keeping talented executives in control of the subsidiaries and did not assume to know how to run those businesses. In comparison, when Sears acquired Dean Witter, Coldwell Banker, and Allstate, with the idea of creating full-service financial centers within their retail stores, consumers recognized the move as ill advised. Consumers did not want to buy these services when shopping at Sears, and revenue levels reflected that problem. The joke became, "Sears is the place to buy socks, jocks, and stocks."

The disparity between Sears and those unrelated businesses was glaring. Sears was known for its internal financing of appliances, catalog sales, repair services, and network of stores. None of that experience convinced consumers that Sears was qualified to provide financial services. The acquisition could have worked if done differently. Perhaps the timing was poor because the acquisitions happened shortly before major reforms in the early 1980s that affected investment companies. Perhaps the acquisitions could have been managed in a different way. The idea of having those services *in* retail stores may be what doomed the decision. More than anything else, public perception hurt Sears. At about the same time, Sears began experiencing difficulties in its customer service levels. Anyone who had to wait many weeks working with the repair service division, or who had problems with the catalog division of Sears, would not have much confidence working with an in-store stockbroker.

Lateral growth is not a simple matter for big companies. Even with adequate capital to buy new subsidiaries and cover cash flow requirements, companies have to enter into the move with a specific plan, an understanding of the new market, and a retention of capable executives who understand their markets. So investors should be suspicious of companies acquiring anything in sight, and they have to make sure that acquisitions make sense. A big retail organization like Sears can succeed in selling and financing refrigerators, but when it comes to stocks, insurance, and real estate, they were left out in the cold. Successful lateral growth requires more than financial resources. The right management has to be in place, and the company needs to market its newly acquired subsidiaries in the right manner. Thus, Altria Group allowed Kraft Foods and Miller Brewing to continue in their own industries without overlaying the tobacco imprint, whereas Sears made a strategic mistake by placing financial services within their retail stores.

THE TRACK RECORD REQUIREMENT

A sensible way to judge companies in their lateral growth program is through studying their track record. Has the company acquired other concerns? What is the revenue and earnings history of (a) the acquired companies and (b) the consolidated corporation? A track record that demonstrates the company's ability to manage newly acquired subsidiaries well is one sign that it has undertaken acquisitions for the right reasons, such as to increase revenues and profits through lateral growth.

As with other financial disclosures, it is the company's reporting responsibility to disclose how and why it undertakes acquisition activity. If a high cost is associated with an acquisition, the corporate report should include a plain-English discussion of management's justification for the investment. If a large number of acquisitions occurs within a relatively short time, management should carefully explain the reasoning behind that program. The corporation is responsible to report to its stockholders, not to hide its reasons in obscure and highly technical language. This is a part of the new culture that investors need to insist upon:

Acquisition activity can fall within one of three broad classifications.

1. *To consolidate with and eliminate a competitor.* This is a traditional reason for acquiring other companies within the same industry. The idea that one bigger company can operate better than two small ones has been demonstrated many times over and in many industries. Operating in a competitive environment becomes expensive, especially if a large portion of the cost of sales is being spent on advertising and promotion—in other words, in an attempt to capture or maintain market share. By joining forces with a competitor, the costs of marketing can be virtually eliminated between the two companies. At the same time, a larger company can compete better with the remaining companies within the same industry. This concept works as long as it does not draw the opposition of government antitrust forces.

2. *To improve overall capitalization.* A fundamental standard for acquiring other companies is that the purchase should improve overall capitalization. If an acquisition adversely affects working capital, then it does not make sense. The well-managed corporation will spend time and resources to acquisitions, ensuring that (a) working capital will be maintained or improved (there is no purpose in acquiring a company whose working capital is so poor that it will drain existing resources), (b) operating margins will be improved rather than reduced, (c) the company will gain a clear, bottom-line economic advantage beyond merely eliminating competitors (for example, a company manufacturing a product might acquire its vendor, thus eliminating the markup

in high-volume merchandise), and (d) stockholders will be rewarded with higher dividends and/or earnings per share in the long run, so that long-term growth will be based on enhancing quality of earnings.

3. *To create high quality of earnings through lateral growth.* Lateral growth also achieves diversification of market and capital resources. The quality of earnings test is straightforward. Does an acquisition maintain or improve net earnings? The corporation needs to provide full disclosure, not just a skillful manipulation of the numbers. The sensible acquisition diversifies products or services while establishing real, long-term growth. So one way to define quality of earnings—perhaps the only way that makes sense—is to list its attributes. Growth should result with the same or higher gross margins and net profits. It should improve cash flow, not impede it in the long term. It should eliminate costs, such as between a company and an acquired vendor or service provider. Ultimately, it should also make sense in terms of marketing. Again, consider the case of Altria Group's well-managed acquisition of new product lines versus the Sears debacle in trying to overlay financial services on retail stores.

To many nonaccountants, the procedures and motives of acquisitions are complex and difficult to comprehend. Investors cannot reasonably be expected to learn all about this area of corporate activity. In the 1980s, acquisitions took on a negative reputation for continued growth and were often short-term in nature. Leveraged buyouts were undertaken so that corporate assets could be sold at a profit. This activity robbed employees of jobs and careers, and while compensating investors to some degree, the strategy did away with the concept of buying other companies to *improve* long-term prospects, which are at the heart of most investors's stock selections. In the '90s, skilled CEOs and CFOs discovered acquisitions as a means of falsifying the books and creating revenues out of thin air. So what is in the future for corporate acquisitions?

The corporation must convince investors that proposed or newly completed acquisitions make sense. This means a different format for disclosure that boils down highly technical forecasts and communicates them efficiently and effectively. It will prove unrealistic to expect investors to improve their technical financial knowledge or for them to depend on money managers or stockbrokers. Many investors want to be able to buy and sell stocks on their own, but they need to be given understandable information to make their decisions.

The process of change will be slow, because individual investors represent only a very small portion of total dollars going into the market. The majority comes from institutional investors like mutual funds, big pension plans, and insurance companies. However, individual funds go into those institutional accounts, and it will become increasingly difficult for funds and other institutional investors to maintain capital levels if individuals continue to believe they are being left out of the process. Some of the softening in institutional assets began in 2002, and institutional investors will struggle to maintain their holdings if individual investors lose faith. Ultimately, less investment will continue the bear trend and keep prices soft. The market will finally demand that corporations change the way they undertake and disclose acquisitions. Because the individual works indirectly—more through mutual funds than direct ownership, for example—the reform will take time. We must remember that the market does not like change. It took more than 300 years to replace the eights-reporting (⅛, ¼, and ½) system of exchanges with a more sensible, decimal-based system, so investors have to understand that needed reforms will not take place overnight.

At the same time, you have the right to be impatient with corporations that drag their feet in improving their disclosures. After all, they have at their disposal countless resources in accounting, public relations, customer relations, and other departments; they should make improved disclosure a high priority. Those that do not deserve to lose your confidence and, as a direct consequence, market value in their stock.

You should also be impatient with a brokerage business that resists change, especially a firm that continues to operate with glaring conflicts of interest, pretending to offer you good investment advice while also profiting from investment banking.

Finally, you should also be impatient with regulatory agencies and politicians unwilling to fund enforcement and oversight of the industry. Even though new laws have been passed, the real test of effectiveness will be in their application. The SEC has been underfunded for many years and had virtually no staff increases from 1992 to 2000, even though markets expanded significantly. Thus, the SEC has able to pursue only high-profile cases of insider trading and high-dollar cases of accounting fraud.

It is not enough to understand and apply the fundamental tests well known to analysts and experienced investors. Everyone has to depend on the integrity of the numbers, so a reformed, independent auditing industry needs to regain the public confidence it once held. This change is likely to occur fairly quickly, if only out of necessity (not to mention a new federal law that restricts auditor conflicts of interest). Investors also depend on a more proactive regulatory environment rather than the chronic system of "winks and nods" that permeated the industry in the past. The traditional brokerage industry needs a major overhaul as well. However, the most important changes are likely to occur within the corporate culture itself. Once corporate management realizes that investors will demand accountability, this change will come about. Aided by the requirement that corporate officers certify their reported numbers, real change will take place when corporations realize that the market now demands better disclosure and explanations.

8

TECHNICAL INDICATORS
Useful but Limited

Analysis traditionally has been broken down between fundamental and technical. However, in the minds of some market watchers, the distinction is a cloudy one. Some analysts profess to follow the fundamentals faithfully but turn around and talk about the rise and fall of the Dow Jones Industrial Averages (DJIA), one of the more popular technical indicators.

The confusion between fundamental (financial information) and technical (future-looking and price-related indicators) is harmful in some respects. If you begin with the premise that financial statements and related information serve as the basis for making decisions, then technical indicators are not useful in a direct way. In fact, they often obscure the matter rather than support an informed decision.

This is not to say that technical indicators should be ignored. They can be used in many ways, within an integrated program of analysis, to aid in the ultimate decision. However, technical indicators should not serve as the sole means for picking stocks.

PROBLEMS WITH THE DJIA

The market averages that provide a daily "temperature" of the market—the DJIA as well as the Nasdaq, S&P 500, and others—are useful for quick, sound-bite views of what is taking place on the public stock exchanges. Any other method of communication would be too complicated and obscure to report on television and radio, where most investors get a fast take on the market.

People understand point systems. When "the Dow" goes up or down, it is easy to conclude that it was a good day or a bad day, and financial reporters have become efficient at explaining point changes in brief phrases. *Profit-taking, consolidation, reaction to political or economic news, soft earnings*—all of these phrases are heard daily. This method of scorekeeping for the market as a whole is easy and efficient.

It is also unreliable. As a means for judging general market mood in a very short period of time, within a single day, for example, Dow watching does provide the quick look so desirable to journalists. However, for the long-term investor, a number of things are wrong with paying attention to daily movements in the DJIA.

- *It is a short-term indicator.* Because only a single day is being reported, the index's movement—even a large one—is not meaningful in the longer term. The market is chaotic, and price changes are a summary of potentially hundreds of factors, many inaccurate, that go into the supply and demand cycles for stock. Even under the Dow Theory, short-term changes are recognized as unreliable for any form of trend analysis. Thus, the daily changes in the DJIA, although widely reported and a convenient tool for drawing conclusions on the evening news, should be largely ignored.

- *It is entirely technical.* The fundamental analyst should recognize that the DJIA is far removed from any financial information. Certainly, an individual stock's price will change in reaction to an earnings report or to news affecting a particular company's product such as, for example, FDA approval of a new drug. However, the DJIA is a collection of different corporations in dissimilar industries. Because the averages are based entirely on price—affected, in other words, by much more than earnings and product news—the collective movement in the DJIA is completely technical in nature and unrelated to a company's fundamental information.

- *Changes in DJIA levels are not useful, even in the long term, for determining whether or not to buy or sell individual stocks.* The trends in the DJIA and other market indexes provide a broad overview of general market mood, at least as measured by the structure of the index itself. That mood is confirmed when several different indexes move in the same general direction over time. However, marketwide trends do not always indicate a specific stock's activity. On the contrary, the fundamental information of a specific company might not be reflected at all in the larger indexed movements of the overall market. In a fundamental sense, the value of shares of stock is *not at all* related to index movement. Furthermore, index changes do not provide you with any useful information concerning the timing of a decision to buy, hold, or sell shares.

- *The DJIA itself is not representative of the whole market.* Even if the DJIA is given serious attention among fundamental investors, it is still a combination of only 30 publicly traded companies.[1] Because markets change, some companies are removed and replaced periodically. However, the DJIA becomes distorted over time by these replacements, and the more this occurs, the less reliable the DJIA becomes as a means for historical tracking of market trends. It may serve as a better instrument than other indicators, and it certainly has become widely accepted as "the market," but its basic inaccuracy should trouble any serious investor.

- *The DJIA is weighted so that some companies count more than others.* One troubling aspect of the DJIA is that components are price-weighted. This means that some companies with higher stock values have greater weighting in the Average than those with lower prices.

- *Value distortions occur when the averages include inflated stocks.* The replacement of one company with another can distort the DJIA and other indices. For example, in 1999, Enron was included on the Dow Jones Utility Averages indexes. In fact, Enron's weight value was higher in February 1999 than that of any other listed company; it alone represented more than 10 percent of the total index. Now that we know Enron's financial results were distorted, as was the stock price, it is troubling that a single company held so much weight on one of the three Dow averages. A similar concern should be applied to the industrial, transportation, and of course, the composite averages as well. The industrial averages are so widely watched and followed, even in the fundamental camp, that any serious distortion of the averages on the part of one or two heavily weighted stocks could mislead the investing public.[2]

DRAWING THE WRONG CONCLUSIONS ABOUT THE MARKET

How do investors get information about the condition of the market? The broadly defined ideas of bull and bear trends in the market are, of course, price related and purely technical in nature. However, even if you correctly identify the overall market trend, how does that help you to draw accurate conclusions about (a) the accuracy of an individual stock's current market value, (b) the timing of a decision to buy or sell shares, (c) the effect of overall trends on individual stock price changes, either short term or long term, (d) the safety of invested capital, or (e) the performance of an individual stock compared to the market as a whole.

Even with a thorough analysis of these issues, the larger question remains: how do you pick stocks and determine whether to hold those stocks or get rid of them? The accuracy of a stock's price reveals whether you hold shares at bargain prices or inflated value. The timing of decisions is all-important. Obviously, it makes sense to buy shares when prices are low and sell when prices are high. However, this strategy requires placing money at risk when most people are worried about further price deterioration, and it means selling when the mood is closer to euphoria. One bit of market wisdom states, "The market is not controlled by bulls and bears but rather by chickens and pigs."

A lot of study is dedicated to the idea that an individual stock's price reacts in predictable ways to larger market trends. The *beta* is a value assigned to a stock's historical movement. Thus, if beta is high, the price of the stock is likely to move more than market averages, and if beta is low, the stock is less responsive. We suggest that this approach is misguided and that a more sensible method—one based on solid fundamentals rather than on technical formulation—is to test intrinsic value and determine whether today's price represents inflated value or a bargain. This approach takes the investor back to the fundamentals and requires analytical study, rather than depending on relatively simple (but often misleading) formulas based on price trends.

Following on the argument that intrinsic value should dictate how you buy or sell, it makes sense to evaluate the risk of being invested. The safety of capital cannot be studied just on the basis of price levels or volatility but should be based on fundamental information, financial trends, quality of earnings, and related hard evidence. A serious flaw in many approaches is that the proven scientific method is so often ignored or discounted. True: the hard work that goes into a scientific approach to value identification is not as exciting as applying a simplistic formula. However, the important thing is that identifying value is not easy, or everyone would do it with every market decision they make. Developing a sound fundamental plan for trend analysis and value assessment is not difficult or especially time consuming. However, the traditional market culture has been to rely on predictions by analysts, whose basis for their recommendations often has been suspect and whose track records have been dismal.

Accepting the fundamental value argument, can you discount the overall market entirely? In other words, does the overall market affect stock price values? It does, of course. A mood, whether optimistic or pessimistic, will directly affect stock prices, often broadly. However, recognizing the unreliability of short-term pricing trends, the cool-headed, analytical investor will also recognize that those effects are not based on fundamental value but rather on immediate perceptions that are marketwide. So sudden changes in a stock's market value that are a part of a marketwide reaction (especially on the downside) are opportunities, especially true when the fundamental attributes of a company are unchanged but its stock falls as part of a broad market movement. A broad movement is one in which several indexes move significantly in the same direction and average prices per share marketwide—a little-followed but important indicator—move substantially in the same direction. At such times of downward movement, buying opportunities are numerous but brief. So the speculative investor can make a quick move to take advantage of the momentary change, and the serious, long-term investor can time purchases of additional shares of favored companies.

COMBINED INFORMATION—THE PE RATIO

The thoughtful investor realizes, of course, that technical indicators should not) be dismissed out of hand. Valuable information from a variety of sources, including fundamental and technical, adds together to create an informed base of data—and better decisions.

One indicator, the price/earnings ratio, is particularly interesting because it combines fundamental information (earnings per share) with technical information (current market price). The PE ratio has become popular not only because it represents a crossover between the two major theories about analysis, but also because:

- *It is a simple formula, easily comprehended by most people.* The essence of good information is its simplicity. Esoteric, complex formulations do not reassure investors, who are already uncertain about where to find good information. The PE calculation is well known and well understood.
- *The PE, while simply stated, provides a valid means to compare different stocks.* Most investors want to be able to make valid comparisons, and that desire serves as the basis for their analytical approach to stock selection. The PE ratio is valuable because it helps investors to quantify current price as it relates to the latest reported earnings. However, "typical" PE levels often vary from one industry to another. Therefore, as a means for comparison, the fundamental characteristics, especially as they relate to earnings, should be similar for stocks being compared. Dissimilar industry comparisons could be misleading.
- *The PE ratio can be tracked over time as part of your trend analysis.* The process of analysis should always include long-term trend analysis rather than singular indicators to make value determinations. As price comes to represent ever changing multiples of earnings, you can draw conclusions about the stock's value based

on market actions. PE enables you to track these trends without a complex series of obscure analytical tools.

The PE ratio also presents several problems for investors. Use PE analysis with these limitations in mind.

- *The likely range of PE ratios varies across different market sectors.* The PE analysis will be most valid and useful when you compare market value of stocks within a single industry sector, or among stocks sharing similar earnings characteristics. The most applicable of these characteristics is the net operating margin. So two stocks in different sectors that have traditionally earned very similar net margins over many years can be compared using the PE ratio.
- *Earnings inaccuracies will distort the PE ratio.* This is a problem whenever evaluating the market, and it applies to both fundamental and technical indicators. If the company has overstated earnings, then earnings per share *and* current market value probably are distorted. Thus, the PE ratio will be unreliable as a long-term indicator without going back and adjusting the trend.
- *Earnings adjustments will affect the PE ratio.* Because one of the two components of the PE ratio is earnings per share, any nonrecurring items or adjustments will throw off the ratio. If the company acquires another company during the year and its earnings reflect an increase as a result, then the PE ratio trend will also be distorted. The trend has to be adjusted to reflect these nonrecurring effects on net income.
- *Changes to the number of shares outstanding will affect the PE ratio.* If the number of shares outstanding are changed significantly due to new issuance, or due to the company buying back its own stock on the market, the PE ratio will change correspondingly. This is because earnings per share will change as the number of shares changes.
- *Timing of the latest reported earnings is a serious problem in the accuracy of the PE ratio.* One side of the ratio, price, is always current. However, earnings per share is based on the latest reported financial results. Two problems are associated with this system. First, the latest earnings report could be up to three months old, meaning that the current PE uses outdated information. So the farther

away in time from the latest reported earnings, the less reliable the PE ratio.

- *Seasonal changes in a company's revenues and profits distort the reported PE.* Some changes in the PE ratio reflect seasonal variation rather than significant changes in perceived market value. A seasonal operation has high-volume and low-volume times of the year, and cyclical stocks tend to operate on predictable, longer-term cycles that may involve several quarters or even years. Outside economic, cyclical influences will affect earnings and should be kept in mind as a part of interpreting changes to PE ratio.

- *Investors often misunderstand the meaning of PE.* As a general rule, PE is recognized as an expression of the market's perceived future value. Because price is expressed in multiples of earnings, the PE ratio demonstrates how much value the market assigns to the company's potential for future growth. Of course, if a company has not earned a profit but has reported a loss instead, there can be no PE ratio, so comparing profitable and unprofitable companies cannot be done using PE. However, the perception about future value goes even deeper. Generally speaking, lower PE stocks are considered to be out of favor and not representing much future potential, whereas higher PE stocks are the current hot issues that attract investors due to greater growth potential. However, based on several long-term studies of market trends, the opposite is true. Lower PE stocks tend to be more profitable than average, and higher PE stocks tend to be less profitable than average. So when it comes to using the PE ratio as a test of growth potential, it is a mistake to steer toward those with higher PE levels.[3]

USEFULNESS OF CHARTS

The PE ratio serves as a useful and informative combination of fundamental and technical information. Even with its limitations, the PE ratio should be one of the primary indicators for your analysis.

Because the PE ratio represents a combined look at fundamental *and* technical factors, it is one of the more interesting indicators. In comparison, a purely technical tool is the stock price chart. This serves not only as the centerpiece for the technical analyst, but it is also a helpful way to review price history.

Anyone who has watched the evening news on television or looked through *The Wall Street Journal, Barron's,* or *Investor's Business Daily* is familiar with the stock chart. These are also widely available free of charge online.

Charts often show two statistical summaries of price: actual price levels (by day or week, for example) and a moving average. The price level represents the closing price for the reported period, and the moving average is a line. The combination of these two helps you to understand how prices have changed over a period, and when the stock chart shows a 12-month period, you can quickly understand the market price trend for a particular stock.

Charts serve functions on two levels. First, as a backward-looking review, the chart helps you to understand price history as well as volatility. The broader the range of movement during the past year, the more volatile the stock. However, a price range can mean many things, especially if there was a short-term price spike during the year. A singular event like that distorts the true history, especially if the price aberration was based on rumors that did not materialize. Thus, the chart can be useful in making an informed judgment about a stock's true price volatility. If the pattern has been strongly downward during the year, charts can help identify a bottoming-out. By the same argument, if the trend has been upward, the price eventually will begin to level out.

The historical analysis of stock price trends is useful even to the fundamental investor, who needs to identify recent patterns for a number of reasons: to understand relative price volatility, to identify and remove exceptions in the price pattern, and to compare price patterns to the market as a whole—even if only to time a purchase or sale decision. The second purpose for charts is more purely technical in nature. The *chartist* is a technician who believes that price movement can be anticipated and predicted through a study of recent price movements. Of course, identifying the significance of price movement when reviewing historical trends is easier than predicting the future accurately.

Chartists put a lot of effort into trying to recognize specific patterns. To the extent that charting is used to predict the direction of future price movement, it is often a futile exercise. Pricing is, in fact, a response to a combination of factors: earnings reports, product and industry news, economic and political change, sector and competitive forces, and in combination, a perception in the market about value. The chartist rejects all of these fundamental and social forces, preferring to believe that price changes in an almost conscious manner and that movement is predictable based on recent patterns.

From the chartists' efforts, however, some very useful tools emerge that everyone can use. The market perceives value of stock to exist within a specific range of prices, called the trading range (see Figure 8.1). For the price of a stock to move above or below that range in a dramatic way requires a change in overall perception. A trading range may inch upward over time due to strong and consistent earnings and competent management, or downward over time as internal controls deteriorate and corporate capital strength begins to fail. A study of trading range can, therefore, produce an understanding of price trends that are directly responding to financial information. So consistently produced profits, careful management of debt, high-quality earnings, well-planned acquisition programs, effective management at the top, strong competitive and marketing programs, and other fundamental and executive features are expressed in terms of trading range of the stock. A deteriorating profit history, rising debt as a percentage of total capitalization, low-quality earnings, poorly planned acquisitions, weak management, declining competitive position, poor marketing, and other negative features will show up in a downward trend in the trading range.

FIGURE 8.1 *Trading Range*

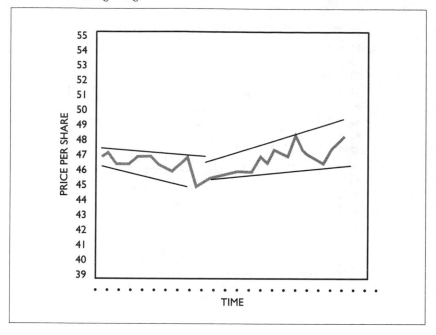

Chartists give names to the top and bottom of the trading range: *resistance level* at the top and *support level* at the bottom (see Figure 8.2). Chartists have observed, correctly, that the resistance and support levels may be "tested" without the price moving above or below the range. The idea of these barriers being tested implies a consciousness on the part of price patterns, but in fact, chartists assume that the resistance and support testing is done by investors. This is unlikely. To manipulate a stock's pricing pattern to that degree would require a coordinated program among many large institutional investors. The market is somewhat more chaotic than the chartist would prefer to believe.

Even so, the concepts of resistance and support are useful in anticipating possible trading range changes. As the tests of resistance occur, a breakout may take place. A *breakout* is a new pattern in which the price exceeds the previously established trading range and moves upward. Likewise, if the support level is tested and passed, then price patterns go through a downward breakout.

Figure 8.3 demonstrates how a breakout appears on the chart. This shows an established trading range followed by a downside breakout

FIGURE 8.2 *Support and Resistance*

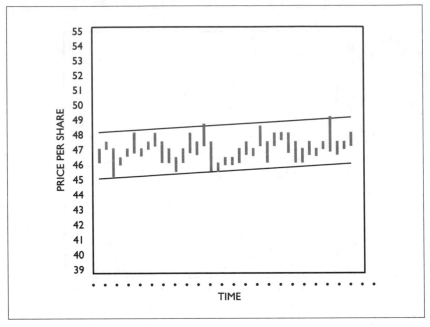

through the support level, establishment of a new trading range, and finally, an upside breakout through the resistance level.

While recognition of these patterns is useful in many respects, the fundamental analyst recognizes that these changes in pricing occur as a result of other forces, often related to earnings (which, most analysts will agree, drive price more than anything else). Other factors would include mergers and acquisitions, new product announcements, insider trading news, and other significant and fundamental information. The price itself does not move predictably enough without external reasons for investors to depend solely on price patterns as a predictive tool.

TESTING STOCK PRICE VOLATILITY

Being aware of price patterns—at least to the extent that they help you to know the current status of the company in the "mind of the market"—is useful, and investors often use charts to identify buying opportunities. Of course, an examination of the quality of earnings, capitalization, competitive strength, and other factors should accom-

FIGURE 8.3 *Breakout Pattern*

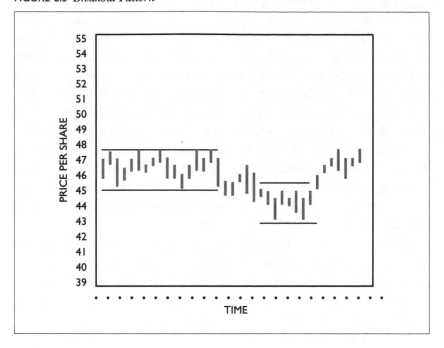

pany the chart study. Remember, there could be a number of reasons that a particular pricing trend has taken place; you can only identify the actual reason and how that will affect your decision by returning to the fundamentals.

For example, a particular stock might be exceptionally volatile in its price. Given that the primary price driver is earnings, why the volatility? Is the movement of stock price a reaction to fundamental information, or are other forces at play? Most investors use price volatility as a primary test of market risk. As a general rule, investors like predictable but consistent growth, even if that expectation is not realistic. In the chaotic world of corporate finance, fundamental volatility—widely ranging sales and profits—will inevitably lead to market price volatility as well. Lower predictability translates to greater chaos in the market, as in all things. However, volatility by itself does not always define the situation in the same way. A more critical test of volatility—aided by a view of a 12-month chart, for example—often shows that nonrecurring activity should be *removed* from the analysis to get the real picture.

Example. A company you are thinking of investing in has historically low volatility in its stock price, with a history of gradually rising prices in a 10 to 15 point range per year. However, during the past year, price ranged from a high of 125 to a low of 60, an exceptionally broad trading range. When you study the stock chart, you realize that the high range was atypical. The stock traded for most of the year between 110 and 125 and fell to 60 when the market went through a very broad decline. The exceptionally low price range corrected within one month.

In this example, the seemingly broad volatility was related to a broader market sentiment and, in your opinion, had no relationship to earnings news or other negative forces. The fact that the aberration corrected very quickly supports your belief that the company's shares are undervalued.

This example is a simplified version of how volatility can be distorted by nonrecurring events like marketwide euphoria or panic which, in its extremes, often is short-lived and tends to distort prices in either direction. While price distortions may be buying opportunities or chances to take profits, the trends themselves are not permanent. For the purpose of analyzing a stock's price volatility, departures from the established trading range should be removed from your analysis.

The traditional method for identifying volatility is simplistic when you consider the possible causes. The difference between the 12-week high and low is divided by the 12-week low, and the result expressed as a percentage. In the example given above, the volatility would be:

$$\frac{125 - 60}{60} = 108.3\%$$

This is an exceptionally high level of volatility. However, when the untypical decline is removed, there remains the more reasonable trading range between 110 and 125. Removing the aberration, recalculated volatility would be:

$$\frac{125 - 110}{110} = 13.6\%$$

Removing the decline-return pattern makes a considerable difference. When you view a range of volatility, exceptionally high levels can
be explained by a number of factors.

- *Market price instability.* It is possible—and should be assumed as a
  starting point—that the stock's price is actually quite volatile. This
  may be caused by fundamental (earnings) volatility. In fact, as corporations begin to operate under greater scrutiny and auditing
  firms have their own liability on the line, investors might see
  greater volatility in listed companies's earnings.
- *Upward trend in pricing.* High volatility is not always a negative. A
  fast-growing organization may experience high volatility as part
  of a strong upward trend in its stock price. This is quite different
  from fundamental volatility; in fact, the earnings trend could be
  quite strong and consistent in this situation.
- *Downward trend in pricing.* High volatility could also represent a
  deteriorating situation in price, again related to a leveling out or
  decline in earnings, or due to weakening capital position (i.e.,
  growing debt capitalization and/or decline in cash flow).
- *Nonrecurring price variation.* As shown in the previous example,
  seemingly high volatility could be caused by price spikes in either
  direction. If these are caused by nonrecurring events, such as
  short-term, marketwide movement that is quickly corrected, then
  the aberration has to be removed before volatility is calculated.
  This suggestion conforms with an important statistical principle:
  in testing a range of outcomes, the highest and lowest outcomes
  are removed so that a more representative sample is tested. Of
  course, if a particular part of a sample seems to contradict the
  remainder, it does not make sense to count that part in the average. The same rule should be applied when testing stock price
  volatility.

A word about the idea of fundamental volatility: in practice, sales
and profit levels tend to be far more chaotic than Wall Street would
like. It has become commonplace for corporations to use acceptable
accounting decisions to smooth out actual results and, to some extent,
investors (especially institutional investors, who better understand how
these matters work) accept the practice of accruing and deferring, or

what is known as managing earnings. However, this "understanding" has always been based on the premise that reported earnings are reasonably accurate, given that adjustments are made from year to year and do not overstate results in the extreme. Obviously, some CEOs and CFOs took advantage of such overstatements to enrich themselves at the expense of investors. However, in judging the quality of earnings, investors will need to accept a higher level of fundamental volatility. Perhaps tests of capital strength and competitive posture should take greater prominence in the decision-making process, and predictions about next quarter's earnings should not play as great a role in the future as they have in the past. If financial statements are less manipulated in future disclosures—due to a combination of CEO and CFO personal liability and a more stringent regulatory environment—then you will have to accept more uncertainty and unpredictability in the financial reports of publicly listed companies.

WORTHWHILE TECHNICAL INDICATORS

Charts serve a useful purpose, even for fundamental investors. However, just as the interpretation of the PE ratio is limited, charts have to be used cautiously as predictive tools.

Some other technical indicators can provide value as well. These include insider buy and sell information as one of the more important clues you can gather. An insider—corporate executives and board members, major stockholders, and anyone else who is in a position to have more or faster information than the general public—is allowed to buy or sell shares of stock as long as they are not responding to insider information.

Insider trades are registered with the SEC each month, so it is easy to find out how many insiders have executed trades and whether those were buy or sell orders. A retiring executive might decide to exercise stock options and sell shares as part of a retirement program. In fact, Robert Olstein makes the point that selling and buying by insiders have to be viewed quite differently:

> Insider selling can be unrelated to any issues relating to a company such as personal financial planning . . . Insider buy-

ing, on the other hand [requires coming] up with capital to buy shares. Usually insiders know where the company is going in terms of earnings and sales and are not likely to buy stock unless they are reasonably certain that the company's operations are moving up.[4]

However, insider trades can mean other things as well, some more sinister than others. A case in point: Martha Stewart is alleged to have sold shares of ImClone when her broker's assistant told her that the FDA was about to turn down the company's application for Erbitux, its cancer drug. Stewart not only sold 2,000 shares of ImClone stock the day before the FDA announcement, but she also sat on the New York Stock Exchange board. One consequence of her trade has been a significant drop in market value of Martha Stewart Living Omnimedia, so that her losses in Omnimedia stock have far exceeded her gains on ImClone stock.

The potential penalties for illegal insider trading are severe. ImClone CEO Sam Waksal, also charged with conspiracy in that case, could face up to five years in prison and a $250,000 penalty for each count, plus up to ten years for securities fraud. Martha Stewart could face similar penalties under federal statutes forbidding insider trading.

A distinction has to be made, of course, between the illegal insider trading described above and legitimate insider selling of shares or exercising stock options or, similarly, the buying of shares by executives. For the observant investor, single decisions on the part of insiders may not be significant, but a trend could be revealing. If a large number of corporate insiders begin buying shares, that activity could mean that the market price is low; if a large number begin selling off their holdings for no apparent reason, it could be a red flag. Another form of insider trading—corporations buying their own stock on the open market—could also indicate that the current price is low. When corporations buy their own stock, it is permanently retired and classified in the net worth section of the balance sheet as *treasury stock*. The higher the purchase of treasury stock by a company, the better. It means that the company (a) has cash flow adequate to invest in permanently retiring its own stock, (b) is confident that the decision will be profitable, and (c) believes that current market value probably is low.

Another useful technical indicator is the new high and new low price ratio. The financial press tracks statistics and reports on those stocks reaching 52-week new high levels as well as 52-week new low price levels. To compute the ratio, the number of issues having reached 52-week new high prices is divided by those reported as new lows. A higher than average positive ratio is considered optimistic, and a lower than average negative ratio is pessimistic. Because the ratio is based on 52 weeks of price activity, this indicator is longer term than most technical indicators, which tend as a group to be short-term in nature unless applied to a longer moving average trend.

A related study involves tracking the trend in advancing issues versus declining issues. A moving average following the trend also indicates market mood, so when an upward or downward trend dominates, investors can conclude a lot about the general mood and direction of the market. The advance/decline line is a progressive track of the trend, with each day's net difference added to or subtracted from the previous day's cumulative number.

Both new high/new low and advance/decline analyses are far more revealing than the relatively uninformative point changes in the DJIA and other selective indexes. Of course, technicians are like fundamental investors in one respect: their emphasis is on price and price trends. Whether you base your analysis on financial results or patterns of price change on charts, the analysis all comes down to the question of whether market price is going to rise or fall. However, an often overlooked technical factor worth examining is trading volume.

Volume, by itself, is not very useful as an analytical tool. It has to be studied in light of how prices change on the same day. Volume is most applicable to individual stocks. You would draw a different conclusion when a high-point price movement is accompanied by heavy volume than when volume was relatively low for the day. The variation in volume could be caused by institutional volume, by widespread investor interest (or disaffection), and also by broader market trends. The point is, volume has to be viewed in the context of both the broader market volume and the stock's price movement on the same day.

Any study of volume is most useful when the trend (higher or lower daily trading volume) is compared to the same day's price activity. An increase in daily volume that is not accompanied with significant price change could be a technical trend that *anticipates* price change in the near future, according to some technicians. However, volume can also be deceptive, considering that the most market trading is done by institutional investors. Thus, mutual funds can distort a study based solely on volume, because their trades involve large blocks. One 100,000-share trade by a large mutual fund will dwarf trades by individuals between 100 and 1,000 shares.

You can judge institutional influence on daily volume by watching a technical indicator, reported daily in *The Wall Street Journal,* called the large block volume ratio. A large block (a trade of 100,000 or more shares) could distort your study unless you understand how it compares to volume as a whole. To calculate, large block volume is divided by the same day's total volume, and the resulting ratio isolates the percentage of trading made up by large blocks. This indicator is useful for excluding trades that are exceptionally high. A contrarian point of view is to see the large block ratio as an opposite indicator. If one believes that institutional investors usually buy or sell at the wrong time, then the large block indicator can serve as a useful reverse signal. As the percentage rises, the contrarian would want to sell shares in that company; its fall could serve as a sign that it is time to buy.[5]

Because mutual funds represent such a large percentage of total daily investing, some fund-related technical indicators are useful as well. The cash to assets ratio—a test of the amount of cash funds have on hand—is one such indicator. As funds invest in shares in large volume, they drive up prices because shares become more scarce (to express the cause and effect of market decisions simply). Of course, if funds decide to sell, the greater availability of shares tends to soften market price. So mutual fund decisions can influence price, perhaps as much as earnings reports in the short term. The cash to assets ratio is, again, usually viewed as a contrarian indicator. When funds are close to fully invested, that is seen as a sign that stocks are priced too high; when funds are holding back and keeping a larger portion of assets in cash, the contrarian sees that as an optimistic sign. The belief, again, is that the mutual fund position is the reverse of what it should be, because fund managers are more often wrong than right.

The purpose of tracking fund trends is not just to provide a means for comparing or selecting funds; that topic is not applicable to my discussion of technical analysis. The purpose is to use mutual fund statistics in a contrarian manner to time buy or sell decisions.[6]

SENTIMENT INDICATORS AND THEIR USE

Another specialized grouping of indicators is the so-called *sentiment* indicator group. These indicators are more closely associated with technical than fundamental analysis. By definition, they are remote from market price and fundamentals and more closely reflect overall market mood.

A favorite sentiment indicator is called the short interest ratio, the number of shares sold short on the market. Short sellers, of course, expect and hope for price declines, so that positions can be closed out at a lower price and produce a profit. This is often used as a contrarian signal, in the belief that short sellers's volume increases at times when prices are likely to rise and falls when prices are likely to go down. In other words, the contrarian believes that short sellers, like fund managers, are more often wrong than right.

In comparison, the members's short index is a similar indicator but is limited to short interest among stock exchange members. These individuals are thought to be more knowledgeable than average, so short interest among members is seen most often as a reliable indicator. As members's short interest increases, the signal is bearish; as members's short interest decreases, the signal is bullish.

Sentiment indicators encompass a broad range of economic signals as well. These include indicators not directly connected to the stock market in any way, except to the degree that changes affect market prices. These include the Gross Domestic Product (spending in the United States) and a measurement of economic output, generally but inaccurately called "productivity." As the U.S. economy becomes predominantly service oriented and less based on manufacturing and production, the GDP as measured may become obsolete. The major components of GDP are demand for goods and income.

The Producer Price Index is similar to the better-known Consumer Price Index but is calculated at the wholesale level. Along with GDP, PPI is considered one of the major economic tests for measuring inflation and economic conditions.

Personal Income and Expenditures measures worker income and spending each month, also known as personal consumption spending, for both durable and nondurable goods. The balance of trade is another major economic test that is given a lot of play in the financial press but, for the most part and in most sectors, has little direct effect on market pricing.

Also followed by economists are a combination of several other indicators, called the Index of Leading Economic Indicators. These "leading" indicators are believed to predict economic trends. They include unemployment, production worker hours, building permits, manufacturers's orders, new contracts and orders for plant and equipment, the money supply, and stock prices for 500 common stocks.

For most fundamental investors, sentiment indicators and economic indicators are too far removed from the market itself to be of any direct value. While the trends they identify might be important in the long term, most fundamental investors will prefer to concentrate on financial information specific to individual companies.

9

ATTRIBUTES OF CORPORATE MANAGEMENT

The culprits in the majority of corporate scandals have been top managers—the very people entrusted with protecting stockholders' interests. This has caused investors, regulators, Congress, the SEC, and Wall Street to take another look at corporate management, with the idea of reforming the way we pick our free enterprise leaders.

The dilemma is a serious one: how do you rein in corporate leaders and control their behavior so that no more Enron-type abuses occur *and*, at the same time, keep in place the competitive freedom that has always characterized American business? This is the big question. Where is the line between aggressive (or creative) leadership and outright fraud? Unfortunately, the line is not clear and sharp but broad and very fuzzy, made up of many incremental parts. The many decisions made on the way across the line might individually pass the test but, added together, they fail. Executives, in some cases, have found themselves on the wrong side of the law, not because of a single decision made in one moment but as the consequence of many decisions made over months or years.

WHO ARE THE LEADERS?

When investors consider purchasing stock, they would like to look at all of the facts. However, how can you know the quality of top management? Looking at past results is one way to discover the effectiveness of the management team. However, even an impressive financial past does not ensure that the same people are in charge today.

The problem with the traditional corporate structure has been that leadership is not accountable to investors. Thus, you would have no way of knowing whether the board of directors exercised any control or oversight at all or merely provided the appearance of managing the company. Likewise, you could not know whether the audit committee had any real influence with the board or whether the CEO and CFO were acting ethically. Are they working in their own interests or those of their shareholders?

The textbook role of top executives is to run operations. So, while a board of directors "reports" to investors, executives report to the board and ensure a smooth, well-controlled internal operation. The operations team reports to the CEO and the financial team reports to the CFO. That is the theory.

In practice, executives and boards have in many cases inflated market value of the corporate stock with their own stock option values uppermost in mind. With higher stock prices driving incentive-based compensation, a clear conflict of interest has been built into the entire financial reporting structure. As Gretchen Morgenson, a financial markets columnist for *The New York Times,* said in a speech at New Mexico State University on September 30, 2002:

> Like all roads leading to Rome, today's corporate greed
> originates in stock options. Put another way, the love of stock

options is the root of all evil in corporate America. Stock options were crucial to both the misrepresentation and the enrichment that have caused a crisis of confidence in business and financial markets. Options are doled out as free money to executives and are the force behind the increasingly lucrative compensation packages at American companies. Because they are tied to the company's performance, they can be powerful incentives for executives to make results look better than they actually are and cook the books. Because of the way options are treated in financial statements, they help executives shade the truth in two ways. First, they allow companies to overstate their earnings because the costs of the options are not deducted from a company's revenues as salary or compensation. In addition, options generate significant cash flow from employees that has nothing to do with day-to-day operations. They also help companies pad earnings by reducing and even eliminating taxes owed to the federal government. Since executive pay is often linked to a company's earnings, the overstatements that stock options produce can mean fatter paychecks for management. Sanford C. Bernstein & Company reports that the value of option grants at the 2,000 largest companies rose from $50 billion in 1997 to $162 billion in 2000. As options have become more popular, their beneficial effect on company earnings has done so as well. Bernstein estimates that if the nation's 500 largest companies had deducted the cost of options from their revenues, their annual profit growth from 1995 to 2000 would have been 6 percent instead of the 9 percent these companies reported.

When employees exercise options, the tax they owe on the transaction becomes a deduction for the company issuing the shares. As a result, profitable companies that are heavy users of options, like Microsoft, Cisco Systems, and Dell Computer, have erased much if not all of what they owed to the federal government in taxes in recent years. At Enron, for example, deductions for stock options helped eliminate more then $625 million in taxes that the company owed the government from 1996 to 2000. Companies reap another benefit when their employees exercise options. An employee pays the company to buy the shares outright. That generates excess cash flow, which only attentive investors will see has nothing to do with day-to-day operations. At WorldCom, for example, half the company's free cash flow in 1999—$886 million—came from workers exercising options.

What started out as a tool for corporate good has really ended up in many cases as just another instrument to allow the siphoning of wealth that belongs to shareholders to senior management. One of the reasons that options are so pernicious is that they encourage executives to do whatever they must to keep their stock prices up and their options valuable. It has become distressingly clear that the pay-for-performance philosophy that was supposed to align executives's interests with shareholders's has been badly distorted. "Pay for pretense" may be a better name for it, given some of the accounting shenanigans that have emerged. The fact is, chief executives have pulled off one of the greatest heists in history: the transfer of wealth in clear light of day in recent years has been nothing short of amazing.

As long as CEOs and CFOs were willing to adjust financial results to maximize current-year reporting income, investors could not depend on those reports. To the extent that outside auditing firms went along with questionable policies, the problem became worse throughout the middle and late 1990s and exploded suddenly in the early 2000s with a steady stream of massive bankruptcies and disclosures of corporate misdeeds. These problems did not arise suddenly. They developed gradually over time, caused by conflicts of interest on the part of corporate officers as well as accounting firms.

All of the problems rest, ultimately, with the board of directors and its audit committee. One frustrating element disclosed in the scandals has been the complete failure of boards and the lack of influence on the part of audit committees. Investors have believed in the textbook version of how corporate organizations function without realizing that, for some executives, the whole plan was self-serving, an opportunity to enrich themselves with investors's capital. A number of important reforms have been instituted through the stock exchanges and the

Securities and Exchange Commission, and while these changes will take time, they will soon change the way that corporations work.

Bill Miller, CEO and fund manager with Legg Mason Funds Management, explains the change needed to solve the board problem:

> The basic issue is that boards of directors are fiduciaries. It's their legal and moral duty to put the owners's interests ahead of their own personal interest or the interest of management.[1]

The purpose of reform should be to prevent future executives from misusing their positions to enrich themselves, by abusing stock option grants, for instance. It will be necessary to separate out the compensation decision at the board level by placing it in the hands of a compensation committee comprised entirely of independent directors (those not tied financially to the corporation). At the same time, executives will continue to earn incentive-based pay in the form of bonuses and stock options, but safeguards to prevent abuse must also be introduced. Two important additional reforms will help prevent misstatements of financial results that are motivated solely by incentive pay. First will be the requirement that the audit committee act as sole contact with the outside auditing firm (the committee also will select the auditing firm without approval of the CEO or CFO). Secondly, the executives themselves will be required to certify the accuracy of results.

These changes are forcing a return to the textbook version of how management is supposed to work. Instead of CEOs and CFOs acting as hucksters, marketing the corporate stock and imposing their will on accounting decisions, they will be required to concentrate on good, traditional *management* of the internal organization. In the minds of investors, effective management determines the level of earnings and, specifically, defines the quality of earnings. In the new corporate environment, executives are removed from the self-serving roles that developed in the recent past and are placed in the position of overseeing internal operations.

What should management do? How do we define quality of leadership? Clearly, these questions have been lost in the scandal-ridden environment of recent years. It is doubtful that leaders of Tyco, Enron, or WorldCom will ever be viewed as effective managers in the real sense of the word. They may be remembered infamously for their actions, and much as art forgers are recognized for their talent, many corporate executives will be immortalized for their accounting abilities—even though they misused them.

CORPORATE ETHICS— THE CHANGED ENVIRONMENT

Investors have the right to demand ethical leadership in publicly listed companies. This should mean much more than just the appearance of ethical behavior. The decision by some business schools to add or beef up courses on management ethics is a lame response in terms of solving the greater problem. In fact, most investors recognize that changing the curriculum at the college level will not really make any long-term difference, if the corporate environment is not changed at the same time.

The free enterprise system requires that management has a certain degree of freedom to compete effectively, respond to ever changing market conditions, and develop product marketing ideas that are better than the competition's. The freedom to operate in an effective way has to be left in place, because management cannot operate in such a restrained environment that it can't make important decisions rapidly. If regulation creates reporting layers, committees, and excessive bureaucracy to monitor the CEO and CFO, then the whole operation will be bogged down. While these changes may prevent abuse, they would also undo the essence of the free enterprise system.

What is needed instead is a series of regulations that provide *real* oversight by an independent board of directors and audit committee. Decisions relating to working with outside auditors and development of executive compensation have to be removed from executive control. Executives should be restricted to running the operation, while questions of how the numbers get reported and how executive incentive compensation is structured are left to others. These significant changes will create a healthier environment, because conflicts will be removed as far as possible and CEOs and CFOs will operate only on the internal level, where they should operate.

Does this environment create a more ethical management team? It might, but it's not the whole answer. We cannot replace ruthless, competitive managers (the kind we all want heading up corporations in whose stock we invest) with saintly, passive managers who are afraid to act in investors's best interests. The middle ground is to impose regulations and exchange rules that limit management's participation in financial reporting, compensation programs, and decisions at the board level. In one sense, this changed environment makes the executive task easier. They can't affect accounting decisions made by independent auditors, because proposed changes are negotiated between the auditing firm and the board's audit committee. Additionally, while executives are given incentives based on profits, the only way they have an impact is through managing the company well—the way that incentive plans are supposed to work.

One lesson to be learned from the scandals that came to light in early 2000s is this: if you deregulate to the extent that corporate executives are given complete freedom, some will abuse that freedom. Enron's mantra demanding deregulation, for example, really meant rejecting any form of transparency, creating a fog of obfuscation behind which they could work their self-serving schemes. The trend toward deregulation created opportunities for corporate fraud and, along with weakened accounting rules and standards, produced the devastating, broad-based loss of investor confidence. The weakness of the early 2000s stock market can be traced to several causes, but their cumulative effect was to undermine the level of confidence of the investing public. The fact that over 700 companies had to restate their earnings between 1997 and 2002 also undermined investor confidence.

To investors, it doesn't matter whether the companies in which they invest are led by more ethical people or whether regulation and oversight is improved. For investors, the key questions will be:

- Can I trust the numbers reported by the company?
- Is management working in my interests or their own?
- Is the internal organization properly structured?

Each of these questions will define investor confidence in the long run. Confidence in the numbers requires a meaningful increase in corporate transparency, a changed independent accounting environment, honest management, and greater power and independence on the board of directors and its audit committee. Management will be required to work in the interests of investors, once it has been removed from the audit itself and can no longer influence the accounting decisions. Proper internal organization should include a specific exclusion between internal operations and operational oversight. Thus, the CEO and CFO have to operate solely on the corporate level, while the board and audit committee have independent authority to represent investors's interests.

An environment in which obvious conflicts of interest are absent can certainly be called more ethical, regardless of how it comes about. Corporations will have to earn investor confidence back, and that will probably take time. However, whether that confidence returns due to better ethics on the part of management or an improved regulatory environment, the result will be the same.

Investors have come to realize that ethical behavior is not easily assumed by corporate officers or professionals. Most organizations have a code of ethics. Accountants, lawyers, real estate agents, and even corporations publish very specific guidelines defining ethical behavior. However, anyone who has complained about professionals knows that, except in extreme cases, trying to get justice often is a joke. The code of ethics often is more public relations tools than hard and fast guideline, put forth to reassure the public rather than to create an environment of good behavior. Unfortunately, human nature requires that we expect ethical behavior and back it up with the threat of real and severe penalties, plus restricting access to those who might be tempted to misuse the system. Remember, even Enron required new employees to sign and agree to a code of conduct, obviously for appearances only without on-the-job application for top management. Not all corporations have the same degree of problems, to be sure. The worst cases were the best publicized, and the picture is not universally bleak. However, new standards are being applied across the board to ensure that abuses do not recur.

Creating an ethical environment requires cutting off management's access to boards of directors, independent auditing firms, and the body that decides its incentive compensation. Only then can investors expect ethical behavior from management. Investors and management alike can then compare performance based on financial results. Improved sales volume and profit, maintained market share, financially viable acquisitions, and other decisions ultimately define the quality of management, and these facts are needed by investors so that they can decide who is doing a good job. Once the accounting and compensation decisions have been separated out, quality is far easier to determine.

HOW MANAGEMENT REPORTS TO STOCKHOLDERS

One area where investors have felt isolated has been in trying to understand the technical reporting of financial results. Clearly, financial statements are often difficult to understand, and many entries in the books are subject to interpretation. For example, profits can be increased simply by making a series of positive assumptions about the future: higher investment return, lower bad debts, less inventory obsolescence—all increase profits and are within the GAAP rules.

However, the Sarbanes-Oxley Act of 2002 will put the burden on management to explain results better to investors. At the crux of reform is the idea that it is not the investor's job to become a better analyst but rather the corporation's job to explain itself better. Executives must concentrate on making the numbers clear. This requirement is enforced by a significant new rule:

> The CEO and CFO of each issuer shall prepare a statement to accompany the audit report to certify the "appropriateness of the financial statements and disclosures contained in the periodic report, and that those financial statements and disclosures fairly present, in all material respects, the operations and financial condition of the issuer." A violation of this section must be knowing and intentional to give rise to liability.[2]

Penalties for "material noncompliance" with these new requirements specify that a CEO or CFO must pay back any incentive-based or equity-based compensation within one year of a false report. The SEC may also bar an offending executive from acting as officer or director of a company, either temporarily or permanently.[3]

The changes in corporate reporting address the disclosure rule, a fine beginning. However, management should also be required to hold more stock in the company. In other words, instead of being given open-ended stock options, managers should be required to hold those options for some period of time. This would prevent the problem of insiders taking short-term profits when, perhaps, they should act in the interests of shareholders over the longer term.

The Financial Accounting Standards Board (FASB) is studying methods for treatment of corporate stock options. Corporations have resisted suggestions that they should treat options as expenses, with good reason. Overall profits among S&P 500 companies would have been reduced by about 20 percent in 2001 if their corporate stock options had been expensed.[5]

The debate has been whether or not to *require* corporations to expense options. Traditionally, the real cost of granting options to executives and employees remained invisible, at least until those options were cashed in; as a result, the financial picture was disclosed only in the footnotes. That might seem like a small distinction, but earnings per share for many companies is significantly lower when options costs are subtracted. For example, Microsoft's earnings were reduced 35 cents per share for 2002, IBM's by 30 cents, and Cisco by about 20 cents (to a small net *loss* per share rather than a profit).[6] Options given to top executives have grown at an annual rate of 19 percent, certainly outstripping earnings per share for the vast majority of companies.[7]

The extreme cases of abuse, such as Ken Lay's Enron deal—he sold off $20 million while telling investors that all was thriving at the company—took place without disclosure, and that secrecy was within the rules. While the SEC has significantly tightened up reporting rules for insider trades, it is like closing the barn door after the horse has escaped. A lot of damage has been done by executives at Enron and elsewhere.[8]

Several major companies have announced that they will expense options. Of course, this probably means that options given to employees will be cut back. What has been treated as a growing employee benefit will be treated somewhat differently when it affects the bottom line. The list of companies leading the trend toward expensing options includes General Electric, General Motors, Bank One, Coca-Cola, and Proctor and Gamble.[9]

In November 2002, General Electric CEO Jeff Immelt and CFO Keith Sherin announced that the company will begin immediately limiting options sales by executives:

> GE will implement a holding period on stock option exercises for senior officers; they will be required to purchase GE stock with option gains and hold that stock for at least one year. Senior officers also will be required to accumulate and hold GE stock equal in value to a specified multiple of their base salary for as long as they hold the position.[10]

As seriously as stock options will affect reported profits, this raises a different and more troubling question: are corporate officers being compensated too highly at the expense of shareholders? If one year's stock options represent one-fifth of total profits, stockholders have to question the practice. Investors' relatively minor dividend payouts do not compare well with what, in effect, is a 20 percent yield on profits, paid to top executives via their options.

Some corporations have announced their intention to begin expensing options as a part of a new trend toward fully transparent reporting. This is a positive change. Although stock options will reduce profits, future option levels will likely be reduced as well, due to a combination of the effect on profits *and* visibility to stockholders.

Not only top executives share in the effect of stock options. Many companies provide stock options to a number of employees as part of an overall benefits package, with increased vesting granted yearly in the same manner as other retirement and savings programs. Full vesting usually occurs within five years for employee plans. However, changes in the accounting treatment of options, whether paid to employees or management, should include full disclosure to shareholders as well.

CHANGING THE BOARD STRUCTURE

Investors have depended on boards of directors to ensure that executives did not violate their interests. However, in many of the well-known cases, such as Adelphia Communications and Enron, the boards clearly did not perform their duties. Troubled investors have to wonder how many other weak boards are failing to keep an eye on executive behavior.

Corporate audit committees are supposed to be at the core of the financial reporting standards within a corporation. The audit committee is supposed to make recommendations to the board to ensure accurate reporting, compliance with both GAAP and federal laws, and cooperation with independent auditing firms, who are also supposed to be critically examining the accounting policies. In some cases, the whole structure failed miserably.

For example, Arthur Andersen cautioned Enron's audit committee in February 1999 that the company's accounting policies were dangerously aggressive and close to violating the rules. As alarming as that conclusion was, none of the audit committee members objected, questioned Andersen's conclusions further, or sought a second opinion. More to the point, none recommended the board adopt less aggressive policies. Similar warnings went unheeded for the next two years. Enron's board of directors later took the position that information was kept from them and that they were lied to by executives.[11]

The board members, often paid six-figure salaries, have been exposed to no real liability under the law for failing to exercise their oversight responsibilities. In practice, boards act too often as rubber-stamp approval systems for management, and audit committees are ignored or have failed to disclose concerns about errant accounting practices. The, "Ask me no questions, I'll tell you no lies," approach to corporate management has aided executive misdeeds at the expense of stockholders. The vague "duty of care" standard applied to directors has had no real teeth. That standard requires that a director discharge duties in good faith, with the care of an ordinarily prudent person, and in a manner reasonably believed to be in the best interests of the corporation. Clearly, this generalized standard leaves a great deal of room for misconduct, and in extreme cases like Enron, even this standard was not followed. The $750 million in cash bonus payments the board approved—more than three-quarters of its reported net income for the most recent year—is one glaring example. The $77 million Kenneth Lay removed through his $7.5 million line of credit and the failure by the audit committee and the board to look into allegations of wrongdoing are further examples of the complete lack of oversight by the Enron board.

Are other corporate boards doing as poor a job? If so, what should the penalties be? Board members face virtually no liability for wrongdoing, as they are protected both by corporate rules and state laws. The only recourse for shareholders is to sue board members, a step that has already begun. The mess under existing laws has to be straightened out between the courts and insurance companies as stockholders file suits. Public pressure to create change may ultimately resolve this problem. Those corporations who have not been caught up in the bad publicity need to reform their boards, so that more responsible oversight becomes a reality.

Reform must be substantial and real, so that the existing boards give up their power to be replaced by more independent boards. Liability, too, should be real for board members as well as for corporate officers. Only then will it be possible to change the system and fix the problem. Charles Royce, of Royce & Associates in New York, proposes creating a class of independent directors as part of the board, similar to the way that mutual fund boards operate:

> There's a relatively simple reform: a very precise definition of what an independent director is. In the mutual fund industry, the definition of an independent director is built into the regulations. It's someone who has no business relationship with the company.
>
> As a second part, there should be a class of companies who say they are going to sign on to the idea of having a portion of their boards as independent directors. They would be responsible for hiring accounting officers, setting compensation and options, and disclosures of management pay and benefits.[12]

Some companies have begun taking steps in this direction, recognizing that the Enron matter serves as a warning signal not just for specific companies but for the entire system. The problem is that finding talented, capable individuals to serve on audit committees and boards of directors could be challenging. Most audit committee chairpersons get $10,000 per year, and even proposals to increase that to $15,000 may not be enough to attract top financial talent. The compensation question also raises the potential problem that higher pay creates additional conflicts of interest.

A board with a majority of independent members would be a positive step in erasing the conflict of interest. Coupled with real liability, changes would help to ensure that boards of directors function as they are supposed to—overseeing the executive management of the company for the benefit of stockholders. Going beyond the board members, audit committees need to communicate better with boards, and their recommendations have to be taken seriously as well. As the case of Enron has shown, this has not always occurred.

Audit committees should be comprised of individuals with financial talent, of course, but who also do not have conflicts of interest with the company. Thus, someone who works for the corporation, or who is employed by an auditing firm also working for the company, is clearly not qualified to act as an independent committee member.

Among the needed reforms are:

- Audit committees rather than management, should select independent auditors.
- Committee members should have no direct financial ties to the company or to the auditing firm.
- Audit committee reports should be disclosed to investors as part of the financial report.
- Meetings have to occur frequently enough to ensure that boards are given timely information, especially concerning problems in accounting practices undertaken by management.
- Audit committees should be the contact for outside auditors in resolving any accounting decisions that arise. Management—whose compensation often is incentive based—has a conflict, because their personal interest lies in reporting the highest possible net income.
- Given the above recommendation, no audit committee member should also be in a position to earn any incentive-based pay from the company.

The Blue Ribbon Committee on Improving the Effectiveness of Corporate Audit Committees (made up of exchange and industry experts) issued a series of recommendations in 1999 to phase in over 18 months. Former SEC chairman Harvey Pitt asked for additional recommendations from stock exchanges. The original recommendations included a definition of an *independent member* of an audit committee:

> Members of the audit committee shall be considered independent if they have no relationship to the corporation that may interfere with the exercise of their independence from management and the corporation.[13]

The report further recommended that a listed company with market value above $200 million should have audit committees comprised solely of independent members.[14]

The report contains additional recommendations for reporting and disclosure, designed to permit investors to understand how accounting oversight was achieved. These recommendations also deal with the relationship between the audit committee and the board on the one hand and with the auditing firm on the other hand.

In response to former SEC chairman Pitts's request, the NYSE Corporate Accountability and Listing Standards Committee issued a June 6, 2002, report, providing additional suggestions for improving audit committee performance. These recommendations were designed to be incorporated into the NYSE listing standards. They include:

> Recommendations to the NYSE Board of Directors . . .
> (6) Add to the "independence" requirement the following new requirements for audit committee membership at listed companies:
>
> - Directors' fees are the only compensation an audit committee member may receive from the company.
> - A director who meets the definition of "independence" mandated for all audit committee members, but who also holds 20 percent or more of the company's stock (or who is a general partner, controlling shareholder, or officer of any such holder) cannot chair, or be a voting member of, the audit committee.
> - The audit committee chair must have accounting or related financial management expertise.

. . . (7) Increase the authority and responsibility of the audit committee, including granting it the sole authority to hire and fire independent auditors, and to improve any significant nonaudit relationship with the independent auditors.[15]

The same report recommended specific improvements in Board of Directors' structure as well and included a requirement that independent directors be given increased authority. The report said that independent directors should comprise a majority of the board and recommended the creation of a compensation committee.[16]

The changes in the NYSE report are significant because they have become *listing standards* for publicly traded companies. Accordingly, companies listed on the NYSE have to comply. The reforms are designed to take away control from insiders and do away with the "buddy system," in which board members have paid themselves and their friends exorbitant salaries and bonuses. It is likely that similar standards will be adopted by NASDAQ and other public exchanges as well, resulting in new, uniform requirements.

At the core of the reforms is the audit committee. Clearly, the NYSE committee recognized the need for accounting skills as well as a powerful voice and proposed the creation of an audit committee structure that would have significant influence with the board as a whole.

Creating a working audit committee structure at the heart of a board of directors would require changes in the existing corporate culture, in which the top executives compensate themselves at high rates while also making accounting decisions, all at the expense of shareholders and employees. A worthwhile standard for the audit committee, in summary, would be to respond affirmatively to the three key questions that Warren Buffett expects an audit committee to consider:

1. If the auditor were solely responsible for preparation of the company's financial statements, would they have been done differently?
2. If the auditor were an investor, would he have received the information essential to understanding the company's financial performance during the reporting period?
3. Is the company following the same internal audit procedure the auditor would if he were CEO? If not, what are the differences and why?[17]

Part Three

YOUR ACTION PLAN IN THE NEW MARKET

10

STRATEGIES FOR MANAGING YOUR PORTFOLIO

For most individual investors, the entire stock market has changed. The approach to determining risks, the scope of those risks, and in fact, whether stocks continue to represent a viable long-term investment plan all have come into question. For many people, especially those hoping to build equity over many years, stocks now seem quite different than they did a few years ago.

To some extent, the market has changed. However, some risks were always there but were not apparent during the boom years. Anyone who has read a prospectus for an IPO or mutual fund already has seen the disclaimer: investing is characterized by certain risks, and everyone accepts those risks when they invest. Thus, market forces may cause a stock's value to fall significantly, without obvious warnings. That type of risk has always been accepted, because investors have known that stocks can also rise in market value, again without obvious predictors.

A second form of risk has taken investors by surprise. This includes the risk that an esteemed auditing firm would know about serious accounting misrepresentations and approve the financial statements anyway, that corporate executives would take millions from their companies and enrich themselves at the expense of their shareholders and employees, or that accounting gimmicks could go on for many years undetected (or detected and unreported). Such aggressive and often fraudulent accounting decisions include offshore partnerships and subsidiaries, off balance sheet liabilities, capitalized expenses, and booking revenues that do not exist.

In this troubling environment, how can you decide whose financial statements can be trusted? How can you ensure that your investment capital is reasonably safe? How do you know that, at the very least, corporate officers and accounting firms are not providing completely false accounting information?

These troubling questions have to be addressed on a number of fronts. The process of fixing the problem has begun already. However, while regulators and the industry itself can do a lot, you also need to change your basic approach to investing. With new laws that curtail the conflict of interest previously associated with auditing firms, a major flaw in the reporting system has been rectified. No longer can auditing firms perform "independent" audits *and* offer consulting services to the same company. In addition, senior auditors have to be rotated off of accounts in five-year cycles, so that an auditor will not get too close to management and lose objectivity. While accounting firms have long been a recruiting ground for financial executives, the new laws also forbid previous accounting firm employees from serving in many corporate positions for a long time. Corporate officers now must certify financial results, and if those results have to be revised later, officers stand to lose their incentive pay or may even be subject to lawsuits and other penalties. In extreme cases, they could be banned from employment at other public companies. More power has been given to independent directors and auditing committees to work with outside auditors.

All of these changes go far toward fixing the problems that came to light in recent years. However, you should never depend entirely on new laws or on regulatory agencies to protect you completely. And certainly you cannot depend on industry associations to provide effective self-regulation to the degree that you would like. The truth is, you have to take steps to review your assumptions, reevaluate risks, and in many cases, to change the basis for your analysis of a company.

THE BASIC DECISION TO BUY OR SELL

The process should begin with these very basic questions. How do you determine whether or not to buy stock in a particular company? For stocks you already own, what indicators signal that you should sell?

In looking back at some of the well-known companies experiencing trouble with their accounting, the essential question is: would your analysis have uncovered those problems and protected you from losing money? Unfortunately for most investors, the answer is no. This includes many mutual funds, whose management includes well-paid professional analysts who examine corporate finances continually. If professional money managers, mutual funds, Wall Street analysts, and individuals were all taken by surprise, how can individuals, who lack the services of a professional group of advisors, undertake an effective analysis of a company?

Some basic tools associated with trend analysts continue to serve as valuable methods not only for identifying viable candidates for your portfolio but also for spotting danger signals. Studying historical growth rates and comparing them to rates predicted by the company can help you to identify disparities. Robert Olstein cites Cendant, which was involved in a high-octane acquisition program in the early to middle 1990s. The company was reporting 30 percent earnings growth rates to shareholders, yet his analysis of the footnotes were indicative of internal growth rates in the 4 to 5 percent range.[1]

If you trust your trend analysis and you see a departure—especially in projections—you may have found a red flag. When corporations confuse their operating profits with nonoperating profits (often based on projections and assumptions), trouble may follow. For example, the practice of including pension fund investment income in net earnings is questionable. Companies can simply increase their assumptions about future earnings to accrue income in the current year. This practice has enabled many companies to abuse the system by overstating their estimates, often without any justification based on historical results.

What is needed? Corporations need to report their operating profits separately from nonoperating items. Investors need to be able to review operating results by themselves. The concept of *core earnings* has to be used not only by analysts and investors but also by corporations as a matter of policy. Pension income should be removed entirely from operating results and, instead, reported as a completely separate entity outside of the corporate financial report. Otherwise, investors cannot make valid assumptions and comparisons. Some corporations have recognized the need for transparent reporting and have already taken steps to improve the information conveyed to investors. However, a universal change in GAAP and reporting policies within publicly listed companies is needed to ensure that financial statements are complete, accurate, and reliable—the very least that investors expect.

When corporations include pension income in their earnings, those earnings include assumed returns from investment in the company's stock. So the greater the dollars invested, the higher the risk. If rosy assumptions are included, but the stock's market value falls, losses in the pension fund will cause lower corporate earnings. Everyone understands that lower than expected corporate earnings cause a fall in the stock's price. However, for many corporations, the reverse has become normal, and this is troubling for everyone. The pension income has to be removed from corporate financial statements before investors will regain confidence. The problem is potentially severe enough to bring down more corporations. For example, American Airlines and Goodyear Tire reported pension fund deficits that *exceeded* the companies' net worth in 2002. Losses in those pension funds were so severe, that the companies do not have the equity to cover them.[2]

Those are glaring examples of problems faced by some companies. Pension funds have to be funded adequately to pay retiring employees; however, a falling stock market places the pension fund at risk as well as the corporation itself. By the same argument, when a company lists an unending series of acquisitions, or when balance sheet account ratios begin spiraling out of control, that is a danger signal. If the company is overstating revenues, capitalizing expenses, or misusing reserve accounts, these problems show up in the ratios.

With this in mind, the decision to buy stock—or to continue holding stock you own—should be based on trend analysis, at least in part. If bad debt reserves fall in relation to accounts receivable levels, or if a lot of deferred charges appear on the balance sheet, the company could be reporting its transactions more aggressively. When reserves are reduced below realistic levels, such underreporting of likely future bad debt increases income. When deferred charges appear on the balance sheet, what does that mean? Is the company capitalizing expenses that should be written off this year? Or are current expenses simply being spread over an unrealistically long period of time to increase reported revenues? Robert Olstein gave a good example: "AOL Time Warner was taking their marketing costs and deferring them over a 2-year period, when in fact the churn rate was 90 days."[3]

Such practices certainly deceive investors. As long as accounting decisions are made to inflate reported earnings, that deception carries through to earnings per share and, of course, directly to the stock's market value. Thus, short-term financial reports can be made to look unrealistically positive, but deceptive accounting practices show up in the ratios. This is why basic trend analysis of accounts relating balance sheet items to profit and loss accounts is so valuable. The adjustments have to be put somewhere; so when revenue is inflated or expenses deferred, the offsetting entries show up in the balance sheet. Typically, the ratios will be off in:

- *Working capital.* The adjustments made to bad debt reserve, for example, will decline in relation to the accounts receivable asset account. At the same time, bad debts as a percentage of charge-based sales will decline as well. If historical bad debt levels justify the historical bad debt reserve levels, then the ratio should remain the same.
- *Deferred asset accounts.* When a corporation books revenue before it is actually earned, the offsetting entry is made to an asset account, usually in the deferred assets section of the balance sheet. When deferred assets grows out of proportion to total assets, the company could be booking revenues that have not yet been earned.
- *Unusually low depreciation rates.* The guidelines for depreciating various classes of assets are spelled out by the IRS, and this information is available to anyone. So it is fairly easy to compare gross asset values to accumulated depreciation for the current year. Compare that ratio to previous years's, and identify aberrations in the trend. Corporations are allowed to elect longer depreciation periods. However, when a company uses those longer periods, are they accurate? If the recovery period exceeds the realistic useful life of an asset, income levels are distorted. The company

will have to replace those assets before the depreciation period has run, meaning that the reported period is unreasonably long.[4]

- *Liability account changes.* In extreme cases, companies have posted loan proceeds as revenue. This classifies a liability as revenue, so that income is overstated while the company's debts are understated. Look for unexplained changes in revenues and in working capital ratios.

These are only starting points. As stocks rise in a bull market, companies are more likely to look for ways to adjust their reported earnings upwards to justify excessive valuations. But remember the observation from Robert Olstein: "At the end of bear markets, companies come clean, and investors who believed the fantasy accounting are left holding the bag."[5]

In a bull market, it is not necessary to adjust the books because stock values are rising, so the observation above has significance in light of recent events and also for predicting the future. Perhaps the revelations of 2002 were a signal to investors that the bear market was coming to an end. The majority of disclosures came about from one of two causes. First, changes in management revealed the practices of the previous group of executives; and second, the ever increasing financial practices could no longer be sustained. As the stock market begins a long-term, upward trend, the quality of earnings also improves. Quality of earnings is, of course, a reference to the *real* operating earnings of the company versus pro forma earnings that included exaggerated investment income estimates, nonrecurring charges, adjustments to reserves, extended depreciation terms, prebooked income, and other questionable practices.

REDEFINING RISK TOLERANCE

Some investors, recognizing the complexity of past problems, will just give up on direct ownership of stocks and entrust their investments to mutual fund managers with a decent track record. While this approach is not necessarily a poor one, it is not the only solution. Many investors will want to continue buying stocks directly but in a more informed manner.

Your *risk tolerance*—The amount and type of risk you are willing to take and can afford—might need to be redefined. Clearly, you face a different set of risks when you include those not previous known or revealed. These include:

- *Accounting policy risk.* The risk that a particular company has made aggressive policy decisions that may distort and overstate earnings. To the extent that such policies affect stock prices, buying or holding shares in the company increases the better understood market risk—that the stock's price will fall. If the company is exaggerating revenues, the stock price will eventually fall to reflect when the inflated values cannot be sustained.

- *Pension fund risk.* The risk that a corporation will not be able to fund its pension fund requirements due to a falling stock market. When a company invests its employees's pension assets in the stock market and that market falls, the pension fund will have losses. Losses are especially severe when those investments are *not* diversified but are invested primarily in the company's own stock. So a company like American Airlines may end up with a deficit in its pension fund that exceeds the corporate net worth. Investors need to pay attention to the very serious investment risk associated with companies whose ever growing pension obligations suffer in down markets.

- *Audit risk.* The risk that an independent audit firm will (a) not find accounting errors or fraud, (b) will find those errors but ignore them, or (c) will have such a close association with the client that they place themselves in a conflict of interest. While this range of risks has been addressed strongly in new legislation (see the Appendix for a summary of the new laws), investors need to view independent auditing practices with more suspicion than ever before. Contrary to what investors have believed historically, the once revered profession is not above yielding to temptation.

- *Management risk.* The risk that management will enrich itself at the expense of investors and employees. Again, new laws have increased the liability of CEOs and CFOs who abuse their trust, and improved rules for audit committees and the makeup of boards of directors will help as well. Responsible corporate management will also take voluntary steps to improve its communica-

tion with its investors. However, investors clearly cannot simply
trust management or boards of directors to protect their interests. The policy of "trust but verify" has to be used, at the very
least, to ensure that management is not abusing investors by providing itself with exceptionally large salary and bonus packages
when the performance of the company does not justify them.

- *Diversification risk.* The risk that an individual's holdings are too
  concentrated in one sector or type of investment. Diversification
  is usually thought of in a limited way: spreading investments out
  over more than one stock, for example. However, you need to
  evaluate other forms of risk exposure and use more advanced
  forms of diversification to protect yourself: investing in industries
  that do not experience the same economic cycles, placing funds
  in investments outside of the equity markets, providing greater
  liquidity in your portfolio, reevaluating risk exposure with different types of risks in mind, and redefining risk tolerance levels as
  your personal circumstances change.

For most investors, *risk* is understood in only one or two of its variations. So, when you ask yourself, "What is the risk of owning stock?"
the answer is likely to be that you could lose money if its market value
falls. You should keep other risks in mind as well, of course, because a
falling stock market also means your capital is tied up indefinitely, pension assets decline (perhaps to the point of corporate insolvency), and
potential management misdeeds come to light and reveal that the stock
price was vastly inflated to begin with. Falling market value is only one
symptom of a far broader range of risks. Owning stock has always been
thought of as a relatively safe way to allocate capital. Of course, cyclical
losses are expected, and you have always known that markets rise and
fall. However, recent events have shaken up the market in a more significant manner: now you see that in some cases, corporate managers were
willing to rob their shareholders, fraudulently report earnings, and use
creative methods to continue their fraud over many years. If you invest
money in the markets, these reported problems are not only a wake-up
call but a warning that you need to pay close attention to several forms
of risk.

THE CYCLICAL HISTORY OF THE MARKET

Ironically, while relatively young investors may believe that recent events are the first instances of corruption in publicly listed companies or in the stock market itself, history shows otherwise. The stock market has seen an almost cyclical pattern of financial abuses and periodic speculative frenzies. Thus, you should expect that, as in the past, the expensive and painful lessons that came to light in early 2000s will be followed by a period of improved conditions. This will be true partly because some of the worst offenders will be imprisoned, and partly because lesser offenders or those who might be tempted into wrongdoing are too frightened to abuse the rules. In the new environment, in which a call for transparent reporting is the battle cry, corporations, their executives, auditing firms, and investors are taking a far more conservative approach to financial reporting and corporate governance.

Stock market activity has gone on in some form for nearly 300 years on this continent. Beginning with exchanges of basic commodities, one-on-one deals for prices were arranged as the origins of an auction marketplace. The first big losses recorded in the market involved shares of the First Bank of the United States. It issued its first shares in 1791 at 100, and speculators drove market prices up to 195. As profit taking began, the value fell back to 108 in less than a single month. The losses—blamed on speculators—led to widespread lack of interest in stocks following the initial post-Revolutionary War foray. In the 1830s, the country experienced a fever of land speculation, and financial institutions loaned large sums of money to fund purchases, augmented by credit supplied by European banks. Railroad, bank, and utility company shares tripled within a few months until, in 1836, prices collapsed. Many bank failures followed, and some states were unable to honor their debts; once again, stock markets fell out of favor.

The California gold rush once again sparked speculative fever. Brokers were able to secure $300,000 lines of credit with as little as $1,500 in deposits.[6] By 1853, the market had crashed once again. Banks called their loans, many of which defaulted, and market activity fell to nearly nothing. Two years later, the market was once again robust and earnings high. However, in another two years, values fell once again, largely due to highly leveraged bank policies.

The Civil War era saw new high levels of speculation, especially in gold and other metals. Confederate victories increased gold's market value and, although Congress made the sale of gold above par illegal, the law was ignored. The Gold Bill of 1864 prohibited speculation in the metal, but when the price of gold continued to rise, the law was repealed two weeks later.[7]

The first big Wall Street scandal took place in 1869 when Jay Gould, a well-connected speculator, tried to corner the gold market. September 24, 1869, came to be known as Black Friday. Gould was betting that the U.S. government would not sell gold, but when it did, prices fell. Many failures followed, including Gould's broker, Albert Speyer, who assumed responsibility for the transactions and went bankrupt as a result.

The period from the end of the Civil War to 1900 was characterized by speculation and manipulation of the markets, including outright fraud in many cases. Many railroad bankruptcies occurred in the panic of 1893, followed by a period of growing speculation in the market. Another panic, called "the rich man's panic" by some, took place in 1907 when bank runs and failures were common.

As World War I began, the New York Stock Exchange closed on concerns about the war's effect on stock prices, and it remained closed for six months. Although trading was slow upon reopening, the market recovered quickly. After the war, the economy picked up and the 1920s saw unprecedented economic prosperity and stock market growth. Margin lending rose to new levels. Stock prices rose remarkably through most of 1929 to all-time high. The well-known crash that October led to many reforms, which continue to dominate the market to this day. Investigations revealed widespread fraud, highly leveraged market trading, and abuses on the part of market insiders. From these investigations came four significant new laws: The Banking Act of 1933, the Securities Act of 1933, the Securities Exchange Act of 1934 (including creation of the SEC), and the Public Utility Holding Company Act of 1934. These laws created a system of federal oversight of exchanges and the brokerage business. By 1935, the stock market was once again robust, with daily trading volume tripling from February to November; NYSE stock values rose in the aggregate 46 percent from April 1 to December 1.[8]

The beginning of World War II was followed by losses in 1940 as Axis powers had one victory after another. Two years later, the news changed and so did market sentiment. A new bull market began and continued for four years. The postwar market had its share of more modern cycles along with moderate reforms in market practices. In

1987, the largest, single-day point drop in market history reminded investors that nothing kept going up forever, not even stock prices. More recently, the late-90s dot.com phenomenon showed, once again, that inflated values eventually have to be reconciled with reality. Many companies that had never shown a profit rose to ridiculous levels only to fall drastically. Many investors, especially inexperienced first-timers, lost most of their portfolio value. Part of the problem was the lack of fundamentals, lack of diversification, and lack of market for many of the newly formed, Internet-based companies. As in every previous speculative period, the frenzy completely overlooked the economic realities of the moment.

In modern investing, a lot has changed. The Internet might have as much influence on the way Americans invest as did the telegraph and the telephone in the 19th century and the computer in the 20th century. The short-lived fad of day trading was followed quickly by the odd phenomenon of the unprofitable but wildly speculative dot.com industry.

We may look back at the Dutch tulip mania in the 17th century as nonsense.[9] However, market frenzies often are characterized by similar behavior. A few years ago, it made no sense to invest large sums in new companies that had never shown a profit and were involved in a relatively new technology (the Internet), which was characterized by a lot of competition and low barriers to entry. However, many investors did just that. Human nature is to follow trends, even when those trends are unsupported by logic or science.

Apart from the investing practices, up and down cycles of the market, and other realities of Wall Street history, scandals are particularly disturbing. The revelations of the early 2000s were the culmination of many years of financial practices that involved not only "creative" accounting but, often, outright fraud. The corporate culture allowed top executives to enrich themselves and provided incentive-based pay for maintaining ever higher stock prices. The temptations were great, and conflict of interest extended beyond the executive and board level to encompass "independent" auditors as well.

Recent legislation as well as industrywide reform—imposed as well as voluntary—may represent change as significant as that after the 1929 crash. We have already seen the requirements change for CEO and CFO responsibility, for the construction of boards of directors, and for limitations on the activities of outside auditing firms.

THE NEW ENVIRONMENT— SAFER THAN BEFORE?

It would be naïve to expect the problems of corporate executive misdeeds simply to disappear because of new laws. No matter how careful the wording of new laws or regulations, a small number of executives, brokers, financial planners, and others will always see a way to make a lot of money by breaking the rules. At times—the recent scandals being a good example—the financial skill required for some of these schemes is considerable, and some very capable individuals decided to use their skills to steal more money than they could ever need. Investors have to apply caution in dealing with their investments. It has always been so, and it always will be.

Even with that warning, I expect a period of relative quiet on the scandal front. As the Justice Department, SEC, and state agencies continue their investigations and offenders are brought to justice, others will retreat from their misdeeds. At the same time, the new laws do have teeth and will prevent many abuses. Most notably, auditing firms are required to perform either audit work or consulting for a client, but not both; corporate officers are certifying results with incentive pay and, perhaps, with their careers on the line; and a changed environment for boards of directors is removing many of the conflicts of interest previously seen.

As new laws and changed exchange listing requirements have gone into effect, I expect a period of relative quiet. The practice of controlling reported profits by journal entry is being toned down, because even though those practices are allowed under GAAP, corporations do not want to be viewed as deceiving their shareholders. Transparency is extending beyond mere disclosure of accounting decisions; the cookie jar approach to accounting is no longer acceptable.

We can expect somewhat greater volatility in the numbers, as sales and profits are reported on a more realistic basis. Some investors do not like the higher levels of fundamental volatility, and their displeasure is reflected in more volatile stock prices. This "brave new world" is, by necessity, upsetting to many, notably analysts who have built their reputations on the black art of prediction.[10]

In recent times, the culture of Wall Street has rested primarily on the revered earnings estimate. Analysts were often amazingly accurate

The **E**xperts **S**peak

Robert Olstein suggests that the entire methodology involving analysts needs to change. He explains, "Analysts should be looking at accounting; they should value companies; they shouldn't be setting price targets."[11]

in guessing to the penny how much a company's earnings per share would be—they simply reported what management told them, and in turn, management produced the result by making a few journal entries, with blessings from GAAP and the auditing world as well. The self-fulfilling prophecy had become the cure for all the ailments and uncertainties of investing, while analysts, money managers, and individual investors took comfort in the illusion of certainty they built for themselves.

Now for reality: earnings per share and other future numbers are far from certain. The value of a prediction is limited unless some alterations take place in the reporting of those results. The comforting (and all too accurate) earnings predictions are being abandoned in favor of a more scientific evaluation involving the true quality of earnings. The market in this new, postscandal era is basing its operating mode on reality rather than the surreal "cloud cuckoo land," in which analysts were able to predict outcomes to the penny.[12]

The entire system that involved giving out advice in the market (see Chapter 11) is being overhauled. Considering the track record, why should investors trust Wall Street analysts? Clearly, analysts have not acted scientifically but have become "nothing but management stenographers,"[13] reporting exactly what management has reported to them. In other words, when analysts "predict" in that manner, their predictions are worthless.

The modern investor recognizes the foolishness of earnings predictions and of the culture that emphasizes their importance. Analysts often do not base their predictions on fundamentals, quality of earnings, or other sensible criteria. The financial press adds to the problem when it compares outcome to prediction. If a company's earnings per share miss the mark by a few cents, the stock's value falls; if earnings exceed the predictions, the stock rises. This simplistic cause and effect approach to valuation creates problems for investors, because it creates a false sense of predictability. Anyone who has ever worked on a company budget knows that forecasting sales, costs, expenses, and profits is an extremely difficult task and should serve as a goal-setting tool. On Wall Street, however, the model had become an attempt to predict the future with precision. Rather than recognizing earnings for what they meant for the company itself, the outcome was measured against the prediction. Beat the prediction equals good; miss the prediction equals bad.

How do you identify companies on the basis of their earnings? First, don't evaluate results on the basis of how well companies met or did not meet analysts' predictions. That is a backward way to invest. Second, look at long-term quality of earnings as a means for evaluation, rather than basing portfolio decisions on quarter-to-quarter earnings.

Investors need to examine how they view earnings reports. If you have believed in assessing companies based on how they compare with analysts' predictions, then it is time to implement a different approach. The value-oriented advisors today agree that long-term evaluation of quality of earnings is the only fundamental approach that makes sense. The flaw in past thinking has been that investors—including those who consider themselves faithful to the fundamentals—have been distracted by technical indicators like the Dow Jones Industrial Averages and short-term price movements but, even more, by what I call false indicators, specifically the predictions offered by analysts.

The financial press invariably is attracted to simple, easily understood measurements, because they are easier to report and easier to comprehend. So the favorite tools for reporting on Wall Street include the DJIA, price point movement, and of course, comparisons between prediction and final quarterly earnings results. For American investors, accustomed to keeping score on a straightforward basis, these tools have a lot of appeal. However, investing is not baseball, and realistic investors need to dig deeper to succeed.

The fundamentals are not exciting, as any financial journalist will tell you. Accountants are not the life of the party, either, so listening to a complex accounting analysis of the numbers is far from fascinating. Thus, the importance of studying ratios's long-term trends is all-important, although far drier than a simplistic prediction. The financial press has done a great disservice to investors in its approach to market information. Investors have to look beyond the rather shallow, simple reporting they get from radio and television reporters and, to some extent, from newspapers and magazines. While the print media are bet-

The **E**xperts **S**peak

Robert Olstein emphasizes the need for long-term point of view rather than short-term accuracy in predictions. "There's too much concern about timing, and being exactly right . . . The horizon has come down to three to five days instead of three—five years; that's the biggest fault."[14]

ter able to devote space to in-depth analysis, and do so in many cases, the whole culture of Wall Street is to worship predictions and respond without understanding their basis.

A good example is the host/interview format so popular on those television and radio financial shows. The pattern seems to be to enter into serious discussions with guests about the fundamentals of companies and to identify some stocks for the week, then to end the show with a prediction game involving the Dow Jones Industrial Averages. Apparently, the format is designed to appeal to a wide audience. First, the analytical investor is given some fundamental analysis of companies, but then the technical side is used to liven up the end of the show. However, predicting the DJIA is far from a science. The weighted average can change for a complex variety of reasons, not the least of which is the possibility that some components of the industrials are occasionally removed and replaced. The criteria for those decisions are not publicly disclosed. However, the change in Dow components is itself troubling to analytical observers, because it means that long-term DJIA analysis is flawed. The weighting method further distorts the outcome, yet, for many, the 30 industrials have come to represent the market itself.

So in the brave new world of investing, what should you expect? First, we will probably experience a period of relative safety due to new laws and regulations plus heightened prosecution of lawbreakers. Second, analysts may (and should) fall out of favor to the extent that they predict outcomes in the capacity of what Robert Olstein calls "management stenographers." Third, serious investors will have to accept the possibility that future corporate sales and earnings will be more volatile than in the past. Fundamental volatility is a reality, because sales occur in a more chaotic manner than has often been reported. Cookie jar accounting is accepted under GAAP but not accurate, and accepting such practices without comment has become a long-standing practice among auditors. While you may not like fundamental volatility, it does more accurately reflect what really takes place. Analysts will certainly not like it, because pegging earnings right to the penny will no longer be possible. Then again, everyone should question the culture that expects analysts to be so accurate. They would better serve the market by becoming skilled in studying the accounting fundamentals and identifying long-term value.

Investors, too, have to change the type of information upon which they rely. So much of the earnings predictions are altered through the use of pro forma forecasting, and those reports should be taken for exactly what they are: unrealistic. A change in perception is called for. Investors need to realize that looking beyond the immediate horizon is the only sensible way to analyze a company's value. The current period's earnings *are not important* in the sense of how they affect the company's long-term growth prospects, and they have little to do with current value, either. Quarterly results are not audited, they may include interim estimates or allocations that affect the report itself, and they may reflect seasonal changes that will even out over the year. Companies can use pro forma forecasting to arrive at any conclusion they want; competent accountants can force budget numbers within the company, and they can do the same to present a rosy picture to investors.

DIVERSIFICATION ON SEVERAL LEVELS

While it is essential that analysts change their whole approach, investors need to examine their role as well. The importance of diversification cannot be emphasized too much. However, many investors, understand this topic only on a rudimentary level. True diversification needs to go beyond the idea of owning several different stocks.

The purpose of diversifying, of course, is to spread risks among dissimilar investments or investment types, so that the portfolio will not suffer sudden, catastrophic losses due to a single incident, such as a broad-based fall in stock prices. To really diversify, you need to consider how to invest capital in the following ways:

- *Basic diversification.* Most investors are familiar with the concept of spreading capital among many different stocks. The most efficient way to do this is through mutual funds. Many investors take this a step further by investing in directly owned stocks as well as mutual fund shares, a variation on the basic theme. However, knowing the concept and practicing it are two different things; consider how many investors lost the lion's share of their capital by overinvesting in single dot.com companies in the late '90s.

- *Sector and characteristic diversification.* Sectors, of course, are defined not only by their primary type of business but also by their market characteristics. So utility companies tend to be sensitive to long-term interest rates; retail concerns have specific annual cycles; and oil companies' values are affected by world oil prices, politics, and international economics to a greater degree than those of many other firms. Diversification requires placing capital in sectors with dissimilar economic and market attributes. If you purchase shares of companies sharing the same attributes, then your portfolio will likely experience similar movement in all of your holdings in response to the same influences. Taking this a step further, consider how different sectors react to specific news. If you invest in two or more sectors, but the stock prices react to specific events in the same way, then you have not achieved adequate diversification.

- *Equity diversification.* Considering the risks associated with the stock market, it is also necessary to invest a portion of your capital outside of the stock market. Anyone buying their own home has already diversified their equity holdings; for those with enough income, investing in rental real estate or undeveloped land might be appropriate as well. You can also diversify holdings in other ways. For example, you might invest in rare coins or stamps, precious metals, commodities, antiques and other collectibles, sports memorabilia, or vintage automobiles. Those highly specialized areas require experience and knowledge to avoid making mistakes, in the same way that stock market investors need to know what they are doing. If you have a profit sharing or pension plan, you can augment that with IRA investments or, if self-employed, with a variety of other tax-advantaged retirement investments. Finally, you should also have some portion of equity in a highly liquid account: savings, short-term money market accounts or funds, short-term bond funds, or cash.

- *Nonequity diversification.* In addition to stocks, real estate, and other equity markets, don't overlook the diversification you gain from investing in debt instruments. Most investors do not want to buy bonds directly, so they purchase shares of income or balanced mutual funds, which hold both stocks and bonds. You also can invest in mortgage pools through GNMA or FNMA or the mortgage-backed mutual funds that hold these securities. Investing in the debt side of real estate further diversifies the debt side of your portfolio.

- *Intangible diversification.* Investors with adequate knowledge and experience may also consider more advanced forms of investing through options or futures. Listed options can be used in a variety of ways, including protecting long or short equity positions, a sophisticated form of diversification. Straddles and hedges can be formulated to take advantage of short-term price movements, and the speculative purchase of calls or puts can provide short-term opportunities, even if your primary emphasis is more conservative. Futures are highly speculative and require specialized knowledge. However, if options and futures are suitable for you, they represent forms of diversification worth considering. If you want to invest in futures or options but don't have the time or expertise to do so, you can invest in a managed futures/options pool or hedge fund that can do the work on your behalf.

- *Fundamental diversification.* This involves tracking of several different financial attributes. You need to diversify your analysis so it goes beyond comparing earnings per share, watching PE ratios, and studying balance sheet accounts. As necessary as those factors are, you should also consider a larger view of the state of the economy, the geopolitical situation, a study of specific business cycles, mood of the market, and factors unique to a specific business or sector (such as annual seasonal changes among retail stocks, for example).

- *Market risk diversification.* This is separate from buying different stocks or spreading capital among sectors. Market risk specifically is associated with price volatility. Thus, if you buy only those stocks with high price volatility, your portfolio is not diversified enough to avoid severe consequences due to market swings. Analysts also call this *beta risk,* because highly volatile stocks (those with high betas) tend to move with the market but to a greater degree. The same problems are associated with an overly conservative approach, buying low beta stocks. These will tend to move in the same direction as the market but to a lesser degree and thus, when the market is moving upward in general, your portfolio may underperform.

- *Inflation and tax risk.* Some investors overlook the double effect of inflation and taxes on their profits. Thus, if you are so conservative that you avoid all other forms of risk, you still stand to lose purchasing power. For example, if you place all of your capital in insured accounts yielding very little, the effect of taxes and inflation will together offset the minimal gains you earn and, perhaps, even exceed them. To calculate after-tax breakeven, divide the assumed inflation rate by the inverse of your effective tax rate (combined federal and state rates).

The after-tax breakeven calculation helps you to identify the real value of a specific rate of return. For example, if you assume that the coming year's rate of inflation will be 3 percent, how much do you need to earn to break even after taxes? Assume that you pay an effective federal tax rate of 33 percent and an additional 8 percent effective tax rate to your state. Your combined effective tax rate is 41 percent. The breakeven formula is:

$$\frac{3\%}{(100 - 41)} = 5.1\%$$

You must earn 5.1 percent on your investments just to break even after inflation and taxes. Thus, if you place your entire portfolio in an insured certificate of deposit yielding 3.5 percent per year, you will lose purchasing power. Avoiding all other forms of risk exposes you to inflation and tax risk.

A chart for the calculation of breakeven interest is provided in Figure 10.1

Too much diversification can undo the intended purpose, however. If you spread out your risks too greatly, then you also stand to miss opportunities in the market. As the chart demonstrates, if your yield from investments is below the after-tax breakeven yield, you lose spending power. An overly risk-sensitive approach to investing does not solve

Figure 10.1 *Breakeven Interest*

Tax Rate	Assumed Rate of Inflation			Tax Rate	Assumed Rate of Inflation		
	1	2	3		1	2	3
21	1.3	2.5	3.8	36	1.5	3.1	4.7
22	1.3	2.6	3.8	37	1.6	3.2	4.8
23	1.3	2.6	3.9	38	1.6	3.2	4.8
24	1.3	2.6	3.9	39	1.6	3.3	4.9
25	1.3	2.7	0.4	40	1.7	3.3	5.0
26	1.4	2.7	4.1	41	1.7	3.4	5.1
27	1.4	2.7	4.1	42	1.7	3.4	5.2
28	1.4	2.8	4.2	43	1.8	3.5	5.3
29	1.4	2.8	4.2	44	1.8	3.6	5.4
30	1.4	2.9	4.3	45	1.8	3.6	5.5
31	1.4	2.9	4.3	46	1.9	3.7	5.6
32	1.5	2.9	4.4	47	1.9	3.8	5.7
33	1.5	3.0	4.5	48	1.9	3.8	5.8
34	1.5	3.0	4.5	49	2.0	3.9	5.9
35	1.5	3.1	4.6	50	2.0	4.0	6.0

the problem of risk avoidance, and excessive conservatism destroys your portfolio value.

For some, the goal in investing is to preserve spending power. Thus, achieving breakeven is adequate in the sense that it protects against inflation and taxes. However, for many others, the goal is to have capital appreciate over time. The best way to achieve that is not through taking ever greater risks but by reinvesting earnings.

INCOME REINVESTMENT— INDIVIDUAL DIVERSIFICATION

Anyone who owns mutual fund shares knows that one of the first choices made after opening an account is what to do with the earnings. You can draw them out or reinvest them in additional shares. Most investors understand that reinvestment is one of the key methods for gaining compound returns over time—as opposed to removing the cash and having to invest it elsewhere.

Even if you own shares of stock directly, you can reinvest your dividends by participating in a dividend reinvestment program (DRIP), which many publicly listed companies offer. Under this system, you take dividends in additional partial shares rather than in cash. While this approach does not change the taxability of dividend income, it does create compound rates of return on dividends. For many investors owning only a few hundred shares of stock, the relatively small dollar amount of dividends is a problem. How do you put such small amount of capital back to work?

If you participate in a DRIP program, it is best to have your original shares registered in your own name (as opposed to a street name at a brokerage firm, for example). If you register shares through a brokerage account, you could be charged a sales commission when your DRIP plan goes into effect. The program is relatively simple; by signing up for DRIP participation, the company issues partial shares instead of sending you a check for your dividend income.

Reinvesting earnings is the primary way that capital grows over time. If you have read any mutual fund sales literature, you have already seen how reinvesting income and capital gains works. You have probably seen the typical example that reads, "If you had invested $10,000 in the fund 30 years ago, it would be worth $43,219 today." While that might seem impressive on the surface, it represents annual returns averaging only 5 percent. So even in those funds performing only at (or even below) overall market averages, you can experience significant growth in the dollar value of your portfolio when all income and capital gains are reinvested.

You might think of dividend reinvestment as a variation of diversifying your holdings. If, instead, you remove income and place it elsewhere, you will need to match or beat the rate or return on your original investment to do better, so reinvesting makes sense as long as your investment choice is wise. Shares of stock in a well-managed company with high quality of earnings are expected to increase in price, and that certainly is one way to achieve growth, even given interim market fluctuations. Combined with long-term growth, reinvested dividends can augment overall return and increase your growth even more.

While reinvesting dividends is not actually a form of diversification, it does diversify your return by creating a two-way income, from increased market value and from compound earnings on the dividends themselves. The advantage of owning mutual fund shares, in addition to the built-in diversification among stocks or bonds, is the ability to automatically reinvest earnings, but you can often do the same thing when you own stocks directly. The trend today is toward more and more publicly listed companies participating in DRIP plans. It makes sense for the company as well as for the investor. By providing partial shares instead of cash payments, corporations can declare dividends while preserving a higher level of their operating cash flow; so as DRIP participation increases, everyone can benefit. Corporations desiring to declare dividends often have a problem, because payment would drain working capital. The DRIP alternative solves the problem, and the more individual investors take part in a DRIP program, the greater the advantage.

USING OPTIONS FOR PORTFOLIO INSURANCE

A limited use of listed options helps to diversify your portfolio further while also mitigating risks in other positions. For example, if you wish to hold onto stock, you can buy a put for every 100 shares you own. The put is a form of insurance to protect the value of your stock against short-term price declines.

If the stock's market value falls below the put's striking price, then the put will increase in value one point for each point you lose in the stock. So the cost for this insurance is the premium paid for the put. This strategy is appropriate only for the short term, however, because puts expire quickly.

An opposite strategy can be used, employing call options when you are in a short position in stock. If you have sold short, the risk is that the market value will rise rather than fall. In that case, you eventually have to buy out of the position at a loss or wait out a turnaround in the market. In cases where a stock's value takes off in a big way, short selling is very high risk. A possible solution is to insure the short position by buying 1 call for every 100 shares sold short. For every "in the money" point of increase in the stock's value, the call will also rise by one point.

Calls and puts can be used to insure either short or long positions. By exercising the option, your losses are offset, because the option sets the price for the 100 shares at a fixed striking value. Alternatively, you can also sell the put or call and take a short-term profit. That profit would offset the paper loss in your stock position.

As another form of diversification using calls and puts, you can use a portion of your capital to speculate. For example, if you believe that shares of a particular stock will rise in the near future but you do not have the capital to invest, you can buy calls. If you are right and the value rises, you can exercise the call and buy shares below market value, or you can sell calls and make a nice profit in a few months, sometimes in a matter of only days or weeks.

If you happen to believe that the market value of a stock will fall, but you do not want to sell short (recognizing the high risks of short selling), an alternative is to buy puts as a form of speculation. If you are right, your puts will increase in value as the stock falls, and you can sell the puts at a profit. Buying options as speculation is recognized as a high-risk investment and is an appropriate diversification only if you know the market well.

In some cases, you expect a big point move, but you don't know for sure which direction it will take. A variety of combinations called spreads and straddles can create profits no matter which direction the stock's price moves. However, the risk is that price movement would not be enough to offset your costs, so again, using options to speculate on short-term price movement is high-risk. Fortunately, buying options limits your loss to your purchase price. A far different picture comes into play when you go short in options.

Selling calls or puts is an interesting strategy, because it presents the widest possible range of risks. The high-risk strategy is selling "naked" or "uncovered" calls. You sell a call when you do not own shares of the underlying stock. If the price of stock does not rise, the call can be sold at a profit; or it can be closed at purchase and the difference between initial sales price and final purchase price is profit. Uncovered call selling has potentially unlimited risks. If the value of the stock takes off, your call will be exercised, and you are required to make up the difference between the current market value and the lower striking price.

Selling puts is somewhat different, because the potential risk is more limited. In theory, the maximum risk is that a stock becomes completely worthless. However, more limited losses are more likely. If the buyer exercises a put you have sold, you are required to purchase 100 shares at the striking price, which would be higher than current market value. However, if you consider the striking price to be reasonable, selling puts is a viable strategy. If the put's premium value falls before expiration, you can purchase the put to close the position and take a profit or allow it to expire worthless.

A final strategy worth mentioning is the most conservative, selling "covered" calls. A call is covered when you own 100 shares for each call sold. There are three possible outcomes. First, the call could be exercised and 100 shares called away. Second, the call could lose value, and you can close it out by buying it for less than you originally sold it for. Third, the call could expire worthless, meaning you keep the entire premium as profit. Covered call selling succeeds when you select calls that would produce three-way profit in the event of exercise: from capital gains (meaning you should have a paper gain in the stock you own), dividend income, and call premium. The double-digit returns likely from selling covered calls are offset only by potential lost opportunity. If a stock's market value soars and your stock is called away at the fixed striking price, you lose out on the profits by being committed to a short position in the call. However, that potential "loss" is future-looking and does not undo the value of covered call writing.

Using calls and puts as a form of diversification has many benefits. You can insure and protect other long or short positions, speculate for short-term gains, or enter into a covered call program to reduce your basis in stock while realizing double-digit profits.

NEW APPROACHES TO PORTFOLIO MANAGEMENT

In the new investing environment, you are like to hear three terms that you might not have heard before, but they will dominate methods of fundamental analysis. These terms are *core earnings, quality of earnings,* and *intrinsic value.*

All of these refer to the same idea. The idea is not new, but the importance of identifying and defining earnings has never been greater. Historically, corporations could manipulate their earnings with accounting tricks and control long-term trends to some degree. To corporate numbers watchers—the analysts—the important thing was to be able to predict earnings per share, preferably down to the penny. So whatever it took to achieve "accurate" predictions in a sometimes deteriorating corporate world was acceptable to internal accountants and financial executives and, more troubling, acceptable both under GAAP and in the auditing world. Investors always believed in the purity of the independent audit and in the integrity of auditing firms. However, the news in the early 2000s demonstrated that a more precise definition would be needed in the future to describe what a company really earns.

In other words, investors have discovered what CFOs and auditors have known all along: accounting is not a clean, simple, or attractive matter. It involves estimates, forecasts, and any number of accruals subject to interpretation. Investors have also discovered that auditors and executives cannot be trusted to protect their interests, and they have learned that analysts often do not understand accounting but have all too often served the interests of management over those of investors.

With these stark realities upon us, the importance of better identifying earnings has risen to the top of the fundamental priorities list. Today's value investors—those who seek bottom line fundamental facts—consider *core earnings* to be the essential starting point in evaluating companies. First Eagle Sogen Funds copresident Jean-Marie Eveillard defines core earnings as being "as close as possible to economic truth" and distinguishes those earnings from what he calls "accounting profits."[15] Another expert, Charles Royce of Royce & Associates in New York, observes, "Everybody says they're a value investor. Some are overvalued investors."[16]

If we distinguish between core earnings and accounting-based earnings or profits, we can understand not only how accounting entries may distort operating profits, but also how we can evaluate corporate outcomes. If the corporation itself does not take the time to explain its core earnings to investors in the spirit of complete transparency, then investors may need to make their own adjustments.

The "core" is the operating net income. This includes sales, costs, and expenses related directly to the primary business. It must exclude all nonoperating profit and loss items, such as pension income, interest income and expense, nonrecurring adjustments and extraordinary items, and capital gains from the sale of assets. It should also exclude the addition of income from acquiring other companies as well as written-off reserves associated with acquisitions from past years. None of these is included in core earnings, because none is related to the primary activity of the company. When all of the extras are stripped away, you end up with the basis for a real comparison from year to year. Core earnings is the number investors deserve to be given for means of comparison and evaluation, and it is the responsibility of management, their accounting executives, and independent auditors to report realistic earnings based on this idea.

The adjustment is not complicated. In fact, the entries that alter core earnings are actually the complications. Core earnings may also have to be adjusted if depreciation has been spread out over too long a period, if certain expenses have been amortized that are more properly included in the current year, or if other current-year adjustments have been made to accounts receivable and inventory loss reserves. Reserve adjustments should be made where established ratios have not been followed and management has not provided explanations for the departure. Balance sheet ratios invariably reveal any "funny business" the company has undertaken, because alterations to income, costs, and expenses should show up in the asset and liability sections. Robert Olstein summarizes the importance of these tests as looking for "fishy items on the balance sheet which seem to indicate that the earnings are not in accord with economic reality."[17]

The next term, *quality of earnings,* is another concept that can fine-tune your program of fundamental analysis. We have all discovered that fundamental analysis is worthless if it is based on unreliable financial information. So, in addition to the basic detective work involved in locating variations in balance sheet ratios, it is also important to examine the mix of revenues and profits reported by the company. This mix reflects the quality of earnings.[18]

A study of ratios does reveal the deterioration from artificially inflating revenues or from taking a more aggressive accounting interpretation of the numbers. If core revenues begin to level off or fall, adjustments can be made in bad debt or inventory loss reserves to decrease expenses, or current-year expenses can be capitalized. A change in these ratios is an important signal of lower quality of earnings.

Looking to the income statement, the relationships between sales and costs (the gross profit margin) and the actual net operating profit trend itself, which would be expected to remain relatively constant over time, can be revealing as well. Assuming that the net operating profit is consistently reported from one year to the next—essential for meaningful analysis—you can identify poor quality of earnings when the ratios begin to change. For example, booking revenue before the applicable period—without corresponding costs, for example—distorts the gross margin and helps identify unrealistic accounting adjustments. Some companies have been found to book revenues that were, in fact, not revenues at all, but pass-through accounts (money received but payable to a third party). Such a practice, at least questionable and perhaps fraudulent, distorts the established gross margin, often significantly. Other companies have taken the more blatant step of recording loan proceeds as revenue, which is clearly false reporting and distorts outcomes on the income statement.

Robert Olstein points out that higher revenues by themselves do not equate to a positive change in the fundamentals, in spite of what the Wall Street culture wants to see. Olstein explains that "investors, in most cases, are confusing the expansion of an industry with profitable growth."[19]

To those not familiar with how expansion occurs, ever higher numbers seem advantageous, but the important question to ask relates to quality of earnings or profitable growth. It matters little that sales and profits are reported at record levels if, in fact, adjustments this year mandate a big (and unexpected) loss in the future. Such losses, often the result of manipulation of the numbers, cause sudden drops in stock values. The quality of earnings has deteriorated, and growth is neither sustainable nor legitimate.

Quality of earnings are also degraded when companies make more subtle decisions about how and when to book revenue, or what accountants call "recognizing" when sales occur. Robert Olstein explains, "They can change their sales recognition policies by accelerating, instead of booking revenues on shipment, on manufacture."[20] If a company determines to recognize revenues in a different time period from one year to the next, it certainly distorts not only the gross and net margins but the accounts receivable relationship to sales as well. If a company books revenues when goods are manufactured rather than when shipping, the effect could be to move considerable revenues into the current year that should be recognized in the following year. At the very least, the prebooked revenues will have to be overcome in later years, meaning future surprises for investors. Booking revenue at the point of manufacture means that a sale, by any definition, has not occurred yet, so those "earnings" are of low quality, perhaps even nonexistent.

Another subtle trick, again involving a change in accounting assumptions, is to change accounting methods for recognition of revenue from the *completed contract* method to the *percentage-of-completion* method. Under most situations, revenues are supposed to be recognized when a customer places an order and that order is shipped. This makes sense. It is a consistent method for recording revenues in the proper and appropriate period, and it conforms with the definition of a sale as taking place when a customer incurs the responsibility to pay. Thus, order and shipment constitutes a bona fide transaction.

The percentage-of-completion method is an alternative used in construction and other industries where contracts may take more than one year to complete. Under this system, revenues are booked along with associated costs and expenses based on the progress of a long-term contract. This method is acceptable when, in fact, the company has completed work and received progress payments and has also expended funds to pay for labor, materials, and other applicable expenses. The percentage-of-completion method recognizes income as occurring over a period of time and is more realistic than booking all income, costs, and expenses at the end of the job. If the project took three years to complete, for example, the percentage-of-completion method is not only reasonable but also more realistic.

Problems arise, however, when a company decides to change its accounting methods to percentage-of-completion only for the purpose of recognizing income earlier than usual. This move distorts the year-to-year analysis and is likely to throw several ratios out of whack. The change in accounting is especially troubling when, in addition to more aggressive policies for recognizing revenues, associated costs and expenses continue to be treated under the completed contract method. As a consequence, revenue comes in this year, but costs show up in the following year. The most likely place to spot this type of problem is in the net profit margin, where unusually high returns on sales make no sense.

The return on sales should be consistent. In any given industry, net profit ratios do not realistically climb every year; there is a natural limitation as to how high profitability can go. Thus, a well-managed company will be able to maintain its net margin (and earnings per share). The unrealistic expectation among analysts, and even many investors, is to expect ever increasing earnings per share. Some corporations have responded to this expectation by inflating earnings, using a variety of changes in accounting assumptions, recognition policies, and other devices that translate to lower quality of earnings.

So identifying and defining quality of earnings—based on a true operating income picture—is an important step in any program of fundamental analysis. Net operating income should exclude pension income in all cases. Some companies have included an estimated investment return, often unrealistically high, in reported income, which has been the majority of reported operating income and, in some cases, has hidden an operating net loss. The practice of including pro forma income with actual operating income has to stop if corporations hope to regain investor confidence. Robert Olstein calls pro forma reporting "the biggest joke today," because pro forma disclosures, which originally only dealt with acquisition accounting, today include the elimination of compensation costs and other ordinary costs as well. The Internet companies turned pro forma accounting into earnings before the bad stuff.[21]

The final term, *intrinsic value,* is defined by Jean-Marie Eveillard: "What is the business worth today? I am always surprised when a business person doesn't look at value more as a bridge game—wanting to figure out its real worth—rather than taking a casino approach."[22]

The question of what a business is worth today is a valuable tool. Obviously, intangible assets such as goodwill provide little or no added value to a company other than, perhaps, product recognition, reputation, or other value not directly related to what could be called liquidation value. So the question is, "What would the company be worth today if (a) its current assets were cashed out, (b) long-term assets were sold at current market value, and (c) any carried-over values were acquired by the buyer?" What, in other words, is the true per-share value?

Liquidation value is not entirely accurate in this analysis, because we cannot ignore the very real current value of future growth. However, how do you place a specific value on that? To some extent, the share price working as a multiple of earnings does represent that very value. The PE ratio is, in fact, a reflection of the current market perception of future value. However, given the way that market price comes about (not to mention the equally troubling mix of items in the operating earnings per share), the PE itself is not necessarily a good indicator of liquidation value. If you own shares, you can sell them at today's price, but that price may be far removed from the intrinsic value of the company and its net assets.

The intrinsic value test should not be limited to liquidation value. Some additional value should be assigned to growth potential, of course. However, the approach should be first to identify intrinsic value and then view likely growth trends as a premium to value. To the degree that growth prospects are stronger in one company over another, intrinsic value also represents a more promising long-term investment. It enables you to evaluate companies given (a) a definition of core earnings, used in like-kind comparative analysis rather than distorted by accounting tricks, (b) adjustments to remove low quality of earnings created by acquisition-based income or aggressively booked or questionable revenue sources, (c) removal of nonoperating income sources such as pension fund investment income and nonrecurring or extraordinary items, and (d) the usual ratios that remain at the heart of fundamental analysis.

By applying the established tests and looking for aberrations in ratio outcomes, and by ensuring that the noncore earnings have been removed, it is possible to evaluate a company's intrinsic value better (whether identifying net capital value or, more appropriately, current per share value as a multiple of earnings). The complex reporting methods used by publicly listed companies have been a problem in the past, as has the inclusion in "net income" of many questionable items, aggressively determined valuations, and nonoperating profits of substantial size (for example, from acquisitions and pension fund income). The corporation, with its resource of professional accountants and aided by outside auditors, has the ability to construct complex accounting reports to justify its decisions. In the future, you have the right to expect plain-English explanations and full disclosure—transparency of *all* of the company's dealings, whether they have a positive or a negative impact on earnings per share.

In summary, year-to-year earnings should not determine whether you decide to own shares but rather the dependability of the numbers, consistency of growth, and the quality of earnings. Without these essentials, you have no means for making an informed decision. With properly defined and disclosed results, you can evaluate a company and tell whether its revenues, costs, and expenses are an improvement over the previous year. In a poorly managed company, management has a motivation to obscure. In a well-managed company, management has every incentive to make full disclosure, so the degree to which you understand management's communications may itself become one of the more important fundamental tests.

11

FINDING THAT
TRUSTED ADVISOR

Investors usually enter the market with little or no knowledge about how it works. They assume as a starting point that they need to find someone to guide them. Some go into investment clubs and benefit from the collective experience and knowledge of other members; others simply find a mutual fund and pay someone else to make decisions for them. The lone retail investor—anyone working as an individual without the help of a mutual fund—may seek out the help of a financial planner, money manager, stockbroker, or other "expert" to help them invest their money, or they may subscribe to a service to get market information.

History has shown that, as a rule, those who advise others on investing their money have a poor track record. Most accounts under management lose money, often far more than overall market losses for the same period. The problems of a poor performance record, coupled with glaring conflicts of interest, have taught most experienced investors that entrusting funds to an advisor entails a dangerous risk.

THE IMPORTANCE OF TRUST

If Wall Street establishments have succeeded at anything, it has been at creating an image of trust and experience. Most commercials for these established firms emphasize their reputations for service, market knowledge, and expertise. In reality, the question of whether or not to trust an advisor working on Wall Street should go back to basics. Do advisors know how to study a company and make an informed decision? Do they understand accounting? Are they providing advice based on fundamentals or on something else? Is it appropriate for analysts to predict earnings levels?

A starting point should be to study the basic premise under which an advisor operates. More to the point, what does the investor expect when seeking out advice? Whether an investor uses a one-on-one relationship—with a stockbroker, for example—or trusts advice provided in a newsletter or other subscription service, the first question should be: how was a specific recommendation arrived at?

The problem is not a new one. The conflict of interest for brokers working in firms that also provide investment banking services has been around for years. Robert Olstein's description of this problem in 1977 still holds true today:

> The analysts worry about losing their relationship with management if they criticize a company, and once they recommend a stock, they have an ongoing bias to prove they were right. And now many research houses are part of investment banking firms that obviously don't want to lose their banking clients.[1]

Olstein continues to point out the weak link between analysts and management in the present day. He has observed that:

> Many analysts just repeat what a company tells them and are afraid to stand on their own. I know of several examples of negative repercussions for analysts who contradicted management's rosy view of operations by issuing sell recommendations or lowering investment ratings. The analyst who predicted Dell's sales slowdown received bomb threats, and the analyst

who correctly predicted Boston Chicken's downfall was eliminated from subsequent conference calls and company meetings.[2]

Two years before that, another expert, Charles D. Ellis, observed a similar problem, namely the chronic tendency among analysts to promote buying decisions with virtually no sell recommendations.

> Almost all of the information in the investment management business is oriented toward purchase decisions. The competition in making purchase decisions is too good. It's too hard to outperform the other fellow in buying. Concentrate on selling instead . . . Almost all of the really big trouble that you're going to experience in the next year is in your portfolio right now; if you could reduce some of those really big problems, you might come out the winner . . .[3]

The question of when to buy or sell is one side of the problem; the other side has to do with how investment bankers have often misused their power. Threats and reprisals have been used by companies against analysts who do not parrot management's theme, and by investment bankers and research analysts against companies. In 2002, Piper Jaffray was fined $300,000 for just such a threat. They were accused of threatening to drop research of Antigenics, Inc., a biotech company, if that company did not give Piper its investment banking business. The NASD regulatory unit fine against U.S. Bancorp (parent of Piper Jaffray) was settled without an admission of guilt. The trend, however, is significant. NASD has announced that it is increasing its investigative staff, and Wall Street firms are on notice that they cannot use their research influence to extort companies to send business their way.[4]

The Piper Jaffray story is one of many of Wall Street's dirty little secrets. Often, business decisions have been based not on the best business practices, but as part of a two-way street of influence peddling and, in many cases, threats. On the research side, it is clear that, just as negative recommendations have been used at times as leverage, positive recommendations have been used to attract investment banking business. This reality serves as a wake-up call to investors, who have often believed that analysts and stockbrokers have some special knowl-

K e y P o i n t

If some special secret to making money exists, no advisor will share it with a customer. The truth is, no one will provide an easy way to beat the averages. This truth usually is learned the hard way.

edge or understanding not shared with most other people. This "insider track" doesn't exist, of course. Even if it did, it would be illegal for the stockbroker to give investors that special information, particularly since the passage of SEC Rule FD (Fair Disclosure), which says that all material information about a company has to be released to the public at the same time, not just to special people like brokers or analysts. Unfortunately, the inexperienced investor soon learns—usually through losing money—that no one will really help him to beat the averages. The very analysts and brokers whom investors have always trusted have been busy furthering their own careers and the revenues of their firms, and the investor has paid the price. Using someone else's help, investors often are lucky to achieve just an average track record.

A new investor probably assumes that when a stockbroker or analyst makes a recommendation, it is based on the fundamentals. You might assume that your stockbroker has studied the financial statements of the company, investigated the footnotes, and done their homework to conclude that (a) the stock is underpriced, (b) the company has exceptional prospects for long-term growth, (c) risks are minimal, and (d) this is the among the best alternatives available today.

The analyst or stockbroker probably has not studied the financial statements, at least not from an analytical or accounting perspective. In fact, brokers and analysts often do *not* understand accounting well enough to equate financial statements to the current value of a stock. The majority are trained in basic sales techniques and are glib in the language of Wall Street but have no real depth of understanding and certainly no accounting training or qualifications.

Stockbrokers often use catch phrases like, "This is a real buying opportunity because the stock is cheap today," "This company is an exceptional long-term growth candidate," and similar sales phrases that are not backed up with solid research (or, often, with any research at all). The broker or analyst may not even know what constitutes an underpriced stock in terms of value analysis and may have little concept of comparative risk analysis.

In fact, most salespeople on Wall Street tend to provide advice on the basis on greed (buy when prices are high) or panic (sell when prices are low). So, rather than "buy low and sell high," the real *modus operandi* is the reverse: "buy high, sell low." In an interview in 2001, Charles Ellis portrayed the market accurately with this story:

> . . . a charming, seductive, manic-depressive gentleman named Mr. Market . . . shows up on your doorstep offering to do business with you. When he's manic, he'll offer to buy your stocks or sell you his for absurdly inflated prices. When he's depressed, his prices are ridiculously low. The mistake most people make is answering the door just because Mr. Market knocks. *You don't have to let him in.* Why should you buy just because he's excited? Why should you sell just because he's down in the dumps? A long-term investor shouldn't care about market prices.[5]

Investors trusting a commission-based salesperson in a brokerage firm are in peril. Those using the services of a money manager may also be in peril, unless they have searched for one of the few value investor managers. How do you find one? A lot of money managers will call themselves "value investors" when asked, but very few actually understand accounting or use the analytical skills required to value stocks. The majority operate in the traditional modes of the market, and very few should be trusted to tell you where to put your money.

Another point to be made is this: good advice is not cheap. If you want to subscribe to a service that provides information based on a serious analysis of the fundamentals, and if you want to understand that information, you must invest time and thoughtful research. Successful investors know that they cannot expect someone simply to tell them what to do; the responsibility for knowledge belongs on both

sides. The advisor as well as the investor should understand the fundamentals well enough that they are speaking the same language. When
a value-oriented advisor offers a suggestion, the investor should understand the significance of the reasoning that goes along with that
advice.

Neither advisors nor their investor clients need to become accountants. However, accounting expertise is part of the requirement for determining the value of stocks. So the advisor needs to employ accounting
knowledge and experience to dissect financial statements and find the
key indicators, including identification of truly under-priced stocks *and*
red flags indicating problems.

The level of bad advice, however, may be at an all-time high, if litigation trends are any indication of the overall problem. With literally
trillions of dollars lost in the market, the blame is largely being laid on
analysts and brokers. By the third quarter, 2001, arbitration claims filed
with the NASD were up 25 percent from the previous year, and complaints filed with the SEC were up 58 percent from five years before.
Dollars amounts are on the rise as well, with averages above $500,000
and million dollar-plus claims more and more common. For the first
time, complaints have been filed to recover for conflict of interest on
the part of brokers.[6]

Not only an increase in litigation reflects the trend. Equally important is the fact that the honeymoon between investors and analysts has
ended. Even the Wall Street faithful have come to realize that those
conflicts of interest *do* affect judgment and that analysts in conflicted
positions cannot be trusted. The situation was bluntly summarized in a
2002 article in Fortune magazine:

> Analysts are whores. Yes, incredible as it may seem, people
> sometimes don't have the best judgment in the world if they're
> being paid both to analyze companies and to finance their
> deals. That often happens when securities analysts advise man-
> agement while at the same time evaluating their stocks. Hello![7]

This problem has been around for decades, and analysts have
repeatedly demonstrated that they are not able or willing to fix it without being forced to. Even so, insiders have insisted that the industry can
heal itself if given the chance. In testimony before the U.S. Senate Com-

mittee on Governmental Affairs, Thomas Bowman, president and CEO of the Association for Investment Management and Research (AIMR) said:

> Ethical standards are most effective when developed by the profession and voluntarily embraced rather than externally and unilaterally imposed. Therefore, in drawing your conclusions and making your recommendations to the Senate, we hope that you have confidence in the private sector to solve these problems."[8]

Mr. Bowman's words probably do not impress anyone who has lost money through taking the advice from a broker, without being advised that the broker's firm also provided investment banking services to the company being touted. Basic trust has been shattered, and investors no longer have faith in the big Wall Street firms to fix their problems. Regulation, litigation, and separation of investment banking and research are needed to restore confidence. The new environment has been described accurately as "the new era of investor skepticism, a time when you have to question every pronouncement, every last statement, no matter what the source."[9]

Citigroup, parent of Smith Barney, has set up a "separate" research company within its financial empire, a move designed to separate research from investment banking. However, that offer was made as part of a settlement negotiation with the SEC and the NASD. Furthermore, the move didn't spin off the research completely but kept some ties with Citigroup and Smith Barney. A move toward reform to make investigations go away is *not* the same as self-regulatory steps or self-compliance.[10]

The truth is, brokers have had problems not only for several decades but literally since the inception of the public stock market in America. Even with the industry's insistence that it can change itself, the record shows otherwise. The "new" ratings being used by most firms still show a strong bias, favoring buy over sell with only 3 percent of all ratings in the latter class. For example, as of July 1, 2002, only 5.8 percent of Merrill Lynch's recommendations where to sell, Prudential only 3.5 percent, Goldman Sachs 1.5 percent, Lehman 1.0 percent, J.P. Morgan Chase 0.9 percent, and Credit Suisse First Boston 0.4 percent. The exception to this dismal rating was Morgan Stanley, whose sell recommendations were 20.9 percent of their total. Clearly, the bias remains strongly in favor of overweight or equal weight ratings, even in the face of industry pledges to self-reform.[11]

THE DISMAL HISTORY OF WALL STREET ANALYSTS

The Wall Street insiders—including analysts, money managers, stockbrokers, and others who operate close to them—have historically operated as a good old boy's club. The exclusion of outsiders has created a separation of sorts over three hundred years, giving a different and more cynical meaning to the idea of "Wall Street"—in many respects, the market has always been distinguished by two camps: insiders and everyone else.

The separation goes back, literally, to the 1700s. In the early days, the need for a continuous market was recognized by everyone involved in trading. Without a continuous market, the early market insiders saw, it would be inefficient to move commodities to market, achieve an orderly system for buying and selling, and avoid problems with outside investors. To create the continuous market, the insider was born.

The first insiders were stock dealers who, in 1792, met daily at noon at 22 Wall Street to transact sales through joint agreement between auctioneers and dealers.[12] The early dealers and brokers wanted to break the exclusive power held by auctioneers and entered their own agreement. They began trading near a buttonwood tree at 68 Wall Street, and their agreement came to be known as the Buttonwood Tree Agreement. It established the club:

> We the Subscribers, Brokers for the Purchase and Sale of Public Stock, do hereby solemnly promise and pledge ourselves to each other, that we will not buy or sell from this day for any person whatsoever, any kind of Public Stock, at less than one quarter of one per cent Commission on the Specie value and that we will give preference to each other in our Negotiations. In Testimony whereof we have set our hands this 17th day of May at New York, 1792.[13]

The Buttonwood Tree Agreement established exclusive dealings and minimum commissions among the brokers and dealers. By 1817, more activity led to more formalized rules. The precursor of the NYSE was formed and called the New York Stock and Exchange Board. New members were not admitted easily, and many new applicants were kept out by blackball. In the pre-Civil War era, exchange members saw themselves as an elite and wore silk hats and swallowtail coats at the exchange. Younger men were rarely admitted to "the club," and initiation fees were raised to $1,000. One historian described the situation:

> The old fellows were united together in a mutual admiration league and fought the young men tooth and nail, contesting every inch of ground when a young man sought entrance to their sacred circle.[14]

Have things changed that much from the 19th century to the 21st? In some respects, they have not. While age barriers have been removed, there remains a clear separation between the insiders of the established Wall Street firms and everyone else. The "club" mentality remains and will change only if and when the market decides to unravel their special cloak. The silk hats have disappeared, and Wall Street insiders have learned to be less ostentatious about their financial success, but there remains a true separation between the individual investor and the Wall Street insider, who serves as brokerage analyst, stockbroker, and investment banker.

If anything has changed, the abuses now are shared equally between "old men" and the "young," and the dollar amounts seem to be growing ever larger. For example, in June 2002, one of the most prestigious money managers on Wall Street, Alan Bond, was convicted and jailed for allocating winning trades to his firm while giving the losers to his clients. Bond was previously convicted for cheating clients in a kickback scheme amounting to an estimated $6.9 million. He was living well beyond his legitimate means at the expense of his clients.[15]

Historically, the insiders, seeing themselves as the investment community's true elite, have accepted change only when pushed into it. True reform has never been sparked from within the establishment. Only when big scandals or panics break out and people lose money does the question arise: how does Wall Street operate? We have discovered once again that the insiders have abused their positions at the expense of the investing public. The analysts have been too close to corporate management, often predicting earnings based on what they have been told with hardly a glance at any financial information—and certainly without any independent or critical analysis outside of a martini lunch with a CFO. Management itself has been given great latitude in achieving its earnings objectives by overly liberal GAAP rules coupled with the passive agreement of auditing firms. The extreme cases have shown that the relationships between auditing firms and management have at times been corrupted as well. So conflicts run all the way through the Wall Street establishment: between auditors and management, between management and analysts, and between analysts and their investment banking departments within the same firms.

For the novice investor, how could this establishment help? The reality is, even with important reforms designed to correct the more glaring problems, insiders will always hold an edge over newcomers, and every individual investor, whether experienced or not, cannot trust the advice of establishment analysts.

THE CONFLICT OF INTEREST PROBLEM

The entrenched insider lives in an environment characterized by conflict of interest at every turn. While stockbrokers tell clients to buy shares of today's favorite company, they do not disclose that their firm's investment banking department is making a profit from selling those shares. The morning meeting has traditionally been characterized by giving brokers a list of companies whose shares are to be pushed onto the market that day—not because the fundamentals work but because the firm is underwriting a large block of shares and has to sell them.

With total losses among investors exceeding $7 trillion since the middle 1990s, how can anyone have confidence in insider advice? The losses in pension and 401(k) plans, not to mention personal investment accounts meant for college education and retirement, have been disastrous. To a great extent, the cause of these losses rests with management and its mishandling of its own responsibilities as well as the relationship between management and auditing firms. The lax accounting rules of GAAP have contributed to the problem as well. However, investors have relied upon the advice of so-called experts to protect their interests. Why didn't the Wall Street analysts see problems coming? Hindsight reveals that a careful analysis of the financial statements should and would have revealed the problems, enabling investors to get their money out in time. The problem, however, is that very few analysts looked at the financial statements, were able to understood their significance, or based their recommendations on any fundamental information.

The majority of analysts continued publishing buy recommendations on Enron, for example, even after a $1.2 billion lowering of equity and announcement of an SEC investigation. Jack Grubman, telecommunications analyst at Salomon Smith Barney, put out buy recommendations on practically all of the companies he followed, even while the company was making big money on investment banking fees, often in excess of $1 billion per year.[16] Grubman has referred to accounting as a means for valuing stocks as a "largely backward-looking exercise" that has "no bearing on the fundamental drivers" of the company.[17]

The out-of-step buy recommendations of Jack Grubman became the topic of many investigations from regulators, and pressure led to his resignation in August 2002. In his resignation letter, Grubman offers an understatement of the problem: "I understand the disappointment and anger felt by investors as a result of [the telecom market's] collapse." His compensation averaged $20 million per year for his recommendations. However, the NASD inquiry raises questions about whether he misled investors in the telecommunications sector. Incidentally, Grubman's employer, Smith Barney, was the largest underwriter in the sector during the late 1990s.[18]

Grubman's dismissal of the fundamentals points out the complete lack of science on the part of many prominent analysts. The lack of appreciation for financial information is only one example of how analysts have functioned. Grubman's glaring conflict of interest is not the exception to the rule; it is the norm. The range of conflict was expressed by Lori Richards, director of the SEC Office of Compliance Inspections and Examinations:

> Over the last several years, there has been increased concern regarding the changing role of research analysts . . . While sell-side analysts used to be perceived as objective forecasters of corporate prospects and providers of opinions, they have

increasingly become involved in marketing the broker's investment banking services . . . Some of the key questions raised by
Congress, regulators, the media, and the public surrounding
the relationship between research and investment banking
include:

- Do investment banking interests drive ratings?
- Do the personal financial positions of analysts and the securities ownership positions of their firms impair analysts's
  objectivity?
- Why are there so few sell ratings?
- Why don't analysts change recommendations when there are
  material financial problems affecting the issuer?[19]

The failure by analysts to disclose their conflict of interest aug-
ments the obvious problems. As long as advice is being given by employees of firms whose receipts include large investment banking fees, those
analysts cannot operate objectively. Firms have made some lame attempts to assure regulators and the public that the two functions are
kept separate, but placing the conflicting functions on different departmental levels does not undo the conflicts. No one accepts the premise
that the problem can be fixed without serious reform. Analysts in the
1990s were given such importance that many became well known and
appeared regularly in the media. These stock gurus gained prominence
and held the limelight as long as dot.com and other stocks continued
rising. Few people asked how analysts came to their conclusions. Were
they analyzing accounting reports? Were they investigating obscure
footnotes? Why were the vast majority of recommendations to buy and
almost none to sell?

The conflict includes even more troubling aspects.

- Analysts often issue positive recommendations on IPOs without
  disclosing that they themselves invested in private placements of
  the companies before the public offering was made.
- The contractual agreement to market securities may include the
  promise of a positive research report.
- Analysts are often compensated based on their success in generating investment banking business.

- The issuer often was allowed to review and approve a draft of the research report before its publication.[21]

Most investors are not aware of the scope of these conflicts and should be angry if, in fact, they have relied upon the recommendations of Wall Street research analysts. The better known conflict held by analysts whose firms also provide investment banking is relatively minor compared to these more serious conflicts.

Real reform may rest with large fines and penalties. In 2002, the New York attorney general settled claims against Merrill Lynch for $100 million for its widespread conflicts involving research analysts and investment banking. Total penalties for Merrill were estimated to reach potentially $2 billion or more. Merrill also agreed, as part of the New York settlement, to separate analysts' compensation from investment banking, to appoint a new committee to oversee the objectivity of stock picks, and to install a system to monitor internal e-mail between investment banking and analysts.[22] In early 2003, the New York attorney general, NASD, and the SEC reached a settlement with ten major Wall Street brokerage firms to pay a $1.4 billion fine to cover a plethora of similar abuses.

The SEC has enacted new rules governing research analysts. Provisions include:

- Limitations on communication between investment banking and research analysts in the same firm
- Prohibition on compensating analysts based on investment banking transactions
- Required disclosure in research reports of the firm's investment banking services for a company
- Prohibition on promises of favorable research reports to gain investment banking business

- Restrictions on personal trading by analysts
- Disclosure of an analyst's financial interests in companies
- Disclosure of rating terms and their meanings and the percentage of buy, hold, and sell recommendations
- Disclosure requirements for analysts making public appearances concerning their firms' investment banking involvement in the company they are toting[23]

Robert Olstein would also like to see analysts required to sign a statement as part of their research reports, stating that they had investigated a company's accounting practices, and a second statement that the company's disclosures are sufficient to make reliable estimates of future cash flow.[24]

The market is also beginning to pressure firms to change. Institutional investors exert the most influence on brokerage firms, whose revenues are derived far more from institutions than from retail investor business. State pension funds for New York and North Carolina have announced that they would award brokerage business only to firms that removed conflicts of interest. The two states together control over $170 billion of invested assets, and the threat of lost commissions is sure to speed up voluntary compliance.[25]

The SEC has taken its reforms beyond the establishment of new rules; it also announced that it was undertaking an inquiry of analysts' market practices, looking for three areas of possible wrongdoing:

1. Have analysts issued any recommendations that were fraudulent?
2. Are firms in compliance with the new SEC rules?
3. Are any new rules needed?

INFLUENCE IN THE MARKET: A SCOREKEEPING MENTALITY

Analysts have held high status on Wall Street, especially in light of their uncanny ability to predict earnings down to the penny. Of course, those estimates often parrot what management has told the research analyst, and little fundamental research has been performed beyond that.

Because management is also able to alter accounting outcomes to meet the predictions, the analyst ends up appearing exceptionally skilled.

Every businessperson knows that forecasting is not a precise science but a means for setting goals and then monitoring them. However, when it comes to earnings predictions, the rather mundane business tool becomes a form of black magic. Few have questioned the analysts' ability to peg the numbers exactly. To some extent, investors have willingly gone along with the idea that analysts are simply good at what they do. Corporate performance is measured not by how well a company performs but by how well the earnings report matches the analyst's prediction—even in cases when management fed that number to the analyst in the first place.

Financial writer Michael C. Thomsett explains that:

> Calling the estimates is sort of like predicting the weather. Trying to invest on the basis of how earnings estimates come out is very short-term thinking . . . a game that a lot of investors play, but it says nothing about the fundamentals.[26]

In the scorekeeping world of Wall Street, the analysts came to play a key role by moving away from recommendations concerning long-term value. Once the analyst became a predictive force on Wall Street—coupled with conflicts of interest—their objectivity disappeared faster than stock values in the dot.com sector.

Unfortunately for investors, scorekeeping is a phony game. It is not based on any reasonable study of the fundamentals but on the analyst's ability to predict the company's earnings. Because this game is fixed, it is also invalid. Not only have analysts like Jack Grubman shunned the fundamentals, even corporate management, in some cases, has expressed disdain for accounting as a means for setting value, which defies reason. Amazon.com CEO Jeff Bezos stated that his company was not setting profit goals. "It would be impossible for us to do so," he explained. Robert Olstein disagrees strongly with the point of view that accounting does not matter. He stated that problems with many companies could have been uncovered earlier if analysts had done their job. Olstein explained, "Had Wall Street analysts understood how to read a financial statement and understood the difference between economic

T *he* **E** *x p e r t s* **S** *p e a k*

Robert Olstein observes, "Securities analysts should not be involved with market timing, predicting crowd behavior, or touting quarterly earnings. They should value companies over a period of years, not days."[27]

reality and GAAP, they would have had the early warning signs that all was not well with these stocks."[28]

More to the point, Olstein correctly notes that value—that quality determined through fundamentals—is at the heart of the decision to buy or sell stock. He explains that, "Anyone who writes that value is out of favor does not understand how value is created."[29]

Serious conflicts of interest need to be addressed and then eliminated, whether by enforcing regulations or through market forces. Ultimately, if the market loses confidence in the system because of the conflicts, then the analysts' validity will quickly disappear as well. With this in mind, real reform is likely to be market driven. Conflicts themselves are only part of the problem, however. Equally serious is the problem of analysts predicting earnings. The centerpiece of an analyst's performance is that accurate prediction equates to quality of the analyst; this is wrong. The anlalyst is supposed to help investors identify worthwhile values in stocks. The short-term idea that earnings predictions are the entire issue is misguided.

Investors should determine the basis for an analyst's recommendations before taking them. Does the analyst base recommendations on the fundamentals or, like many, do they shun accounting as a useless or backward-looking exercise? If they do not use accounting as a basis for recommending a company, what do they use? If they rely solely on a stock's popularity (i.e., public perception and favor), then isn't the recommendation a lagging, responsive way to invest? Most investors expect their information to anticipate the future, not to follow the crowd mentality of the investing public. If analysts rely on stock price movement, they have to use information like price history, buyer demand, and charts—none of which is based on fundamentals. That type of indicator can turn around all too quickly, as any past investor has discovered. So what value is an analyst's recommendations unless they are based on the fundamentals themselves? As unexciting as accounting reports are, investors need to rely on accounting expertise to make informed decisions.

HOW THINGS NEED TO CHANGE

The problem with the whole industry of securities analysis is that ironclad standards of good practice for research reports do not exist. "The real problem is the lack of adherence to professional standards of good practice," says Robert Olstein. "Analysts have acted like Wall Street tailors who cut the suit to fit the cloth."[30]

This is the crux of the problem: the fact that analysts have put themselves in the position of setting price targets for companies, often using unrealistic standards or no real standards at all. In some cases, analysts have even claimed that their price targets were increased to keep up with public expectations. If any scientific standards were in play, why would a securities analyst take such a position? The glaring problem has been that the procedures used for setting earnings targets (and thus, stock price targets as well) were based on popularity of the stock, and that popularity often was created artificially by the analysts themselves. The practice was not to study the numbers and value the company on any formula but "to set price targets based on crowd behavior."[31]

Is it the analyst's job to meet popular expectations or rather to guide public perceptions with realistic, forward-looking studies of earnings? What standards (if any) *should* be employed by analysts? Robert Olstein has defined what the analyst's job should be: "to properly value companies, determine when crowd perceptions result in mispriced securities, and alert clients to these potential profit and loss opportunities."[32]

Olstein further defines the standards he thinks should be followed.

- *A stock should be valued according to a model of discounted excess cash flow.* This is, essentially, the cash-based profit and loss of the company—net earnings plus depreciation, less capital expenditures, and plus or minus changes in working capital. This system—a study of cash flows—anticipates how well the company can provide working capital to fund future operations and is a sensible valuation method.

- *Valuation should be coordinated with the date of the analyst's report.* Timing of reports often becomes a problem, especially when a current research report is based on earnings announcements that are out of date. Valuation based solely on PE ratio or comparisons to the broad market are relatively useless, while working out an estimated valuation looking forward two years would better serve analysts' clients.

- *Research should incorporate recent financial statements.* We have seen that analysts as well as some corporate executives dismiss the fundamentals out of hand. However, Olstein suggests that financial statements should be published along with research reports. He recommends that the balance sheet, income statement, and statement of cash flows should be included for the past two years along with three-year projections of earnings, cash flow, and capital expenditures.

- *Research should examine and discuss accounting policies.* The accounting and reporting practices employed by the corporation should be included, as well as applicable liquidity ratios and trends and any material deviations.

- *Do away with quarterly earnings estimates.* Perhaps the greatest problem analysts have exhibited is preoccupation with projected earnings versus actual earnings from one quarter to another. This has become the standard for measuring "good" and "bad" outcome, but the analyst should be valuing the company instead of projecting quarterly earnings. Olstein explains that, "There has been a huge incentive to beat earnings-per-share expectations, even if only by a penny. Thus, there's an equal incentive to manage earnings to please Wall Street."[33]

- *Research papers should not be subject to advance review by the company.* Analysts have become so close to corporate executives, that they often report whatever they are told and subject their research reports to advance review. This should stop.

- *Nonrecurring write-offs should be subtracted from earnings.* Some companies have adjusted previous-year accounting assumptions as nonrecurring adjustments, thus not affecting current-year operating earnings. In valuing a company, those adjustments should be taken from current-year operating results.

- *Price targets should be eliminated.* Analysts should be barred from including stock price targets as part of their research reports. They should concentrate on valuation rather than on the technical aspects of company stock. The widespread practice of price targeting is not based on the fundamentals and should be stopped.[34]

FINANCIAL PLANNERS: WHO ARE THEY?

Investors who use the services of an analyst have often been poorly served, because analysts have concentrated on projecting both earnings and stock price levels without any tie-in to financial reality. Rather than valuing companies to identify underpriced or overpriced situations, analysts have placed themselves in the position of predictors. While this service has come to be seen as valuable, the idea that anyone can set prices is misleading. As long as markets are rising, these predictions become self-fulfilling prophecies. The higher a stock price moves, the higher the analyst predicts the next level. However, the settling of scores is inevitable. Analysts were strongly recommending many of the more popular dot.com companies, even as they started to fall. Most had no profits to report, no long-standing history of performance, and nothing upon which investors should have bought—except for the recommendations offered by analysts. The whole system became a house of cards. When the market reversed in 2000 to 2002 on news of corporate misdeeds, analysts' roles again came into question. Many of the companies in the greatest trouble were being touted by analysts. This industry, whose sell recommendations are less than 1 percent of all recommendations, needs to undergo serious reform.

Analysts working for big brokerage firms are not in exactly the same industry as financial planners, although both may be members of the same industry organizations. Some investors prefer working in a one-on-one relationship with a financial planner rather than buying a subscription service from a brokerage house. The financial planner, like the securities analyst, has functioned in a variety of roles. The whole industry has been so ill defined, that you will find a vast array of individuals calling themselves planners. These include highly skilled financial analysts as well as insurance salespeople. The range of background varies as well.

To select a planner, limit your search to the highly trained, experienced individuals who hold the Certified Financial Planner (CFP) designation. These individuals have undergone an intensive course of education, passed a certification exam, and have no less than three years of experience in financial planning. They also agree to adhere to a code of ethics and are required to undergo no less than 30 days of continuing education each year.

As the Wall Street establishment—including analysts and research departments of the large brokerage houses, stockbrokers, investment bankers, and money managers—goes through a period of reform, financial planners specialize more in one-on-one consultation with clients. Some specialize in working with higher-income clients, while others have general practices and still others work with individuals who are just starting out or who need help with basic money management and planning problems. Given the wide range of possible advisors, you need to make sure the planner is a good match for your needs.

Those planners with local practices usually are not stockbrokers and are most likely to work through a "wire house" to transact stock trades. However, many would-be clients will find that financial planners are better suited for developing a long-term, comprehensive family plan (including investments, insurance, estate planning, etc.) and are less suited to helping with a program of portfolio management. You may want to use the services of a planner for the planning aspects of your financial life but direct your own stock trades, perhaps using a discount brokerage house and trading online. While some planners are well versed in stock market issues, most are likely to recommend buying equities through mutual funds.[35]

Given the disturbing trends of corporate scandals, investors have discovered that trusting executives, auditing firms, and analysts should not be automatic. Clearly, too many market insiders have abused their positions and misled investors on many levels. In the current environment of reform, financial planners are likely to play an important role in helping investors to determine their financial futures, identify appropriate risks, and select investments that are a good match, given the circumstances. As disillusioned investors abandon the Wall Street establishment, dominated by large brokerage firms deeply mired in conflicts, much of the business will fall to the financial planning industry. Thus, it is more important than ever to ensure that a professional is both qualified and experienced and is a good match for you individually.

ONLINE ORDER PLACING AND DISCOUNT BROKERAGE

In addition to moving business away from the larger brokerage firms to financial planners, many investors will also decide to invest on their own. This can be done in several ways. Less experienced investors will likely invest through mutual funds or work with investment clubs. More seasoned investors may use mutual funds to a degree but may also begin investing through a discount brokerage firm. The trading costs are lower, but no investment advice is provided. However, considering the dismal record of the analysts and money managers in the recent past, investors may be better off getting no investing advice.

Using a discount brokerage service or a low-cost, online order placing service is a viable alternative, assuming the following:

- *You have enough experience to make your own decisions.* A newcomer is rarely wise to develop an investment strategy without some form of guidance. The problem, of course, is that advice is generally poor, and Wall Street professionals in brokerage research departments have done more harm than good. Remember, less than 1 percent of all analysts' recommendations were to sell. In such an unobjective environment, what value is advice anyhow? To many people going on their own for the first time, the most difficult aspect will be the idea that no one will be advising them. However, experienced investors probably already know better than anyone else what works for them, what risks are appropriate, and how to locate value.

- *You use a value-oriented subscription service, financial planner, or other source for professional analysis.* Even if you make decisions without direct help, it still makes sense to use a subscription service. For example, the basic, fundamental research you find with a service such as ValueLine or S&P is worthwhile. You also can find most publicly listed company financial statements online.

- *You accept the risks of working on your own and are comfortable with that approach.* Most investors are primarily concerned with managing risks, even if they don't give it that precise name. Concern about the safety of capital is one form of risk aversion, and there are many ways to mitigate that risk. As long as you have the means for diversifying your portfolio, identifying appropriate types and levels of risk, and finding an individual comfort level, you can probably do your own analysis and succeed without the Wall Street establishment.

- *You develop a sensible approach to fundamental analysis.* No one can take the time to study every indicator, and with so much information available, the problem becomes deciding which information to use and which to ignore. The value approach is based on identifying working capital and cash flow requirements as well as closely watching liquidity ratios. The value approach makes sense. Following the fundamental trends having to do with balance sheet accounts also helps identify questionable practices or red flags, and reading and following up on questionable footnotes is essential. With the new theme of transparency in reporting, you are also likely to get more help from corporations themselves in terms of disclosure, explanations, and plain-English reporting.

As long as you are comfortable with the idea of working without an analyst (or at least keeping advice at a distance with well-picked subscription services, for example), there is no reason to go the traditional route. Given recent events, it makes little sense for investors to use stockbrokers who charge full commission and continue to offer advice. Given the conflicts big firms have with the combined business of research/ analysis and investment banking, the order placement arms of those firms are probably the least likely sources for investment advice.

THE HARSH REALITY—NO ONE ELSE WILL CARE AS MUCH AS YOU

The modern investor has been forced to confront this fact: finding objective, honest advice is a difficult task. The Wall Street insider is self-serving and not much of a resource. When you cut through the hype associated with predictions of earnings per share and setting stock prices, you realize that analysts have provided a disservice to the investing public. Their close association with management has tainted the whole industry. The problems include (a) an inclination to let corporate management review research reports in advance, (b) the tendency to include whatever management tells them to say, (c) a disdain for fundamentals or, worse, a complete lack of knowledge about financial analysis, and (d) the failure to disclose conflicts of interest, even when they are severe.

Putting this another way, the industry of securities analysts needs to be overhauled in its entirety. The actual job and objective of the industry has to be redefined so that it is entirely removed from conflicts—not in name only, but in practice. Separating departments within the company is not enough. The conflict has to be done away with completely. Just as auditing firms are now banned from offering auditing and consulting services to the same client, securities research and investment banking services should not be offered on the same securities. It is a matter of common sense.

Another way that redefinition is required is in the reporting disclosure itself. Just as corporate reporting is now required to be transparent, so too should research services. Analysts should be forbidden from making recommendations if they are invested in the company, whether through stock ownership or units of private placements. Why should analysts be allowed to "pump and dump" securities, when anyone else would be subject to criminal prosecution?

Analysts also need to be trained in accounting analysis. The fact that so many analysts ignore accounting as the basis for investment recommendations is both alarming and ludicrous. Investors should be given professional analytical advice based on a study of the fundamentals rather than market hype based on market-response price targets and self-fulfilling prophecies about earnings per share. The popular scorekeeping methods of Wall Street, which obsesses on the Dow Jones

Industrial Averages and earnings predictions, has to be replaced with a more sensible, fundamentals-based approach.

Finally, analysts are providing advice to investors, and if that advice is *known* to be poor, many people will lose their equity. Federal and state regulators need to enforce the laws already on the books for defrauding investors, a trend that has begun already. New York State has aggressively pursued some cases, to the embarrassment of the slower-moving SEC. Analysts should face severe civil and criminal penalties for misleading the public—especially when they knowingly provide false information. This has occurred often enough to require serious reform and enforcement.

For any investor who depends on advice from individual analysts, the very least they deserve is a full disclosure of all relevant information. This includes not only the fundamentals-based facts about the company and value analysis but also disclosure of any conflicts on the part of the analyst. Investors should settle for nothing less.

12

THE IMPORTANCE OF EXPERIENCE AND KNOWLEDGE

The terrible losses suffered by individual investors—as a direct result of abuses by some corporate executives—have demonstrated an even deeper problem. The established insiders of Wall Street—executives, boards of directors, analysts, and auditing firms—became so accustomed to being able to do whatever they wanted without consequence, that such behavior became the norm.

Can we blame the regulatory agencies that have not pursued wrongdoing aggressively enough? To a degree, we can; however, if those agencies are not funded well enough to enable them to chase down every instance of abuse, then they would be unable to afford to right every wrong. This is precisely what happened in the early 2000s. The SEC had not been given adequate budget increases throughout the 1990s, and even though the investing environment changed greatly in that decade, increasing investigative budgets was politically impossible. In addition, it is never politically realistic to increase those budgets during a cyclical bull market. As long as everything is going up, few people look ahead and anticipate future problems. When the problems blow up, they always seem to take everyone by surprise.

Can we blame the conflict of interest that existed between management and auditing firms? Attempts to fix those problems on the part of politicians or regulators were resisted by the strong accounting lobby in Washington, whose interests have normally been to free accounting from excessive regulation. Former SEC Chairman Arthur Levitt noted in 1998 that, "Flexibility in accounting allows accounting principles to keep pace with business innovations. Abuses such as earnings management occur when people exploit this pliancy." The problem of finding the right way to reform this problem area is not easy, however. Levitt explained, "Many in corporate America . . . know how difficult it is to hold the line on good practices, when their competitors operate in the gray area between legitimacy and outright fraud."[1]

The 2002 laws that swept away the most obvious auditing conflict of interest did fix a large part of the problem. However, is that fix on paper only? The new rules have not become effective in every sense, and some accounting firms continue to offer consultation services, including installation of financial accounting automated systems, compensation consulting, litigation support, and more. Even though the remaining Big Four accounting firms have done away with their consulting subsidiaries, they continue earning fees for nonaudit work., with all four firms reporting receipts between $3 and $5 billion as of September, 2002, a year that will still see about half of auditing firms' fees coming from nonaudit sources.[2]

The firms insist they are allowed to provide these services, because the new law specifies and lists only what they *cannot* do. Classifying nonauditing consultation outside of the list gives them a way out. Obviously, the audit reforms will have to be tested before we can really know how effectively this conflict of interest has been removed. For the foreseeable future, legislation will be in its transitional period: the scope of prohibited transactions will need to be defined and tested and the law itself enforced. Certainly clarification will be needed to fix loopholes and to provide protection for investors who rely on the objectivity of audit opinions.

Can we blame executives and weak boards of directors? This good old boys network of rubber-stamp approvals, raiding profits, liberal incentive compensation, and the failure even to question many practices made the whole structure of corporate governance a joke. In the combined regulatory changes in federal law and exchange provisions, we will see a transitional period leading to better controls over corporate behavior, although, again, the scope of the law and associated rules will be challenged and more modifications required.

Perhaps the longest standing problems are found in the conflicts of interest by analysts. Glaring problems, associated with close ties to a firm's investment banking activities and analysts' holdings of equity interests in many firms, have helped to paint the whole industry with the brush of suspicion. Not disclosing these conflicts has only made the problems worse. Unless the big Wall Street firms are willing to accept real reform, as opposed to the mere appearance of fixing the problem, they will end up losing business through mistrust, not to mention incurring the expense of civil suits, which have already begun and will continue as long as the problems persist.

In this environment of transition, in which there are doubts about whether or not the new laws and regulations even go far enough, how can you, the individual investor, protect your capital? How do you know whether or not the companies you select for your portfolio are safe? The problems and accusations of wrongdoing, you should recall, have not been limited to newer, relatively unknown companies. Many well-established companies and their executives, such as General Electric,[3] Xerox, and Motorola, have come under criticism as well as the relatively new ones like Enron, AOL Time Warner, and WorldCom. So the problems cannot be simply assigned to any one class of corporation; they have been cultural and have come from many different conflicts needing a number of solutions. The problems encompass corporate executives and boards, auditing firms, analysts, and other Wall Street insiders, including the big investment banking firms, regulatory agencies, and even Congress for not keeping up with the budget requirements of the SEC.

FINDING THE RIGHT FIX

Do the new laws fix all of the problems? Of course not. Investors should not believe that even the most sweeping changes solve the complex shortcomings of the investment world. Even when we see once powerful executives being taken off in handcuffs, the problems have not necessarily been fixed.

It is not simply a matter of changing the rules or requiring listed companies to follow new, stricter listing standards. To fix this problem, we need to see a broader change in four specific areas:

1. *The corporate culture itself needs to change.* Along with the broad idea of free enterprise is a cherished idea that government and regulators should stay out of corporate business. While this argument has merit, the abuses of corporate executives coupled with weak board oversight has demonstrated that the free enterprise culture has limits. If executives want to minimize the oversight of governmental regulators, they also need to examine the culture itself. Clearly, greed motivated accounting fraud to justify incentive compensation, but executives can no longer treat corporate assets as a poorly monitored source of personal enrichment. Stealing employees' pension fund assets and investors' equity is inexcusable. No matter how many new regulations are put into place, the corporate culture needs to change as well.

2. *Executive compensation has to be controlled.* The huge payments to chief executives of the larger, publicly listed companies have long been the subject of criticism. A counterargument is that, when an executive leads the company to higher profits and stronger competitive position, they earn their pay. However, when investors discover that some of those same executives have falsified accounting to increase their incentive compensation, the question has to be looked at in a different light. Is it proper to provide such large incentives to the CEO that employing "creative" or "aggressive" accounting is a temptation too hard to resist? Even with changes in the rules designed to curtail abuses or, at the very least, to punish abuses, the problem of executive compensation will continue to serve as a debate topic for years to come. The connection between earnings and incentive pay has been at the root of many problems; it has been too easy for executives to alter the numbers—with little fear of consequence—with the obvious motive of self-enrichment.

3. *Can we find corporate leaders who respect the rules?* Investors were understandably troubled to discover that their investment portfolios and 401(k) assets were decimated through the combination of bankruptcies and a weakened stock market. These

problems have been traced in large part to a flurry of disclo-sures of corporate crimes and ethical lapses, and the whole mat-ter raises the question: who should be entrusted with running our publicly listed corporations? We have always expected cor-porate leadership to work on the shareholders' behalf, to act ethically, and to follow the rules. At the same time, we expect tough, competitive leaders. So where is the middle ground?

4. *How do we reconcile tough leadership with the profit motive?* In many respects, the investors place conflicting requirements upon cor-porate leadership. We want the CEO to be ruthless, perhaps, in beating the competition, creating new markets, expanding sales and profits, and of course, causing the stock price to rise. At the same time, we don't want those leaders to use their positions solely to enrich themselves—to pursue their own profit motive. The CEO's job is a difficult balance, requiring tough but ethical leaders, operating in a suitable regulatory environment but not hampered by excessive regulation, whom we reward for good work with handsome compensation but who do not raid inves-tors' or employees' assets to enrich themselves.

This list of requirements is difficult to satisfy. It also points out the difficulty every investor faces in the current and coming periods of transition. While we expect our regulators to punish civil and criminal wrongdoers and enforce tough new standards, we also want to preserve the competitive edge of our free enterprise system. Perhaps abuses will inevitably occur in a free society, and risk is an element of investing that cannot be eliminated. A balance is the way to fix the big problems that have come to characterize the actions of executives, boards of directors, auditing firms, and analysts.

In addition to finding the right balance, investors can speak with a collective voice. The market ultimately dictates whether or not the sys-tem works, and when investors shun corporations that resist appropri-ate change (while rewarding the more progressive ones), the system will respond with changes that protect investors.

The new rules developed by the New York Stock Exchange are also listed in the Appendix.

TRUSTING THE WRONG PEOPLE

Experienced investors recognize that it makes no sense to trust someone else to help develop an investment portfolio, at least not without reservation. Novice investors often enter the market believing that the big Wall Street institutions are beyond reproach. This belief has been shattered—rightly so. Clearly, the big institutions do not protect the retail investor in any sense of the word.

Thus, subscribing to research reporting services run by companies that also offer investment banking services is a mistake. If nothing else, reform needs to require disclosure of analysts's conflicts, so that investors will know about them before deciding to believe what the research report promises. Another cultural change that investors need to demand of analysts is that they cease predicting earnings levels and publishing target prices for stocks. Not only does the practice of prediction give analysts too much misplaced power, given their proximity to corporate executives and investment banking departments; it also provides a service based on little or nothing of value. Many analysts have raised their prediction levels in response to investor actions that drove up prices, which proves the point. When analysts make predictions about earnings but have no accounting knowledge, those predictions are baseless and should be ignored. The investing public—the individuals who subscribe to the services analysts offer—can have a significant impact by canceling subscriptions to any service that makes these predictions. Analysts should concentrate on identifying value for long-term investing, not trying to handicap the market in the next three months.

Investors also need to understand that auditing firms will resist change, because consulting fees represent billions of dollars in annual receipts, often more than auditing fees. The new law prohibits many specific forms of consultation but creates a loophole that auditing firms are already using to redefine their consultation, arguing that these services are not specifically prohibited. Thus, auditing firms will resist the spirit of the law—to do away with conflicts. With this in mind, investors cannot trust auditing firms' opinions concerning the reliability of corporate financial statements without some additional cautions.

- *Corporate transparency.* Those companies that go out of their way to explain the numbers to investors and to disclose all of the news, good and bad, should be rewarded. However, as long as auditing firms continue to offer consultation services, investors need to discount the reliability of financial statements, remembering that the consultation creates a conflict for the auditing firm.
- *Revised reporting methods.* Corporations need to take responsibility for educating investors and for explaining complex accounting decisions in plain English. Besides complying technically with reporting standards, reports need to be augmented with explanatory notes that everyone can follow.
- *Elimination of nonoperating items from operating profits.* Perhaps the biggest required change is the revision of reporting norms for operations. In an accurate income statement, all nonoperating income or loss should be reported *below* the line of net operating income. Unfortunately, corporations often include nonrecurring items, write-offs of prior year reserves, income from acquired companies, and pension profit or loss. The latter has often had a big impact on reported operating results, even masking net operating losses. Until accounting changes, corporate financial statements will remain unreliable, making company-to-company comparisons meaningless.

How can investors trust any of the traditional sources for information? Corporations themselves, auditing firms, analysts, and money managers have failed the investing public. Investors are left with few objective sources for reliable information. In fact, investors either need to locate a reliable and independent research service and be willing to pay for it, or trust no one and apply their own fundamental analysis to identify value.

The first choice will be expensive, and the second requires analytical skills and hard work. However, nothing has really changed. The unending quest for easy answers or the inside track does not yield profits and never has. Corporate scandals have been expensive reminders that, in fact, those with the power and control do *not* work for or protect the investor. When you place capital at risk, you are on your own.

Does this make the stock market exceptionally risky? No—the risk elements have not changed. However, beyond the well-known market risks, investors also need to recognize the risks associated with auditing firms and their conflicts of interest, as well as the question of how self-serving management and boards of directors are in their procedures. While the stock market continues to offer substantial opportunities, it also is characterized by specific risks. The wise investor accepts these risks and uses risk elements as selection criteria in identifying investment candidates.

ESSENTIAL ANALYTICAL TOOLS

The theory of investing has always been based on a few assumptions, including the idea that an orderly market depends on the reliability of financial statements, the honesty of corporate executives and boards of directors, and the expertise of analysts.

With all of these assumptions proved wrong in the recent past, how do you know which companies are relatively safe, long-term investments? What position do you assume as an investor in studying the fundamental volatility of a company's reported sales and profits? Investors have often taken comfort in the predictability of company reports, not questioning the accuracy of reported sales and profits that exactly match analysts' predictions. So to a degree, investors have accepted the premise that GAAP provides flexibility and, to a degree, have expected corporations to even out their revenues and profits.

In the future, we should expect less flexibility in GAAP procedures, because the very flexibility that enables companies to remove volatility has also opened the door to excess. The line between year-to-year evening out of reported results and outright fraud is a difficult one to identify. It consists not of a single instance or decision but of a series of layers of corporate activity. Because latitude allows abuse, investors must accept more fundamental volatility in the future. To the extent that less reliable reporting may also create short-term price volatility, investors will need to accept that as a reality. The market cannot be completely controlled if we also expect integrity in the numbers. So a natural conflict exists between the desire for low volatility and the need for full disclosure and honest accounting.

Investors cannot be expected to acquire an accounting education to properly analyze a company's value. However, a review of a few of the basic trends and balance sheet ratios explained in this book can and does reveal a lot about a company's reporting. Even the inexperienced investor can apply these tests. The ratios should remain within acceptable levels, even when reported results are more volatile from year to year. In fact, consistent accounting policies are likely to create more reliable fundamental information, whereas aggressive accounting decisions will distort the fundamentals.

The basic tests include accounts receivable tests as a primary means of analysis. Comparisons of accounts receivable with total sales, as well as bad debt reserve levels with accounts receivable, reveal a lot. When corporations recognize revenue in advance of the earned date, it invariably shows up in the accounts receivable balance. So when the levels of accounts receivable are significantly higher than in prior years, the company could be reporting revenues in advance of earning them.

Inventory levels and related reserves for losses should be followed in a similar manner. Inventory adjustments will show up as unusual changes in gross profit margins. Because part of the cost of goods sold includes adjusting for the difference in inventory levels from the beginning of the year to the end of the year, accounting adjustments will also affect gross margin.

Also, look carefully at all deferred asset accounts. If a company has decided to place current-year expenses on the balance sheet, it will amortize them over several years. However, if this technique treats expenses inaccurately, then the company's value has to be adjusted to reflect lower operating profit. A similar argument applies to the account th1at adjusts capital asset values, known as reserve for depreciation or accumulated depreciation. This is a credit balance account in the long-term assets section of the balance sheet. If the company uses excessively long recovery periods, they are understating current year depreciation.

On the liability side, study the bond ratio to ensure that the company does not depend heavily on debt capitalization. As the ratio of debt rises, increasing levels of operating income have to be paid in interest, and less remains to provide dividends to stockholders. Also, check nonliability credits on the balance sheet. When companies want to hold income over to the following year, those holdover amounts often are found in deferred credit accounts. An examination could reveal that the company is trying to level out its reported revenues and earnings.

Remember that fundamental tests should be done as part of an ongoing trend analysis. Any adjustments the company makes to its reported operating results will show up as adjustments in the balance sheet, either to asset or liability accounts. An exception would be off balance sheet items, which should be disclosed by footnote or banned altogether. Some off balance sheet valuation information is valid, of course, such as current market value of real estate, long-term lease commitments, and contingent liabilities that are material in size.

Every investor can perform the basic tests described above, using information found on the financial statements of the company. If publicly listed companies take their role seriously in reporting to investors, and if they truly subscribe to the idea of full transparency, they will go out of their way to provide meaningful ratio analysis to investors. Given the resources companies have at their disposal, they would serve their own interests by helping investors to understand the financial reports. Whether or not companies will be willing to disclose that much remains to be seen.

USING THE INTERNET: GREAT OPPORTUNITIES

In addition to using information supplied by the company in its annual audited statement, you can also check quarterly filings with the SEC. Further information is available online; the Internet is perhaps the fastest and most efficient research tool at your disposal.

You can get annual statements, annual and quarterly financial summaries, and more online. For monitoring your portfolio, virtually every financial Web site offers free quotes and charts, showing current prices and volume as well as moving averages. For either fundamental or technical analysis, online information cannot be matched.

The trend toward investors making their own decisions or investing based on their analysis of subscription-based research is leading to increased use of online order placement. The older, archaic method of using the telephone to place orders through a brokerage firm is rapidly becoming impractical, given the efficiency of the Internet. As today's investor begins to replace the prior generation of investors, who were less computer literate, this trend is likely to become the norm.

Just as the telegraph and telephone significantly changed the way people invested in the 19th century, the computer was a big advance in the 20th century. For the first time, remotely located brokers could report real-time quotes to their customers. And in the 21st century, the Internet will prove to be just as significant an advance as the previous technological improvements. For traders in options or futures contracts, or for those who want to speculate in stocks, the Internet is a natural fit. If you desire to find solid financial information on a company, you can search and instantly find news, published reports, and even a direct link to the corporate relations department of just about any listed company.

The efficiency of the Internet has also made it possible for individuals to gain compound returns on dividend income without needing to invest through mutual funds. A large number of companies now offer dividend reinvestment plans (DRIPs), so that you can choose to take dividends in additional partial shares rather than in cash.

These examples demonstrate the efficiency and practicality of the Internet. Of course, investors also have to be careful when investing on the Web, because its accessibility brings danger, too. Some guidelines:

- *Don't respond to online ads or unsolicited e-mail.* Web sites may have pop-up advertisements, which should be thought of as online junk mail. A sound policy for investors is never to respond to any unsolicited pop-up ad or e-mail relating to investments. If you need anything online, you should generate the search rather than responding to unsolicited ads. This policy will save you from signing up for services that sound fantastic but do not deliver anything of real value.
- *Stay out of investment-related chat rooms.* You might be interested in seeing what is discussed in the chat rooms, but remember that you do not know who the other people are. Never make decisions based on claims, rumors, or alleged insider information you see in an investment chat room. One favorite ploy is the pump-and-

dump; someone buys stock in a company, promotes it heavily in the chat room to drive up the price artificially, and then dumps shares at a profit. The practice is illegal, but it still takes place. The information you read in chat rooms will be unreliable, so you should never rely on it for any decisions.

- *Use secure sites when transacting funds.* One of the greatest dangers involved with online investing is vulnerability to identity theft. Never provide your Social Security Number, credit card number, or other personal information to someone who asks for it, and only provide credit card information or bank account numbers when transacting funds on a secure site. Using a credit card is a wise idea, because your maximum loss in the event of theft is $50 (or zero, if your card provides no-cost insurance as a benefit). This is safer than transmitting your checking account information to buy stocks, for example, because a hacker might be able to remove thousands of dollars using the same information. Of course, an unauthorized removal of funds from your account probably is protected through your institution's insurance coverage, but using a secure site protects you from theft.

- *Know with whom you are transacting.* Before agreeing to transfer money to an online account, place orders, or provide personal information, make sure you know that the site is legitimate. You may recognize the name of a national brokerage firm, but are you sure that you're not dealing with an imitator? A favorite ploy of charity scams is to publish Web sites with very similar names, so that people assume they know the charity and give money more easily. The same could happen with investment sites, so before opening an account, providing personal account information, and sending funds, be sure you are dealing with the real site.

CONTENDING WITH THE ESTABLISHED SYSTEM

Perhaps the greatest danger investors face now and in the future is not whether they find a convenient mode for trading online, whether they can locate fundamental information efficiently, but rather how they deal with the Wall Street establishment. In many ways, every retail investor (individual) is an outsider. The big institutions, which collectively account for the majority of trades on the exchanges, also dominate the supply and demand for shares as well as the attention of the specialists and dealers on the floor.

Recognizing that individuals are in the minority, every investor also needs to understand that whether they live a few blocks from the Exchange offices or in a small town thousands of miles away, they have certain rights as well as limitations.

The limitations are obvious. No one investor will be able to influence the market like a massive mutual fund, and access to corporate information may be limited as well. However, the rights held by every investor are a matter of law. You have the right to access to the markets, to the same information known to everyone else, and to a fair and reliable reporting system. Everyone has recognized that the rules relating to insider trading often are violated, and the offenders are punished if caught. But most people also know that some degree of insider trading goes unreported and unpunished. So the individual who is not also an employee, executive, or board member in a company often cannot really compete with the insiders, who know what is going on in advance of the general public.

Is the stock market an unlevel playing field? In many respects, it is. However, even though the retail investor has specific disadvantages, and even though their influence will never be as significant as institutional investor influence, there is hope. The stock market has traditionally been a source for long-term wealth building for the individual, and it still is. Recent events show that some of the traditional institutions cannot be trusted—analysts, auditing firms, boards of directors, and executives, for example—and that reform requires not only new laws and enforcement practices but changes in the investment and corporate cultures. Change will not take place overnight, and many alterations in the laws and regulations will be required before current problems will be fixed.

Almost certainly, even with the elimination of all of the problems that enabled corporate scandals to take place in the last decade, the future will see a new variation of scandal. The history of Wall Street can be traced almost cyclically from one shake-out to another. Big panic markets have often accompanied revelations of insider misdeeds and, often, have been followed by periods of reform. However, even when reform is swift and effective, real change takes time. We see already that the strong legislation limiting auditing firms from offering consultation has had little immediate effect. Clearly, the profit motive weighs more than any market sensitivity, and the remaining Big Four auditing firms will continue to seek consultation contracts with audit clients, oblivious to the inherent conflicts of interest. Fine-tuning the rules and overcoming political obstacles, as well as changing the accounting culture, are needed to make real change.

Other conflicts of interest will go through similar transitions, with resistance on the inside. For example, while changes to the actions and responsibilities of boards of directors and audit committees will help eliminate the more glaring conflicts and prevent executives from misusing their positions in many ways, variations of misuse certainly will occur. Analysts working in big firms that also offer investment banking services will continue to work around the system, even in the face of strong new restrictions and disclosure requirements. The firms themselves will try to comply in appearance alone without actually removing the conflict. New regulation and enforcement will be needed to bring about real, permanent change.

For any investor with capital at risk in the stock market, the risks are all too real, as many have been discovered at great personal expense. However, nothing has changed; the risks have always been there, and experienced investors knew of them. The difference now is that many more people have had to contend with the reality of the unseen and unknown risk. The fear in this climate is that many more companies have accounting irregularities or executive misdeeds yet to be revealed. Investors fear that other risks are out there, such as illegal actions by some of the remaining Big Four accounting firms, executive raiding of corporate profits, and most of all, potentially false accounting reports on the scale of WorldCom or Enron.

For the individual, referring back to the fundamentals and performing the basic ratio analysis are a smart starting point and, as a matter of practice, a sensible way to track corporations as well as to compare one company to another. We can never eliminate all risks; we have to accept risk as the flip side of investment opportunity. However, every individual has the right to expect honest reporting, transparency in disclosure, and the elimination of obvious conflicts of interest.

Robert Olstein summed up this point nicely in an article he wrote nearly a decade ago:

> I'm a believer that numbers matter. Over the years, I've discovered they're more reliable than corporate management, more reliable than Wall Street analysts. Numbers not only can help investors ferret out value but can also save them from devastating mistakes.[4]

R e f o r m :   N e w
R u l e s   a n d   L a w s

Following is a summary of the new laws, rules, and regulations:

Sarbanes-Oxley Act of 2002

This law:

- Establishes an Accounting Oversight Board to monitor public accounting firms
- Provides for inspection, audit, and disciplinary procedures in cases of violation
- Allows the board to work with professional groups to establish universal auditing standards
- Identifies prohibited activities on the part of auditing firms, including many forms of consulting services performed for audit clients
- Requires rotation of audit partners on accounts every five years
- Prohibits corporate financial officers from serving in their positions if the company's audit firm employed them during the previous year
- Requires company audit committee members to be independent
- Places responsibility for hiring an auditing firm with the audit committee rather than with the executives of the company
- Requires the CEO and CFO of publicly traded companies personally to certify financial results quarterly
- Requires officers to reimburse their incentive-based compensation if financial reports are restated within one year

- Allows the SEC to prohibit an offending officer or director from continuing in their position, temporarily or permanently, in cases of violation
- Prohibits the purchase or sale of stock by officers or directors during blackout periods
- Prohibits companies from granting personal loans to executives
- Accelerates requirements for reporting designated transactions (insider trades) to one day following the transaction
- Requires an assessment of internal controls as part of the annual report
- Mandates conflict of interest restrictions for research analysts
- Establishes new rules of conduct for attorneys practicing before the SEC
- Creates the Corporate and Criminal Fraud Accountability Act of 2002, which defines destruction of documents as a felony when those documents would impede a federal investigation
- Requires auditing firms to maintain all work papers for at least five years
- Protects whistleblower employees from retaliation by auditing firms or corporations
- Imposes penalties for securities fraud of fines and up to ten years imprisonment
- Increases penalties for white collar crime classifications (e.g., wire fraud, mail fraud, records tampering)
- Authorizes an SEC freeze on extraordinary compensation to officers
- Prohibits anyone convicted of securities fraud from serving as an officer or director of publicly traded companies
- Requires certification by CEO and CFO of financial statements filed with the SEC, plus penalties for violations up to $500,000 and/or five years imprisonment[1]

Securities and Exchange Commission—New Rules Governing Research Analysts

On May 8, 2002, the SEC announced new rules governing research analysts, including:

- Limitations on relationships and communications between investment banking and research analysts
- Analyst compensation prohibitions: firms can no longer tie analysts' compensation to investment banking transactions
- Disclosure of compensation: research reports must disclose management of public offerings for firms in their research reports
- Prohibition of promises of favorable research to attract investment banking business (or the threat to withhold a favorable rating or price target)
- Restrictions on personal trading in a firm's securities by analysts prior to initial public offerings, when the company is in the business sector the analyst covers
- Disclosure requirements of financial interests by analysts in covered companies
- Disclosure requirements in research reports regarding ratings: clear explanation of terms is required
- Disclosure requirements by analysts during public appearances, especially of any positions in stock or investment banking activities in a company[2]

SEC Final Rule: Selective Disclosure and Insider Trading

The SEC published in 2002 a "final rule" regarding selective disclosure and insider trading:

- Regulation FD (Fair Disclosure) company officers must publicly disclose insider information provided to securities market professionals.
- Rule 10-b5-1 defines insider trading as when in "knowing possession" of nonpublic information, further defining prohibited insider trades.

- Rule 10-b5-2 improves the definition of insider information by defining three nonexclusive bases for determining that a duty of trust or confidence was owed. This rule is intended to provide better clarity on unsettled issues regarding insider trading.[3]

NYSE Accountability Standards Changes

The New York Stock Exchange has changed its listing standards to include:

- Increased role and authority for independent directors
- Better defined audit committee qualification requirements
- Requirement of good corporate governance standards by listed companies
- Providing shareholders with monitoring participation in governance
- Establishing new control and enforcement mechanisms (e.g., CEO certification of financial statements, disclosure of violations)
- Requirement that boards of directors have a majority of independent members
- Tightening the definition of an independent director
- Empowering nonmanagement directors to act as check on management
- Requiring the nominating/corporate governance committee to be composed entirely of independent directors
- Requiring the compensation committee to be composed entirely of independent directors
- Improving requirements for independent director membership on audit committees, limiting compensation to only directors' fees and requiring financial management expertise for the audit committee chair
- Increasing the authority and responsibility of the audit committee, including sole authority to hire and fire independent auditors
- Increasing shareholder control over equity-compensation plans
- Requiring adoption by companies of a code of ethics

- Requiring listed foreign private issuers to disclose differences in corporate governance practices compared to those of domestic companies
- Requiring each CEO to disclose compliance with NYSE rules[4]

NYSE Recommendations to Other Institutions

The NYSE also issued recommendations as follows.
To the SEC:

- Require public accountants to be regulated by an independent organization
- Require CEOs to certify to shareholders the accuracy of financial statements
- Require reporting of GAAP-based financial information before references to pro forma or adjusted results
- Prohibit relationships between independent auditors and audit clients
- Exercise greater SEC oversight of the FASB and improve the quality of GAAP accounting rules
- Improve Management's Discussion and Analysis (MD&A) disclosures
- Require prompt disclosure of insider transactions
- Evaluate the impact of Regulation FD on corporate behavior

To Congress:

- Allocate additional resources to the SEC to improve monitoring and enforcement
- Authorize the SEC to bar officers and directors from holding positions for violations of the new rules
- Create a public/private panel to review stock concentration in 401(k) plans[5]

Chapter One

1. "Americans Gloomy over Finances," Financial Planning Association news release, 8 October 2002.

2. The FASB, <*www.fasb.org*>, was formed in 1973 as an industry organization to set standards governing preparation of financial reports. These standards are recognized by the SEC as well as the AICPA Rules of Professional Conduct for accountants.

3. "Merck Booked $12.4 Billion It Never Collected," *Wall Street Journal*, 8 July 2002.

4. "Halliburton Faces an SEC Probe of Its Accounting," *Wall Street Journal*, 30 May 2002.

5. "Former Sunbeam Chief Agrees to Ban and a Fine of $500,000," *New York Times*, 5 September 2002.

6. "Adelphia Overstated Cash Flow, Revenue over Past Two Years," *Wall Street Journal*, 11 June 2002.

7. "Cable Family Falls," *Variety.com*, 24 September 2002.

8. "SEC Broadens Investigation into Revenue-Boosting Tricks," *Wall Street Journal*, 16 May 2002.

9. Arthur Levitt, "The Numbers Game," speech at the NYU Center for Law and Business, 28 September 1998, at <*www.sec.gov/news/speech/speecharchive/1998/spch220.txt*>.

10. *Ibid.*

11. Once a company peaks within its primary industry, acquisitions in other industries are a sensible way to achieve lateral growth, enabling

a company to continue expanding revenues and profits. However, astute investors need to evaluate not only the motivation for acquiring other companies but also the volume of merger and acquisition activity. The higher the volume, the more the true financial picture is obscured.

12. A billion dollars is a difficult amount of money to imagine. If a stack of one million in $100 bills is five feet high, then a stack of $1 billion would be one mile high. $19 billion would extend up 19 miles! That's the equivalent height of about 125 skyscrapers of 80 stories each.

13. In negligence law, *duty of care* means the accused party had a responsibility of some type. To win a negligence claim, three things have to be shown: that a duty of care exists, that it was breached, and damages flowed from the breach.

14. "Kozlowski Quits under a Cloud; Worsening Worries about Tyco," *Wall Street Journal*, 4 June 2002; "Former Tyco Chief Is Indicted for Avoiding Sales Tax on Art," *Wall Street Journal*, 5 June 2002.

15. Reuters, "Former Enron Execs Say Merrill Helped Book Profit," 7 August 2002.

16. Wendy Zellner and Michael Arndt, "The Perfect Sales Pitch: No Debt, No Worries," *BusinessWeek Online*, 28 January 2002.

17. *WorldCom Exec Told 'Don't Ask Questions,'* Reuters, 26 August 2002.

18. "High Profiles in Hot Water," *Wall Street Journal*, 28 June 2002; "Handcuffs Make Strange Politics, You Say? But Not in Washington," *New York Times*, 2 August 2002.

19. Five companies comprise the $140-plus billion dollar figure: Enron $63.4, Global Crossing $25.5, Pacific Gas & Electric $21.5, Kmart $17, and Finova Group $14 billion. "Going for Broke," *Fortune*, 18 February 2002.

Chapter Two

1. Arthur Levitt, "The Numbers Game," speech at the NYU Center for Law and Business, 28 September 1998, at *<www.sec.gov/news/speech/speecharchive/1998/spch220.txt>*.

2. Russell J. Lundholm, Jeffrey T. Doyle, and Mark T. Soliman, "Pro Forma Earnings Mislead Investors." University of Michigan Business School, 2002.

3. *Ibid.*

4. Robert Olstein, cited in "When a Rosy Picture Should Raise a Red Flag," *New York Times*, 18 July 1999.

5. Research report, Bear Stearns & Co., Inc., "Pro Forma Earnings: A Critical Perspective," September 2002

6. "Numbers Do Lie," *Kiplinger's Investing*, April 2002.

7. Ron Insana, interviewed in "Looking for Weird," *Money*, April 2002.

8. "Enron: The Lessons for Investors," *Money*, January 2002.

9. "Worried about Corporate Numbers? How about the Charts?" *New York Times*, 15 September 2002.

10. In practice, reserves for bad debts reduce the current asset of accounts receivable and serve as a negative asset. While the result remains the same as though recorded as a liability, understating the amount distorts the true picture and deceives stockholders.

Chapter Three

1. The Racketeer Influenced and Corrupt Organizations (RICO) statute was designed originally to prosecute members of organized crime, especially the Sicilian Mafia. The Department of Justice Web site concerned with RICO *<www.usdoj.gov/criminal/ocrs.html>* explains the functions of the Justice Department's Organized Crime and Racketeering Section (OCRS). The Web site explains, "In addition to its close supervision of all federal organized crime cases, OCRS reviews all proposed federal prosecutions under the Racketeer Influenced and Corrupt Organizations (RICO) statute and provides extensive advice to prosecutors about the use of this powerful statute."

2. "Harvey Pitt on Disclosure Overhaul," *BusinessWeek Online*, 15 February 2002.

3. "Wall Street Story," *Fortune*, 8 July 2002.

4. Regulation FD (Fair Disclosure) provides that when an issuer discloses nonpublic information to market professionals, it must also make public disclosure of the information. SEC final rule announcement at <www.sec.gov/rules/final/33-7881.htm>.

5. NYSE Corporate Accountability and Listing Standards Committee report, 6 June 2002, 25-28.

6. *Money,* 8 November 2002, at <www.money.cnn.com/2002/11/08/news/pitt/reut/index.htm>.

7. "The Reluctant Reformer," *BusinessWeek Online,* 25 March 2002.

8. AICPA, "Summary of Sarbanes-Oxley Act of 2002," at <www.aicpa.org/info/sarbanes_oxley_summary.htm>.

9. SEC public statement op-ed, *Wall Street Journal,* 11 December 2001, at <www.sec.gov/news/speech/spch530.htm>.

10. *Ibid.*

11. President George W. Bush speaking 9 July 2002, cited in "Bush, on Wall St., Offers Tough Stance," *New York Times,* 10 July 2002.

Chapter Four

1. The other four firms are Deloitte & Touche, Pricewaterhouse-Coopers, KPMG, and Ernst & Young.

2. "FASB Facts," at <www.fasb.org/facts/>.

3. Walter Wriston, interview with Lou Dobbs, "The Impact of Enron," *Money,* May 2002.

4. "How a Bright Star at Andersen Fell along with Enron," *Wall Street Journal,* 15 May 2002.

5. John A. Byrne, "Joe Berardino's Fall from Grace," *BusinessWeek Online,* 12 August 2002, at <businessweek.com/magazine/content/02_32/b3795001.htm>.

6. "Adelphia Plans to Dismiss Deloitte," *Wall Street Journal,* 10 June 2002.

7. "KPMG's Work with Xerox Sets New Test for SEC," *Wall Street Journal,* 6 May 2002.

8. "Xerox Holders, SEC Target KPMG," *Wall Street Journal,* 1 July 2002.

9. "Tyco Probe Expands to Include Auditor PricewaterhouseCoopers," *Wall Street Journal,* 30 September 2002.

10. "Accountants Are Reviewing Old Audits," *New York Times,* 7 June 2002.

11. Harvey Pitt, public statement at the SEC Headquarters "Regulation of the Accounting Profession," 17 January 2002.

12. SEC Release 2002-91, "Commission Formally Proposes Framework of a Public Accountability Board," 20 June 2002, at *<www.sec.gov/ news/press/2002-91.htm>.*

13. Robert Olstein, interview with the author, September 2002.

14. *Ibid.*

15. AIPCA 2000 report, 715, cited in "Is There a Gap in Your Knowledge of GAAP?" *Financial Analysts Journal,* September/October 2002.

16. "Is There a Gap in Your Knowledge of GAAP?" *Financial Analysts Journal,* September/October 2002.

17. "AICPA President Calls for Rejuvenated Accounting Culture," press release, 4 September 2002. Address at the Yale Graduate School of Management at *<www.aicpa.org/news/p02090b.htm>* and *<www.aicpa .org/news/p02090a.htm>.*

18. Quoted in "Pushing Accounting into the Info Age," *BusinessWeek Online,* 1 February 2002, at *<businessweek.com/bwdaily/dnflash/feb2002/ nf2002021_8751.htm>.*

19. "AICPA President Calls for Rejuvenated Accounting Culture," press release, 4 September 2002. Address at the Yale Graduate School of Management at *<www.aicpa.org/news/p02090b.htm>* and *<www.aicpa .org/news/p02090a.htm>.*

20. The Securities Exchange Act of 1934 is the foundation of modern securities law. It provided for creation of the SEC and remains today the basis for protecting investors in public companies. For reference to a full text of the 1934 Act, go to *<www.sec.gov/divisions/corpfin/34act/in dex1934.shtml>.*

21. The major provisions of the Sarbanes-Oxley Act of 2002 are reproduced at the AICPA Web site, *<www.aicpa.org/info/sarbanes_oxley_ summary.htm>.*

Chapter Five

1. Sarbanes-Oxley Act of 2002, Section 302 (Corporate Responsibility for Financial Reports), requires the CEO and CFO to certify financial reports; and Sections 304 and 305 define penalties for material noncompliance, including forfeiture of compensation and other penalties.

2. Chuck Carlson, "Liar, Liar," *Bloomberg Personal Finance*, July/August 2002.

3. Roger Lowenstein, "Vanishing Act," *Smart Money*, February 2002.

4. Robert Olstein, interview with the author, September 2002.

5. Robert Olstein, quoted by Elizabeth MacDonald, "Breaking Down the Numbers on Wall Street," *Forbes*, 6 June 2002, at *<www.forbes.com/2002/06/06/0606olstein.html>*.

6. Robert Olstein, *op. cit.*

7. Robert Olstein, interview with the author, November 2002.

8. "Mind Games," *Bloomberg Personal Finance*, November 2002.

9. Robert Olstein, quoted by Elizabeth MacDonald in "Breaking Down the Numbers on Wall Street," *Forbes*, 6 June 2002, at *<www.forbes.com/2002/06/06/0606olstein.html>*.

10. *Ibid.*

11. Jean-Marie Eveillard, interview with the author, September 2002.

Chapter Six

1. Lauren Young, "Value Rules!" *Smart Money*, August 2001.

2. *Ibid.*, citing Leuthold Group.

3. Harris Collingwood, "The Earnings Cult," *New York Times Magazine*, 9 June 2002.

4. In a study conducted in 1966 by Sanjoy Basu, 500 issues were analyzed over a 14-month period. This study confirmed earlier results from a study conducted by David Dreman, who followed 1,200 stocks for the decade ending in 1977. Low-PE stocks yielded an average of 7.89 percent, whereas high-PE stocks yielded 0.33 percent on average.

5. Jersey Gilbert, "Big Is Bad!" *Smart Money*, April 2002.

6. *Core earnings* are "the after-tax earnings generated from a corporation's principal business," as defined by Standard & Poor's Corporation. The S&P definition is expanded to:

> Included in Standard & Poor's definition of core earnings
> are employee stock options grant expenses, restructuring
> charges from on-going operations, write-downs of depreciable
> or amortizable operating assets, pension costs, and purchased
> research and development. Excluded from this definition are
> impairment of goodwill charges, gains or losses from asset
> sales, pension gains, unrealized gains or losses from hedging
> activities, merger and acquisition related fees, and litigation
> settlements."

From S&P news release, "Standard & Poor's to Change System for
Evaluating Corporate Earnings," 13 May 2002, at *<www.standardand
poors.com/PressRoom/Equity/Articles/051302_CoreEarningsPR.html>*.

Chapter Eight

1. Information on weighting methodology and components is
found at the Dow Jones Web site, *<www.djindexes.com/jsp/industrial
Averages.jsp?sideMenu'true.html>*.

2. An interesting historical perspective on the Dow Jones Industrial
Averages, including a complete list of changes, replacements, and addi-
tions, is at *<www.e-analytics.com/dowchang.htm>*.

3. David Dreman, in a study from 1968 through 1977 of 1,200
stocks, concluded that lower PE yields averaged 7.89 percent and higher
PE yields averaged 0.33 percent. A second, 14-month study ending in
1977, conducted by Sanjoy Basu, confirmed Dreman's findings.

4. Robert Olstein, interview with the author, November 2002.

5. The belief that mutual funds and other institutional investors
are wrong more often than right is supported by studies conducted by
Morningstar, Inc. As reported in *The New York Times* on January 11,
1998, only 10 percent of diversified stock funds exceeded the S&P 500
averages for the past year. Between 1994 and 1998, the percentage of
funds performing better than the S&P 500 never exceeded 26 percent.

6. For those interested in comparing mutual funds with all fees and costs adjusted, the Securities and Exchange Commission offers a free mutual fund calculator at *<www.sec.gov/investor/tools/mfcc/mfcc-int.htm>*.

Chapter Nine

1. Bill Miller, "Memo to Imperial CEOs: Party's Over," Roundtable, *Smart Money,* September 2002.

2. Sarbanes-Oxley Act of 2002, Section 302, Corporate Responsibility for Financial Reports, summary at AICPA Web site, *<www.aicpa .org/info/sarbanes_oxley_summary.htm>*.

3. *Ibid.,* Section 305.

4. David Rocker, interview with the author, October 2002.

5. Bear Stearns & Co., Inc., study, as reported in Reuters, "New Option Disclosure Rule in the Works," 15 August 2002.

6. Microsoft and IBM are as actually reported, and Cisco is estimated. Justin Fox, "How Big Is the Options Bite?" *Fortune,* 10 June 2002.

7. Roger Lowenstein, "Runaway Gravy Train," *Smart Money,* July 2001.

8. "Insider Trades—Exposed!" *Fortune,* 27 May 2002.

9. "What the New Options Rules Mean for Your Pay," *Wall Street Journal,* 7 August 2002.

10. "GE CEO and CFO Sign Financial Statements; GE Enhances Commitments to Investors with Actions on Stock Options and Corporate Governance," in Investor Information, November 2002, at GE Web site, *<www.ge.com/company/investor/press/ceo_cfo_sign.htm>*.

11. W. Neil Eggleston, attorney for Enron's outside board members: "This board was continually lied to and misled by management. No amount of further diligence or questioning would have been sufficient to cause management to tell them about these transactions." Cited by John A. Byrne, "Commentary: No Excuse for Enron's Board," in *BusinessWeek Online,* 29 July 2002, at *<businessweek.com/magazine/con tent/02_30/b3793720.htm>*.

12. Charles Royce, interview with the author, October 2002.

13. Blue Ribbon Committee, overview and recommendations, from Recommendation 1, at <*www.nyse.com/content/publications/NT0000AE 72.html*>.

14. *Ibid.,* Recommendation 2.

15. New York Stock Exchange Corporate Accountability and Listing Standards Committee, report of 6 June 2002, in "Recommendations to the NYSE Board of Directors," 11, 13.

16. *Ibid.,* 2.

17. Andy Serwer, "Dirty Rotten Numbers," *Fortune,* 18 February 2002; also cited by Robert K. Herdman, chief accountant, SEC, in a speech at Tulane Corporate Law Institute, "Making Audit Committees More Effective," 7 March 2002, at <*www.sec.gov/news/speech/spch543 .htm*>.

Chapter Ten

1. Robert Olstein, interview with the author, September 2002.

2. American Airlines and Goodyear Tire financial reports, October 2002.

3. Robert Olstein, *op. cit.*

4. Depreciation guidelines are provided in Internal Revenue Service Publication 946, "How to Depreciate Property," which can be downloaded at <*www.irs.gov/formspubs/index.html*>.

5. Robert Olstein, *op. cit.*

6. J. K. Medbery, *Men and Mysteries of Wall Street* (Boston: Fields, Osgood, 1870) 306.

7. Richard J. Teweles and Edward S. Bradley, *The Stock Market,* 5th Ed. (New York: John Wiley and Sons, 1951) 87.

8. Martin S. Fridson, *It Was a Very Good Year* (New York: John Wiley & Sons, 1998) 132.

9. Great fortunes were invested in single tulip bulbs as values rose. Not only the wealthy but the middle class as well considered owning expensive bulbs a sign of good taste. Many became rich until, without warning, the market crashed. Those who had gone into debt to finance

the purchase of tulip bulbs were ruined immediately. Charles Mackay, *Extraordinary Popular Delusions and the Madness of Crowds*, (New York: Harmony Books, 1980).

10. "O brave new world that has such people in 't!" *The Tempest* 5.1.

11. Robert Olstein, *op. cit.*

12. Cloud Cuckoo Land is the city in the clouds in Aristophanes's *The Birds.*

13. Robert Olstein, *op. cit.*

14. Robert Olstein, in Ian McDonald, "10 Questions with Olstein Financial Alert's Bob Olstein," 25 June 2001, *TheStreet.com*, at <*www.the street.com/pf/funds/fundjunkie/1472254.html*>.

15. Jean-Marie Eveillard, interview with the author, September 2002.

16. Charles Royce, interview with the author, October 2002.

17. Robert Olstein, interview with the author, September 2002.

18. The most revealing and valuable of the balance sheet ratios are the current ratio, bad debt to accounts receivable ratio, total accounts receivable to charge-base sales, number of days accounts receivable are outstanding, inventory turnover, ratio of inventory loss reserves to average inventory, accumulated depreciation to long-term assets ratio, and the bond ratio.

19. Robert Olstein, Letter to Shareholders, The Olstein Financial Alert Fund, April 2001.

20. Robert Olstein, interview with the author, September 2002.

21. *Ibid.*

22. Jean-Marie Eveillard, interview with the author, September 2002.

Chapter Eleven

1. "Analysts Who Don't Ignore Bad News," Inside Wall Street, *Business Week*, 6 June 1977.

2. Robert Olstein, President's Message, The Olstein Financial Alert Fund, 3 October 2000.

3. Charles D. Ellis, "The Loser's Game," *Financial Analysts Journal,* July/August, 1975.

4. "Piper Jaffray Is Fined for Research Threat," *Wall Street Journal,* 26 June 2002.

5. Charles Ellis, quoted by Jason Zweig, "Wall Street's Wisest Man," *Money,* June 2001.

6. "Sue Your Broker," *Money,* October 2001.

7. Stanley Bing, "Lessons from the Abyss," *Fortune,* 18 February 2002.

8. Thomas Bowman's testimony, summarized in *AIMR Exchange Supplement,* March/April 2002.

9. Gerri Willis, "What Evil Lurks in the Heart of Corporate America," *Smart Money,* April 2002.

10. "Citigroup Offers Separate Research Arm in Settlement Bid," *Wall Street Journal,* 30 September 2002; "Possible Salomon Settlement May Change Wall St.," *USA Today,* 30 September 2002.

11. First Call, cited in "Should You Trust Wall Street's New Ratings?" *Wall Street Journal,* 17 July 2002.

12. F. L. Eames, *The New York Stock Exchange,* (New York: Thomas G. Hall, 1894) 13.

13. *Ibid.,* 14.

14. Henry Clews, *Fifty Years in Wall Street,* (New York: Irving, 1908) 7.

15. "Alan Bond Is Convicted of Investment, Mail Fraud," *Wall Street Journal,* 11 June 2002.

16. "The Betrayed Investor," *BusinessWeek Online,* 25 February 2002, at *<businessweek.com/magazine/content/02_08/b3771001.htm>.*

17. Cited by Elizabeth MacDonald, "Breaking Down the Numbers on Wall Street," 6 June 2002, *Forbes.com,* at *<www.forbes.com.2002/06/06/-6-6olstein.html>.*

18. "Salomon's Grubman Resigns; NASD Finds 'Spinning' at Firm," *Wall Street Journal,* 16 August 2002.

19. Lori Richard, "Analysts's Conflict of Interest: Taking Steps to Remove Bias," speech at the Financial Women's Association, New York, 8 May 2002.

20. David Rocker, interview with the author, 22 October 2002.

21. Lori Richard, *op. cit.*

22. "New York's Bubble Boys," Review & Outlook, "How Spitzer Pact Will Affect Wall Street." Both in *Wall Street Journal,* 22 May 2002.

23. Lori Richard, *op. cit.*

24. Cited by Elizabeth MacDonald, *op. cit.*

25. "Two Big States Tell Wall Street: Reform, or Else!" *Wall Street Journal,* 7 June 2002.

26. Michael C. Thomsett, quoted in "More to Companies than Earnings Estimates," Sergio G. Non, *c/net,* 8 June 2001, at *<news.com.com/ 2100-1017-268538.html>.*

27. Robert Olstein, "Fixing the Analyst Problem," *Bloomberg Personal Finance,* October 2001.

28. Cited by Elizabeth MacDonald, *op. cit.*

29. Robert Olstein, in The Olstein Financial Alert Fund Letter to Top Members, April 2001.

30. Robert Olstein, *op. cit.*

31. Robert Olstein, *op. cit.*

32. Robert Olstein, *op. cit.*

33. Robert Olstein, in "A Nose for Value . . . and Nonsense," *Barron's,* 4 October 1999.

34. Robert Olstein, "Fixing the Analyst Problem," *op. cit.*

35. Planners will be likely to recommend load funds, because they will be compensated by way of a sales commission. For individuals who would prefer the no-load approach, it makes little sense to ask a planner for mutual fund advice.

Chapter Twelve

1. Arthur Levitt, "The Numbers Game," remarks at the NYU Center for Law and Business, New York, 28 September 1998.

2. Cassell Bryan-Low, "Accounting Firms Are Still Consulting," *Wall Street Journal,* 23 September 2002.

3. GE's former CEO John Welch came under criticism, when he and his wife divorced and papers filed with the court disclosed that GE had paid big-number living expenses for the couple. (*New York Times,* 6 September 2002). The matter came under investigation by the SEC to determine whether lavish benefits and facilities made available to the ex-CEO and his wife were violations of law. (*Wall Street Journal,* 17 September 2002).

4. Robert Olstein, "Quality of Earnings, The Key to Successful Earnings," in *Barron's,* 2 July 1984.

Appendix

1. AICPA, "Summary of Sarbanes-Oxley Act of 2002," at *<www.aicpa.org/info/sarbanes_oxley_summary.htm>;* implementation described in press release by the Securities and Exchange Commission, "Commission Approves Rules Implementing Provisions of Sarbanes-Oxley Act, Accelerating Periodic Filings, and Other Measures," 27 August 2002, at *<www.sec.gov/news/press/2002-128.htm>,* summary provided by Susan B. Hollinger for Gallagher, Callahan, & Gartrells, "Accounting Industry Reform Act," July 2002, at *<www.glglaw.com/resources/corp_gov/reform.html>.*

2. Lori Richards, director, Office of Compliance Inspections and Examinations, SEC, in a speech, "Analysts's Conflict of Interest: Taking Steps to Remove Bias," at the Financial Women's Association, New York, 8 May 2002, at *<www.sec.gov/news/speech/spch559.htm>.*

3. Securities and Exchange Commission, "Final Rule: Selective Disclosure and Insider Trading," 2 October 2002, at *<www.sec.gov/rules/final/33-7881.htm>.*

4. NYSE Corporate Accountability and Listing Standards Committee Report, 6 June 2002; "Overview and Recommendations" in NYSE Publications, at *<www.nyse.com/content/publications/NT0000AE72.html>.*

Index

Hedges, 174
HFS, 10
Hi-Speed Media, 8
Home ownership, 173
Homestore.com, 8

IBM, 67, 148
IGI Inc., 42
ImClone, 16, 133
Immelt, Jeff, 149
In the money, 179
Incentive-based compensation, 143, 148
Income reinvestment, 176–78
Income statement, 183
Index of Leading Economic Indicators, 137
Industrial averages, 120
Industry expansion, 183
Inflation, 175
Informix, 11
Initial public offerings, 200
Insider buy/sell information, 128, 132
Institute of Management Accountants, 57
Institutional investors, 114
Intangible diversification, 174
Interest coverage, 90
Internal reorganization, 102–3
International Accounting Standards, 59
Internet
    guidelines, 223–24
    information, 222–24
    stocks, 167
Intrinsic value, 185–86
    adjustments of, in footnotes, 72
Inventory, 87, 221
Investor(s)
    confidence, 50, 57, 145–46
    expectations of, 6, 24–28
    knowledge and, 221
    losses, 198
    rights of, 225
IPOs, 200

J.P. Morgan, 195

Kozlowski, L. Dennis, 13, 48
KPMG, 47–48
Kraft Foods, 109

Land speculation, 165
Lateral growth, 108–11
Lawsuits, 32, 69
Lay, Kenneth, 13–14, 148, 151
Lease obligations, 32, 69
Lehman, 195
Leveraged buyouts, 113
Levitt, Arthur, 8–9, 19, 54, 214
Liabilities, 31–32
    disclosure of, 32
    reclassifying as income, 32
Liability account changes, 162
Liquidation value, 185
Listing standards, for publicly traded companies, 154
Lowenstein, Roger, 63
Lucent Technologies, 11–12
Lundholm, Russell J., 20

Management. See also Boards of directors; CEOs/CFOs; Corporate management
    abuse of system by, 22–24, 163–64
    compensation of, 23
    effectiveness of, 140–44
    financial result certification and, 158
    misconduct, lack of internal control and, 27
    oversight, 22
    responsibilities of, 6
    stock options and, 141
Management risk, 163–64
Managing earnings, 132
Market
    analyst predictions and, 121
    broad movements in, 121
    condition, drawing conclusions on, 120–22
    cyclical history of, 165–67
    investment environment, 158, 168–72
    mood, 119, 174
    stock prices and, 121–22

Share the message!

Bulk discounts
Discounts start at only 10 copies. Save up to 55% off retail price.

Custom publishing
Private label a cover with your organization's name and logo. Or, tailor information to your needs with a custom pamphlet that highlights specific chapters.

Ancillaries
Workshop outlines, videos, and other products are available on select titles.

Dynamic speakers
Engaging authors are available to share their expertise and insight at your event.

**Call Dearborn Trade Special Sales at 1-800-621-9621, ext. 4404
or e-mail trade@dearborn.com**

Dearborn™
Trade Publishing
A **Kaplan Professional** Company